The Kids Are Online

The Kids Are Online

CONFRONTING THE MYTHS AND
REALITIES OF YOUNG DIGITAL LIFE

Ysabel Gerrard

UNIVERSITY OF CALIFORNIA PRESS

University of California Press
Oakland, California

© 2025 by Ysabel Gerrard

Library of Congress Cataloging-in-Publication Data

Names: Gerrard, Ysabel, author.
Title: The kids are online : confronting the myths and realities of
    young digital life / Ysabel Gerrard.
Description: Oakland : University of California Press, [2025] |
    Includes bibliographical references and index.
Identifiers: LCCN 2024033108 (print) | LCCN 2024033109 (ebook) |
    ISBN 9780520388079 (cloth) | ISBN 9780520416093 (paperback) |
    ISBN 9780520388086 (ebook)
Subjects: LCSH: Social media and teenagers.
Classification: LCC HQ799.2.15 G47 2025 (print) | LCC HQ799.2.15
    (ebook) | DDC 302.23/10835—dc23/eng/20240820
LC record available at https://lccn.loc.gov/2024033108
LC ebook record available at https://lccn.loc.gov/2024033109

Manufactured in the United States of America

34 33 32 31 30 29 28 27 26 25
10 9 8 7 6 5 4 3 2 1

For Sean Richardson

We haven't got fat computers and Myspace anymore.

CLAIRE, 17

Contents

Illustrations

Preface

Writing this book was tricky, not only because it is tricky to write any book but because of the immense pressure I felt to get it right. A pressure so intense, in fact, that the publication of this manuscript was a little (a lot) delayed. This book tells vivid stories about how young people navigate their identities across social media platforms and about the wider role these technologies play in their daily lives. It shows how, despite the risks, they use social media to evade stigma and achieve feelings of safety. It explores some of the challenges they face as a result of social media, which aren't confined to their smartphones in a binary online-offline sense and therefore materialize at home, along the school corridors, and in many other everyday spaces. This book also sheds light on the socially comparative nature of image-based platforms, particularly when it comes to our physical appearances. Naturally, then, this book covers topics like mental health, bullying, body image, and sexual harassment, along with lots of other issues experienced by today's youth, especially in England (the context from which I write).

The aim of this book is to contribute calm and nuanced evidence to contentious public conversations about young people and social media, which can be heard on the news, in our corridors at work, in the aisles of supermarkets, at our nail salons, among our family and friends, and even from passersby. I was terrified of getting it wrong not on account of my own professional reputation but for the sake of my research participants. I am so lucky to have received funding to go into schools and other learning environments to talk to young people and learn more about their lives. And I am especially privileged to have earned the trust of their educators, who welcomed me with open arms. But the pressure to represent their views and experiences fairly; to write something that would show my immense appreciation for their having given me so much of their time; to avoid writing anything—a rogue sentence, a throwaway phrase—that might be taken out of context and used to harm them was so extreme that I would go weeks at a time without writing anything at all. I don't share this experience to invoke pity or to make excuses. I say it to highlight the responsibility I know I have in writing this book, and to tell my readers, before they even reach the introduction, of my deep gratitude to my participants for sharing their stories. I hope I do them justice.

Acknowledgments

This book is the product of years of support, collaboration, and encouragement (which I often resisted) from friends, family, and colleagues, among many other guiding lights—and its publication is as much their achievement as it is mine. I begin by thanking those who funded or mentored the research on which this book is based. Thank you to my colleagues at the Microsoft Research New England Social Media Collective for my wonderful internship in 2017 and for kindly hosting me again in 2019. I am grateful to Nancy Baym, Tarleton Gillespie, Mary L. Gray, Dan Greene, Sharif Mowlabocus, and Dylan Mulvin for your close mentorship over the years and for encouraging me to wait a little while longer to write the book I really wanted to write instead of more speedily getting out the one I thought I should. Thank you to the British Academy for selecting me as a Small Grant recipient in 2018, and thank you to the Department of Sociological Studies at the University of Sheffield for awarding me with Strategic Research Support funding in 2022. I also thank the University of Sheffield's Faculty of Social Sciences for funding a secondment to the 5Rights Foundation in 2022 and am grateful to their fantastic Policy team—particularly Izzy and Daral—for their guidance.

I also wish to thank the audience members, reviewers, and kind question-askers at the various conferences and events at which I have presented elements of this book over the years, particularly the Association of Internet Researchers (AoIR), the European Communication Research and Education Association (ECREA), the International Communication Association (ICA), Ofcom, along with many others. I thank you for your interest in the work I have been doing and for encouraging me to keep going with this book in the face of obstacles, including the Covid-19 pandemic and suspension of my fieldwork and my yearslong struggle to figure out its throughline. I am so lucky to have colleagues and friends in my field who have guided me through the years, who have either read drafts of this book, reviewed the manuscript and/or the proposal, or have been involved in formative conversations. To Crystal Abidin, Phoenix Andrews, Anna Bailie, Maitrayee Basu, Sophie Bishop, Robyn Caplan, Niki Cheong, Ranjana Das, Tom Divon, Harry Dyer, Anna Gibson, Debbie Ging, Zoë Glatt, Briony Hannell, Tim Highfield, Tama Leaver, Kate Miltner, Tzlil Sharon, Nic Suzor, Katrin Tiidenberg, Jacqueline Ryan Vickery, and my anonymous reviewers: thank you so much for your support and kindness. Tremendous thanks go to my collaborators, whose efforts fundamentally shaped this book and the research on which it is based: Tarleton Gillespie, Anthony McCosker, and Helen Thornham.

When I started my job at the University of Sheffield in 2017, I didn't know where my place would be. I was a non-sociologist embedded within a department of sociological studies, supporting the growth of two brand-new degree programs and given more responsibility than I knew what to do with. But people took me, nearly fresh out of my PhD, under their wings and guided me through my journey in a way I'm still not entirely sure I deserve.

My colleagues are all wonderful, and I feel lucky to work among such genuine kindness and collegiality. But special mention must go to Katherine Davies, Hannah Ditchfield, Kate Dommett, Helen Kennedy, Nathan Hughes, Sarah Neal, Kitty Nichols, and Mark Taylor for their endless patience and wisdom. I also thank my lovely friends for the adventures, laughs, and voice notes that have made everything around my work and this book feel so special: Anita, Bryony, Fobazi, Geoff, Jordan, Katie/Blossom, Meg/Gab/Birdie, Nat, and Victoria. And to Jez: a wonderful friend whose time with us was far, far too short. I also thank my lovely extended families—the Kidds and the Walshes—who have welcomed me with open arms and championed every part of my career since the day we met. To my adventure-loving dad and Milla, who taught me that life is far too short and needs to be lived, preferably in a sunny place and with your next flight booked, and to my wonderful mum and Jonathan, for always giving me a place to rest my head and pour out my soul.

As many of my readers will know, I have never written a book before, and so I feel incredibly lucky that my first experience was steered by Michelle Lipinski. Michelle, you have been the best editor I could've wished for (and made me the source of such envy among my peers!). You have been so patient, kind, and excited about this project, even through the Covid delays and other strange life occurrences, and I thank you wholeheartedly for everything you have done. Crucially, I also thank my research participants, whose words and experiences have made this book a reality. I thank them for trusting me with their stories and letting me into their lives and for giving me hours of joy as they taught me everything I needed to know about social media today. I also thank the educators and facilitators I've worked with over the last few years for introducing me to their students, and for having faith in me to handle the work with ethical care.

I close this section by thanking two people (and some animals) of equal importance, without whom I could not exist on a day-to-day basis let alone write an entire book. To James Lowell Walsh and our four-legged family—Buttercup and Hazel, the kittycats; Willow, the puppy dog; and Billy, the pony (otherwise known as my "serotonin machine")—thank you for teaching me that falling in love is not just something that people in movies do and for always encouraging and enabling me to get this finished. To Elena Rosa Maris, thank you for our cross-continental coworking sessions, which are the highlights of my week and go a long way in bridging an approximately 4,000-mile physical distance. Thank you for making me laugh until my sides hurt, thank you for supporting me without question (even when you really, really should question it), and thank you for being the best friend anyone could ever have.

Introduction

Social Media in Young Lives

Reader, I would like you to meet Bella.[1] Bella is a White, 17-year-old, heterosexual English girl with aspirations—fueled by a deep love of writing and true crime podcasts—of a career in investigative journalism.[2] At the time we spoke, Bella was taking A-Levels—a common qualification in England that can be used for entry into universities—in politics, media studies, and English literature, with the intention of applying for an undergraduate degree in journalism. Bella is a self-confessed extrovert with a magnetic personality, making her well-known among her peers and in certain circles on social media. It seemed like Bella knew everyone and everyone knew her. But this, she told me, was less a blessing than it was a curse, especially for someone who has grown up at the heart of what many describe as the social media age.

I first met Bella in April 2022, during a workshop I led with the students at Jaynes Sixth Form College. In case readers are unaware, colleges in England educate students between the ages of 16 and 18, before they attend university or enter the working world. The college is located in a Northern English city widely considered, with its roots in the Industrial Revolution, to be working class. It has a majority-White population and in the 2019 General Election was a Labour Party stronghold.³ My workshop focused on the promises and pitfalls of anonymous apps: apps that allow you to send messages without revealing who you are; well-known examples of these apps among the English teens I spoke to included YOLO, Sarahah and Tellonym. The cozy workshop included 11 participants, all between the ages of 16 and 18.⁴ I remember sensing Bella's initial skepticism of my presence at her college; she had her walls up and rightly so. After all, what could I—someone who grew up with "fat computers and Myspace," to borrow 17-year-old-participant Claire's words—possibly understand about her life? After a round of introductions and some scene-setting, I began the workshop by splitting participants into small groups and asking them to design their ideal anonymous app. I asked them what app they felt there was room for in the current marketplace, what their app's core demographic might be, and how its users would be protected from harm. Groups were also asked to use large sheets of paper and brightly colored pens to come up with some branding for their proposed app and to consider how its users would navigate their way through the app's interface.

Partway through the workshop, Bella caught my eye and gestured me over to her table. She'd remembered that she once used an anonymous app called YOLO—an acronym for "You only live once"—when she was in her second year of high school. Luckily, I had heard of YOLO. Launched in 2019, YOLO was an anonymous question and answer (Q&A) app that could be embedded into Snapchat: an ephemeral social media app whose users can send images and videos to one another that will disappear within a certain time frame. Snapchat users can also send text-based messages and use popular features like the Snap Map, which displays consenting users' real-time locations on a map. In 2018, seven years after its launch, Snapchat introduced something called the Snap Kit: a developer tool that allows third-party apps to "piggyback on Snap's login for sign up" and integrate elements of their own apps into Snapchat.[5] YOLO was one of the first apps to be built with the Snap Kit, though it was not owned by or affiliated with Snap Inc. (Snapchat's parent company).[6] Rocketing to the top position in US app stores only a week after launching, YOLO users could request anonymized responses to a particular question.[7] Bella started looking through her Snapchat archive to see if she could still access the messages she had sent and received during what she described as her "YOLO era," which took place when she was around 13 years old. I will repeat that final point because it feels important: Bella was *13 years old* in her YOLO era. After a few minutes of scrolling, a wide-eyed Bella gestured me back over to her group's table. She told me she had found some messages from a YOLO-based game she once played called *Amuse Me or Abuse Me*. I'm not sure exactly who invented this game, but to be clear it hadn't been popularized by YOLO and seemed to be an organic social trend. The aim of this game was to invite your Snapchat network, via YOLO, to send you either a humorous message or one that insulted you. The only catch: unless the sender outed themselves to you directly, players had no way of knowing who was saying what. For the locally popular Bella, her many followers included a combination of complete strangers and known contacts, making it nearly impossible for her to de-anonymize her message senders.

I remember watching Bella scroll through her Snapchat archive, reliving the feeling of being called a "stuck up bitch" and a "slut" more times than she could count. I could feel the depth of Bella's sadness for her younger self, something she later reflected on in the interview portion of my research. During our longer conversation,

Bella told me how scared she felt for her younger cousin—who was, as it so happened, age 13 at the time we spoke—about the pressure she might feel to send nudes of herself to boys and about the toxicity she would likely encounter on certain apps, all of which would be underpinned by the "systemic issue[s]" facing attendees of public (non-paid-for) Northern English schools. Bella's walls finally came down, at which point she admitted she was glad she had "made it out [of school] alive." It was—and still is—moving to read Bella's self-reflections, and I feel honored that she let down her guard for me.

I recently shared Bella's story with one of my work colleagues—who herself has two young daughters—and, on seeing her eyes grow wider as I spoke, recall apologizing that my aim was not to scare her or to frame Bella's overall experiences with social media as bad. After all, four years had passed since *Amuse Me or Abuse Me*, and Bella was still an avid social media user who was more than able to critically reflect on her relationship with the apps she was using. And that's just it: whether she likes it or not, my colleague's children will likely want to use social media even if some of their experiences are bad. They will probably want to use it at a younger age than she would ideally allow and, despite her senior-academic-level of knowledge on the relationship between social media and society, she will sometimes struggle to know what to do when tricky situations arise. Her children's activities will also vary according to the apps they use. As Livingstone noted in 2008, "also influencing the balance between opportunities and risks online are the specific affordances of social networking sites."[8] In other words, while they may share unique selling points and borrow from one another's successes, no two social apps are exactly the same, making the catch-all term *social media* somewhat unhelpful in today's technological landscape. But my colleague's daughters will also have a wealth of good experiences; in fact, sometimes they will *need* to take the bad with the good, a notion that entirely underpins this book, in which I foreground young people's own voices and experiences in order to tell stories about their relationships with social media.

I call this concept *the platform paradox*, and it is grounded in a longer-standing resistance among many social science and other academics to frame technologies and their use as either good or bad. As I have spoken to more and more young people through my research over the last few years, I have come to realize that it is not enough to describe their experiences of a given app—or a particular feature within an app—in either-or terms.[9] It is also not quite enough to say that young people's experiences are sometimes bad but sometimes good. Though this statement is true, stopping short at this binary framing precludes a complete understanding of young people's increasingly technology-heavy lives, doing them a profound disservice. This is because, paradoxically, technologies can be experienced as both good and bad at the same time. The hard truth is that, sometimes, it is only by accepting and facing risks on social media that young people can activate pleasures and benefits. Take Bella as an example here: when I asked her why she continued to use YOLO in the face of sexist insults, she said she remained curious about what people might say to her. Put simply, she chose to take the risk because she felt it could pay off in an unexpected way. Bella's experiences of course don't mirror all teens' experiences, and her story reminds me of something Livingstone noted in 2020: that the same activity on social media or other parts of the internet can be felt differently according to a young person's identity.[10] But paradoxical experiences of social media dominated the research findings on which this book is based, and so its contents offer a framework through which we might be able to break down commonplace yet unhelpful dichotomies between good and bad, beneficial and harmful, and pleasurable and painful social media use in contemporary young lives.

This book combines three distinct research projects on young people's social media use. By *young people*, I could of course be referring to a purely age-based categorization: young people are defined by organizations like the United Nations (UN) and YouGov as people between the ages of 14 and 29, the core demographics of many of the world's most popular platforms.[11] However, on social media it is often difficult to ascertain people's ages, and many of the phenomena I describe in this book pertain more to cultures and concerns about *youthfulness* than they do to those who are in an exact age group. So, while this book is primarily based on research from three English schools and features participants between the ages of 13 to 18, it does not always use the term *young people* in a strict age-based way. It also makes distinctions between ages, as being a 13-year-old is, of course, very different from being a 17- or 18-year-old.

My book's central contribution to knowledge is the concept of platform paradoxes as a route into understanding young people's experiences of social media. Its underpinning argument is that young people often negotiate their identities across platforms in highly paradoxical ways—that is, when young people use social media, "polar opposite" experiences "can simultaneously exist, or at least can be potentiated, in the same thing."[12] As Mick and Fournier explained in 1998, such an approach does not attend to either-or outcomes of technological use, as "these categories are overly broad and do not adequately reflect the specific content and pressures of the cultural contradictions of technology."[13]

I am not, of course, the first person to talk about the paradoxical nature of people's technology use; nor are all young peoples' experiences paradoxical.[14] But the word *platform* in the term *platform paradox* emphasizes the role that private technology companies' rules and policies play in shaping young people's experiences of social media. This demographic lies at the heart of anxieties felt in lots of places around the world, and there are efforts across sectors dedicated to ensuring "safer" social media use for those who are imagined to be most vulnerable to its supposed consequences. I am also under no illusion that attending to paradoxes would be an easy task for policymakers, tech workers, educators, parents, families, and lots of other folks who care about our youth. Nor am I implying that we shouldn't be worried about certain things. After all, there are genuine problems in young people's social media use: there are posts that may be difficult for some to see; there are malign actors, both known and unknown to users; and there are plenty of examples where platforms have been used as avenues for bullying. But I have ample evidence to suggest that attending to paradoxes is necessary to breathe empirical life and critical depth into our understanding of the contemporary realities of young lives online.

Social Media in Young Lives, from Networks to Platforms

I grew up on Myspace, MSN Messenger, and Habbo Hotel, which gives you a rough indication of the year I was born and the country I grew up in. While I'm still a young person by some estimations, the generation behind mine—Generation Z—has a unique relationship with social media: one my thirty-something friends tell me they're relieved they've escaped.[15] Members of Gen Z are often described as "digital natives," a term defined by Prensky in 2001 as the "native speakers of the digital language of computers, video games and the Internet."[16] For Prensky, this age-based characteristic meant young people in the early 2000s had a different relationship with information seeking and processing compared with the so-called digital immigrants born before them.[17] Young people were assumed to have comfort and familiarity with digital devices popularized during this era—like gaming consoles and websites—purely because they had grown up alongside them.

However, Banaji, Livingstone, and other scholars have more recently argued against this catchy term and give evidence to prove that age is not the only determining factor in assessing a person's engagement with new digital technologies.[18] We can become skilled; likewise, people who were born into a particular generation do not necessarily have the skills that they are presumed to have (or the financial resources to obtain them). In some parts of the world, young people cite "poor electricity and telecommunications infrastructure, lack of access to hardware, and the cost of connectivity" as some of the key barriers to internet access.[19] No two young people have the same relationship with digital technologies, and the gaps between experiences deepen according to geography and other factors. As Banaji explains, many of the worries we may have in England about youth and digital media are "not immediate hazards" in other places around the world.[20] But it still feels fair to say the youth in my research have a distinctive media landscape and that they engage in some communicative dynamics that people my age did not.

It is difficult (and certainly controversial) to decide what counts as the world's first example of social media.[21] Things like instant messaging (IM) and bulletin board systems (BBS) are social forms of media technologies, and they have been around in many countries for decades.[22] For example, personal computer communications (or *pasokon tsūshin*) emerged in Japan in the late 1980s; *pasokon tsūshin* were "basically bulletin board systems (BBS) that enabled users to seek out information from various news feeds as well as participate in online discussions and send email to other users."[23] While these early systems were not taken up by the Japanese population en masse, they found their place in certain communities—for example, among feminist women and those living with chronic illnesses.[24] But social network sites (SNSs), as we used to call them, came a bit later and offered something more than IMs and BBSs. In what became a go-to source for those seeking a definition of this term, in 2007 boyd and Ellison explained that SNSs were "web-based services that allow[ed] individuals to (1) construct a public or semi-public profile within a bounded system, (2) articulate a list of other users with whom they share a connection, and (3) view and traverse their list of connections and those made by others within the system." As they explained, "The nature and nomenclature of these connections may vary from site to site."[25]

Using the above definition, Myspace would be a perfect example of a social networking site. Founded in 2003, Myspace users were invited to create their own profiles, which displayed a profile picture that users could upload from their computer, along with their name, age, and location. Users could also choose their "Top 8" friends and browse each other's social connections, leave comments on people's profiles, send messages, choose a song to play when their friends opened their profile, and display biographical information. Crucial to Myspace's success, however, was the editability of the profile. "Myspace users needed to learn basic HTML and CSS to creatively customize their profiles": features that are unfortunately "mostly absent" from the platforms young people use today.[26] Like many people my age, I genuinely regret dropping my so-called coding skills when Myspace died.[27] I spent hours figuring out how to hide the comments people left me, list my top four friends instead of my top eight, and prevent people from pausing my profile song (because it was, of course, imperative they heard whatever masterpiece I had deemed worthy). But the functionalities and characteristics of communication technologies have advanced considerably since my Myspace days, alongside relevant social, economic, and other changes. This means we have recently seen a change in terminology from social *networks* to social *media*.

In a shift from boyd and Ellison's crucial definition of SNSs in 2007, no longer do today's youth typically maintain a single profile on a given platform.[28] Most of the young people I have spoken to maintain multiple social media accounts, both within the same platform and across platforms, with the ultimate goal of "compartmentalizing" parts of their lives, to borrow van der Nagel's phrase.[29] Studies conducted by organizations like Ofcom reiterate how common it is for young people to spread themselves across multiple social media platforms, with the four most popular among 13- to 17-year-olds in the UK currently being YouTube, TikTok, Instagram, and Snapchat.[30] The "stranger danger" discourse is to some extent a thing of the past, as young people rarely exclusively engage with networks of known contacts on social media. Instead, they talk to people they've never met in a face-to-face setting, either through accounts depicting their "real" identities or through accounts where they are pseudonymized.[31]

These two shifts are reflected in Burgess et al.'s more recent 2017 definition of *social media technologies*, which they define as "those digital platforms, services and apps built around the convergence of content sharing, public communication, and interpersonal connection."[32] Notably, Burgess et al. foreground the creation and sharing of social media *content* rather than the maintenance of a profile and its showcasing of friends and networks. Often, the visual and text-based posts we want to share are more important to us than the maintenance of our networks and, as I edit this introduction in late 2023, I am seeing plenty of evidence that people are using social media to share content in highly intimate ways.[33] As Humphreys explains, to create and populate an account in today's social media landscape is to suggest a "collection of media traces" that are tied to a person's identity.[34] Humphreys coined the notion of *media accounting* to describe how people use digital technologies, particularly those that are image-based, like Instagram or Xiaohongshu (Little Red Book), to chronicle various aspects of their lives so they can "remember, relive, recount, reconcile, and reckon at future points."[35] This implies a meaningful relationship with longevity, perhaps akin to tangible photo albums, scrapbooks, or baby books. Like their analog predecessors, the call to represent our identities via social media "is always incomplete. Much like housework, it is never done," and the growing use of social media in such intimate ways suggests this work will be ongoing among young people for many more years.[36]

Alongside this definitional shift, within and beyond academic circles, we have witnessed the popularization of the term *social media platforms*. In 2010, Gillespie noted that the largest online communication providers using English as a first language in their marketing materials—including social media companies—were quietly positioning themselves as "platforms."[37] This word could be taken to mean lots of things, but in the context of digital communication, it did not just "drop from the sky."[38] The phrase is used by communication providers to discursively position themselves as "open, flat and neutral spaces open to all comers"—spaces where we may place our content without restriction.[39] When social media (or SNSs, as they were formerly known) found their way into everyday life in the mid-to-late 2000s, academics and public commentators were proclaiming important shifts from our habits of media *consumption* as audiences or receivers to media *production* as users.[40] Participatory media are argued to differ from traditional media because they represent a shift in communication structures, taking us from the one-to-many communicative style of television shows, magazines, and some older websites to the many-to-many participatory dynamics we see in newer technologies like social media.[41] As Livingstone and Das noted in 2013, the concept of the audience was "no longer useful" for some; indeed, the phenomenon was "claimed to be obsolete, or at least disappearing."[42] But within the last decade, this early excitement has been replaced with concerns about media and society relations, as platforms are now more widely understood to be anything but "open, flat and neutral spaces open to all comers."[43]

The word *platform* masks the myriad ways intermediaries intervene in our digital sociality.[44] Gillespie puts it best when he says, "platforms, in their technical design, economic imperatives, regulatory frameworks, and public character, have distinct consequences for what users are able to do, and in fact do."[45] Put differently, we cannot just say and do what we want on social media; there are rules and limitations, which undermines any claims of neutrality made by communication providers. The topics discussed in this book—social media content relating to mental health, harmful messages sent through anonymous apps, policies around naming across social apps, and digital photo editing of the face and body—are considered to be contentious because they break some of those rules (or, at the very least, they tread a fine line). My use of the term *platform* throughout this book foregrounds the fact that young people should not be straightforwardly imagined as avid and unidirectional *users* of social media. We know very well that young people do not freely log in, post, comment, like, share, swipe, tap, and scroll. What they do on social media is heavily curated and governed by the rules and systems set by a small handful of private companies. The publication of this book therefore coincides with an intense moment of public debate in certain geographies and cultures about how young people should be protected from the harms that might befall them on social media, while also asking tough questions about which harms young people may themselves be perpetuating and why they may be doing so.

Social Media: The Teen Era

It has been 10 years since danah boyd published *It's Complicated: The Social Lives of Networked Teens*, and it has been a real pleasure to re-engage with this book while asking about the myths and realities of young digital lives as I wrote my own. As boyd argued in 2014, "Although the specific sites and apps may be constantly changing, the practices that teens engage in . . . remain the same."[46] The issues discussed in boyd's book—like privacy, bullying, and literacy—and their alignment with the ones that arose for my research participants tell us very clearly that teen sociality has not radically changed since 2014. As boyd explained, by the time her book was to be published, "the next generation of teens [would] have inhabited a new set of apps and tools."[47] And while there have been some changes, like the soaring popularity of anonymous apps along with digital photo editing tools, most of the big players for boyd's US-based participants are still going strong in many places around the world.

Social media itself might therefore be thought of as teenaged, and certainly still young. At the time of writing, YouTube is 19 years old, Instagram is 14, Snapchat is 13, and TikTok is 8. That means social media has reached a certain level of maturity now and might, to borrow a Swiftie phrase, be in its *teen era*. So, what does this mean?

In the last decade we have witnessed some spectacular controversies relating to social media, and I am sure readers can name plenty of them. But I would say we've also developed a stronger sense of what to be afraid of, as we have now spent enough time with social media to know what's actually worth worrying about and what might not be, though some questions admittedly still remain unanswered. As boyd told us in 2014, "Many of the much-hyped concerns discussed because of technology are not new (for example, bullying) but rather may be misleading (for example, a decline in attention) or serve as distractions for real risks (for example, predators)."[48] The process boyd described here still happens today: we know now that there are risky and harmful elements of social media use, just as we have come to realize—or, at least, I hope we have—that there are heaps of good things. But what we are perhaps still not reconciling as a society is how these realities work together in terms of social media use: how it has become crystal clear that you can't always have one—the good or the bad, the pleasure or the pain—without the other.

Case Studies: The Worries and Realities of Social Media

This book explores four case studies, each of which presents empirical research from a set of qualitative internet research projects carried out between 2017 and 2022.[49] These projects grew somewhat organically from one another: when I headed to Microsoft Research New England for an internship in the Summer of 2017, I hoped that my digital methods research on the moderation of eating disorder content across three platforms (Instagram, Pinterest, and tumblr) would ignite other work in the youth culture space, which it did. In 2017, when I commenced my lectureship at the University of Sheffield, I worked with our Widening Participation team to promote our new undergraduate degree program to local high school pupils. This work gave me a rare opportunity to talk to teens about social media for hours on end, and it was in their company that I learned about anonymous apps: a genre that hadn't received much academic attention at the time, despite its chokehold on teens' digital lives. In 2018, I was fortunate enough to receive a British Academy Small Grant to conduct school-based workshops and interviews exploring teens' views about anonymous apps. The conversations that took place during the course of this research—especially the tangential ones—grew into a further study, and in 2022 I received pilot project funding from my department's Strategic Research Support Fund to explore English teens' views on digital photo editing.

In the end, I found myself with a collection of studies that focused on social media-based activities widely considered to be risky for young people. The 5Rights Foundation makes a crucial distinction between risk and harm, explaining that a "risk is a harm that has not yet happened," while a harm "is a risk that has been realised."[50] They then divide risks into four broad categories, known as the "4Cs":

1. *Content-based* risks occur when "a child or young person is exposed to harmful material."

2. *Contact-based* risks happen when "a child or young person participates in activity with a malign actor, often, but not always, an adult."

3. *Conduct-based* risks emerge when "a child or young person is involved in an exchange as either a perpetrator, victim, or sometimes both."

4. *Contract-based* risks, also known as commercial risks, focus on children or young people's exposure to "inappropriate commercial contractual relationships or pressures."[51]

While this book is not exclusively about risks and does not focus on younger children, it explores the issues that emerge (or are imagined to emerge) from young people's content, contact, and conduct across various social media platforms, excluding contract-based risks, as they fell outside of my research parameters.

The Kids Are Online carefully and calmly examines empirical evidence to add nuance to current and pressing debates around the risks facing young social media users by unpacking some of the myths and realities of their networked lives. I feel grateful that this work has allowed me to make real-world changes across the public and private sectors and to collaborate with wonderful individuals and organizations in pursuit of the shared goal of making the digital world a better place. In this book, I talk about some of the big debates currently cutting through corridors and the public domain, but the concerns I overhear and engage in are not necessarily echoed elsewhere. As Banaji argued in 2015, "While moral panics about children's addiction to screen media, or vulnerability to online predators are commonplace in the Western press and academia . . . the lives of children with little media access or representation are sparsely discussed and generally theorised uncritically with reference to an assumed (Western) media-saturated norm."[52]

While some of the harms experienced by the 9- to 17-year-olds in Banaji's India-based research share similarities with my findings—particularly with respect to bullying—I agree that it is crucial to avoid universalizing narratives about young people and media.[53] Indeed, "reading a universal relationship between children and ICTs from European and American studies results, at best, in a misrepresentation of global south lives and concerns."[54] For example, in their research on young people's uses of social media in a large Indian city, Sarwatay and Raman identify a "'chain-link' approach to problem solving and risk mitigation" within the multigenerational structure of many Indian families.[55] They found that older family members turned to younger ones "for technological understanding," while "emotional wisdom and civic awareness" flowed in the opposite direction.[56] This example reminds us that there is no singular, dominant adult or youth social media relationship, and yet recurrent narratives from the Global North would have us believe otherwise. Learning from Sarwatay, Raman, Banaji, and many other authors cited in this book, I advocate for the importance of precision and contextual sensitivity when making claims about platforms and society. The social concerns I discuss throughout this book are, to be clear, ones that came out of my own research as well as others'. This work included conversations with English teens, along with research on content posted in English on largely US-founded platforms. I do not wish to generalize from the experiences of young people growing up in England to those living their younger years elsewhere, though I hope the notion of platform paradoxes explored throughout this book may resonate with the realities of those I have not directly researched.

In chapter 1, I lay the book's theoretical foundations and explain how I arrived at the concept of a platform paradox. The chapter goes back in time to revisit academic theories on the relationship between older, pre-digital innovations and youth, assessing the enduring relevance of concepts like moral panics, media panics, and technopanics for understanding the case studies discussed in this book.[57] Chapter 1 historicizes societal responses to the emergence of new technologies, showing how young people, particularly in Western contexts, are "simultaneously hailed as [their] pioneers" and "feared for" as their "innocent victims"; the chapter asks what implications this has for their relationships with social media.[58] It then examines four key academic concepts that have shaped my understanding of the empirical data on which this book is based. While other studies on young people may be better understood through theories on, say, privacy or surveillance, stigma, secrecy, safety, and social comparison are the four that emerged most strikingly from my work. These four concepts have a rich history and the lessons we can learn from each can aid in our understanding of the present and futures of young, networked lives. Crucially, though, these concepts are not felt neatly by young people and sometimes facilitate paradoxical experiences. As my participants might put it: engaging with like-minded, stigmatized others can make me feel less alone while also exposing me to things that make me feel worse; asking for people to tell me their secrets through anonymous apps makes me feel excited while also exposing me to harm; embracing pseudonymity on social media can make me feel safe but also makes me worry about who those around me are; editing pictures of myself can bring me self-confidence while also making me feel bad about myself. The theoretical groundwork I lay in chapter 1 has helped me to contextualize young people's experiences appropriately, in ways that I hope respect the tensions and contradictions characterizing their digital lives.

Chapter 2 asks why young people turn to social media to engage with content about mental health and shows readers what restrictions they face when they do. Most, if not all social media companies have policies on the things people can and cannot do and say in relation to mental health. But these rules are sometimes broken, a reality that has led to widespread social concern that platforms aren't safe enough for young people to use. And there are ongoing, substantive debates about what those rules should and should not be. Chapter 2 therefore interrogates two (of the many) facets of the relationship between mental health and the rules underpinning social media use: (1) people's evasion of platforms' rules to talk about their mental health in the face of enduring social stigma in many places around the world and (2) the automated circulation of mental health–related content via recommendation systems, a process that threatens to undermine the rules platforms have in place to protect their most vulnerable users. The chapter outlines a number of paradoxes that emerge from these two examples. By seeking to minimize harm to their users by having and enforcing rules, platforms can harm those same users, as their rulebooks have the capacity to re-stigmatize particular identities and issues. Further, to exist as helpful spaces for those with mental health conditions, I ask whether social media platforms *have* to be harmful, or at the very least risky, because engaging with mental health–related content is itself a risky endeavor. The realities I outline in chapter 2 suggest we need to embrace paradoxes moving forwards as other modes of thinking and policing in this space—like patchwork technical moderation such as hashtag bans or seeking to prove a causal link between social media and mental health—can be too limiting.

Chapter 3 explores 16- to 18-year-olds' opinions about and experiences of anonymous apps. This genre of social media allows people to send messages to others without revealing information that might identify them, like their legal name. Anonymous apps are extremely popular among teens on a global scale, and while individual apps usually have a short shelf life, the genre has been enduringly popular for over a decade. However, the apps' popularity is accompanied by worries that they are dangerous for young people. While my research is based in England, given the apps' tremendous popularity across the globe, the findings I share in this book have resonance beyond this national context. News media have linked anonymous apps to harms like bullying and suicides, and each app seems to attract a number of high-profile petitions that ask app stores to take it down. But the reality is that anonymous apps play paradoxical roles in young, networked lives: to be pleasurable to teens, anonymous apps necessitate displeasures. Participation in anonymous apps is a notoriously risky endeavor, but it is only by experiencing the displeasures that accompany anonymous app use that users can hope to achieve some benefits. Anonymous apps are risky not only because the content might be harmful but also because teens never quite know if their participation is going to pay off.

In chapter 4, I explore 13- to 15-year-olds' opinions on and experiences of naming practices across social media platforms. Today's networked teens face a conundrum: though social media participation feels much safer when they can use a nickname, opportunities for identity concealment are said to be shrinking. In England and elsewhere, anonymity has become socially stigmatized following widespread concerns that people want to hide their identities for nefarious reasons.[59] Chapter 4 shows how identity concealment, like using a pseudonym, offers teens significant personal and social safety. Social safety is understood here to mean protection from the risks associated with embarrassing identity disclosures among a young person's peers, while personal safety echoes more traditional understandings of what safety means with respect to young people and includes protection from things like threats, grooming, identity theft, and catfishing. The reality is that identity concealment is paradoxical. A common theme across my interviews with teens and adults was that a key risk of online anonymity lies in what other people do—the groomers, the bullies, the catfishers—who present teens with personal safety concerns. Anonymity is therefore both a threat and a method of protection for today's teens, inevitably leading to complex perspectives on its social value. And a standout theme from my interviews with adults was an emphasis on the consequences of teens' social media engagement and how what they post online might affect other aspects of their lives. This has potentially created an opportunity for young people to face an extra level of surveillance from adults, who check in on their content to make sure it is palatable. Paradoxically, this enhances the draw of identity concealment, making nicknames all the more alluring.

Chapter 5 explores 17-year-olds' views on digital photo editing. By this, I am referring to the editing—not via pre-made filters—of images of the face and body via digital tools. The growth, ease of use, and affordability of digital photo editing has led to worries that it is "changing the way we see ourselves."[60] Such concerns are typically applied to teenage girls, in part because they engage in this practice more frequently than other genders.[61] Digital photo editing, we are told, is causing unrealistic expectations of adolescent bodies and is therefore harmful to teens' body images and overall well-being. But as I explain in chapter 5, research in this area produces inconclusive and at times competing findings. And crucial to note is that studies have thus far predominantly "focused on samples of young white women living in Western countries."[62] In my research, I confess I was surprised to find a large degree of acceptance of digital photo editing. The teens in my research inspired me to develop a typology of digital photo editing, which charts both the technical aspects of the editing process (the extent of change within an image) and invokes some moral categorizations according to how socially acceptable the type of editing is. My participants are highly aware of the popularity of digital photo editing and have developed sophisticated techniques for spotting it, contradicting research that claims they have not. They are skillful at compartmentalizing digital imagery from "real life" settings to maintain healthy perspectives on body image and beauty standards and are not, as I argue consistently throughout this book, nearly as vulnerable as is feared. These findings again combine to suggest paradoxical experiences of digital photo editing. My participants indicate that, in order to be helpful, digital photo editing must also be harmful. While light touch digital photo editing can be helpful because it enables you to hide your so-called flaws, masking those insecurities with editing tools makes them less visible to other teens; they thus uphold the same societal beauty standards and social comparisons which informed their insecurities to begin with.

I conclude *The Kids Are Online* by offering some pragmatic recommendations intended to be read by academics, policymakers across sectors, educators, parents and families, and anyone else with an interest in the relationship between young lives and social media. Some of the recommendations I list in chapter 6—like avoiding the use of *social media* as a catch-all term and hesitating to make claims of newness about social media—require more of a discursive shift than others and may be especially relevant for those who think, talk, or write about technology. Other suggestions I share—like working toward future-proofed e-safety lessons for schools or discouraging platforms (especially social apps) from integrating with services that do not meet the same safety criteria—err on the more pragmatic side and are useful for those working across sectors who deal with technology policymaking. Beyond making a set of recommendations, the final chapter of this book reflects on why it matters to move beyond "tiresome binary debates" about social media and young people, along with the importance of embracing paradoxes, however tricky this work may turn out to be.[63] Social media platforms are not either good or bad, helpful or harmful, or positive or negative for our young people, and I thank readers wholeheartedly for their attention throughout this book as I explain why.

1 *From Moral and Media Panics to Platform Paradoxes*

It is quite normal to fear technological development. Concerns about how media might affect, influence, or impact individuals or groups of people have greeted every new technology as far back as the printing press, and it is particularly common to ask these questions on behalf of children.[1] In a 1999 paper on media panics, Drotner argued that social anxieties about the release of new media formats are founded on an "intrinsic historical amnesia," in that each worry about a new technology tends to center on the same thing, including media addiction, the dumbing down of important issues in media content, the perpetuation of narrow body-image ideals, among other examples.[2] As Gruenberg explained in 1935, each invasion of a new cultural invention—the telephone, commercial radio, the automobile, the movie, tabloid newspapers, and even paperback books—finds adults feeling "unprepared, frightened, resentful, and helpless" on behalf of children.[3] These worries can take hold in academia, too. Take the media and eating disorders as an example: research in some academic disciplines from the 1990s and early 2000s asked if women's glossy gossip magazines were partly responsible for causing a rise in reported cases of eating disorders among young women;

we are now witnessing identical questions levelled at content posted to heavily visual social media platforms like Instagram.

Questions about media effects began to fall somewhat out of fashion in media and communications research in the late 1970s and into the 1980s, partly due to the rise of active audience theories. These thinkers moved academic conversations away from linear effects models to ask about the wealth of ways people engage with—and, crucially, resist and circumvent—media texts. Such research reoriented analyses of media toward representation and language.[4] Hall's 1973 encoding/decoding model, for example, emphasized the process by which meaning is encoded into a text and then decoded by an audience.[5] This model of communication tried to synthesize both media power (which produces ideology) and audience power (who resist or negotiate those meanings). Still, some effects-laden questions continue to greet new technological developments into the 2020s—be they about a new social app, a specific feature within a new or older app, or about social media writ large. While in a Western context we have mostly moved on from thinking television dumbs us down or video games cause violence, we've pivoted toward concerns that Instagram causes eating disorders, doomscrolling gives us depression, and that we're addicted to our smartphones, to name only a few of the social anxieties that come to my mind as I write this book.

Although many readers will recognize the concerns I describe here, others may not. As Banaji noted in 2017, there are plenty of parallels between the concerns listed above, which I write from my office in England, with others from around the world, like "infringement of privacy, illegal downloading, cyber-bullying, harassment and exclusion, particularly of girls."[6] However, this set of risks has become "detached, free-floating and *universalised* in literature," which does not acknowledge the many other risks—unimaginable to those reading about them "from the comfort of a digitally connected upper middle class living room"—to young people around the world.[7] In 2015, Nemer and Freeman made a similar argument about social panics around selfies: self-taken photographs, usually via a front-facing smartphone camera, which are often shared through digital communication channels like messaging apps and social media platforms.[8] Selfies were popularized in the mid-2010s due to the global saturation of camera phones (especially smartphones), the marketing and widespread adoption of the front-facing camera, and the growing popularity of photo-sharing apps.[9] Nemer and Freeman note that popular and academic interest in selfies tends to emphasize Western social concerns—for example, that they represent attention-seeking behaviors and imply the taker has self-esteem issues. But this focus misses the other ways people might use and understand selfies in other places around the world. For example, in Brazilian favelas, teens' selfies are not "a shallow way to show narcissism, fashion, and self-promotion and seek attention"; instead they are used to exercise free speech and talk about violence in their area, document their own lives, improve their literacy skills, and let their parents know they are safe.[10] Within this chapter and throughout, I therefore do not intend to suggest a universality to people's worries about social media use among young people (in other words, I don't claim that everyone worries about the same thing the world over). I instead position my research participants' words and experiences within specific geographic, cultural, and social contexts.

In this chapter, I explain how I hope you will come to the material I present, as well as how I hope we as a society will try to think about young people and communication technologies moving forwards. Rather than asking causation-oriented questions about how one may affect or impact the other, the aim of this book is to emphasize the *relationship* between young people and social media: an ethos I hope transcends my geographically situated context. While older frameworks have helped us to understand media and society relations—like moral panics and media panics, which I will discuss shortly—these concepts do not map neatly onto the objectives of this book. I therefore use this chapter to introduce the lens of *platform paradoxes:* an intervention that acknowledges how young people's individual uses and experiences of platforms can be characterized by simultaneous pleasures and harms. Paradoxes also emerge from societal rhetorics; young people are sometimes pushed into behaviors like identity concealment for their own safety, just as those same behaviors are framed in public discourse as harmful. I then introduce four key concepts— stigma, secrecy, safety, and social comparison—each of which has a rich, pre-digital history and aids in my understanding and re-telling of my young participants' relationships with social media.

Moral Panics (and Their Discontents)

Drotner's theory of a media panic, introduced above, can be understood as a subdivision of the older notion of a moral panic, coined by Cohen in the 1970s, first in his PhD thesis and later in a book called *Folk Devils and Moral Panics.* A moral panic is a feeling of fear experienced across a particular group or society, based on an exaggerated or false threat to the members of that group. The supposed "threat" comes from a behavior or cultural group that is deemed to deviate from societal norms. Cohen explained that moral panics occur in stages within societies, and perhaps the most widely cited definition of this process is as follows:

[A moral panic occurs when] a condition, episode, person or group of persons emerges to become defined as a threat to societal values and interests; its nature is presented in a stylized and stereotypical fashion by the mass media; the moral barricades are manned by editors, bishops, politicians and other right-thinking people; socially accredited experts pronounce their diagnoses and solutions; ways of coping are evolved or (more often) resorted to; the condition then disappears, submerges or deteriorates and becomes more visible.[11]

Moral panics tend to converge around a fear of—or on behalf of—The Other, by which I mean social groups that do not constitute the "main powerholders."[12] For Cohen, this focus on The Other comes from concerns that such groups might become "aggressive or be otherwise harmed" by the object of the panic narrative.[13] As Baym notes, the emergence of new technologies often "stir[s] up fears of moral decline" in the Western press, and such discourses tend to focus on protecting "the well-being of children, and especially on the well-being of teenage girls."[14] And yet, as Orben argues, those reporting on or otherwise perpetuating panics about such groups are "interestingly immune" from the consequences of the supposed threat at hand.[15] Where young people are concerned, panics give greater weight to the powers of technologies over their human users, which may be called a *technologically deterministic* approach. Baym explains that technological determinism "positions people as powerless to stop these changes unless they invent new, better, or different technologies or eschew technologies altogether."[16]

Moral panic theory remains highly influential for the study of media and society and has, as McRobbie, Thornton, and Hunt noted in the 1990s, become so far-reaching that it is now quite ironically used as a phrase by the media themselves.[17] Since the mid-1980s, many journalists felt sufficiently comfortable with the term to use it "almost pejoratively" within their writing, casually referring to "the inevitable media moral panic" or "the media-saturated space marked 'moral panic.'"[18] In *Policing the Crisis: Mugging, the State and Law and Order*, published in 1978, Hall et al. argued that moral panics function as a form of social control.[19] They studied the phenomenon of "mugging," unpacking crime statistics to show how the threat of mugging—the act of attacking and then stealing something from someone in public—was over-blown by British news media outlets and those they quoted, like members of the police force and politicians. Hall et al. examined crime statistics relating to mugging and could not find a causal link between the rise in societal panic around mugging (as seen, for example, in news coverage) and actual incidence rates. They there-fore concluded that, by "raising the wrong things into sensational focus," the moral panic around mugging hid and mystified "the deeper cause" of social instability in Britain: issues around eco-nomic uncertainty along with social anxieties relating to race, crime, and youth.[20] British citizens were ultimately persuaded to view mugging as a genuine crisis and to accept the need to deal with the supposed "threat." For Hall et al., moral panics functioned as a means of enforcing social control, which was a different lens from that through which Cohen initially conceptualized them.

While moral panic theory has been invaluable for many seeking to understand the relations between media and society in the twen-tieth century, I agree with scholars like Hunt that writers "need to be more rigorous" in our continued use of the term.[21] I share con-cerns that the phrase has become so far-reaching that it has become a method for dismissing social concerns rather than commanding a deep critique of and intervention into them.[22] While genuine moral panics about young people and social media continue to exist, it is worth remembering that not every worry about them should be described as a moral panic. In their 2012 article, Buckingham and Jensen outlined some arguments toward retiring the phrase entirely, a move I am not entirely convinced by but respect nonetheless. The authors explained that, according to its original definition, moral panics intrinsically involve a form of displacement; social panics are actually about something else.[23] Drotner made a similar argument in a 1999 paper, arguing that worries about the computer, games, and the internet serve as "mental metaphors for discussing and debating wider social concerns."[24] In other words, where children and young people are concerned, panics about new media are actually fears about, say, loss of childhood innocence or adults' inabilities to sufficiently monitor their behavior.[25] But this defining factor of a moral panic "preclude[s] the possibility that people might actually be quite sincere."[26] People "might genuinely be concerned about what they say they are concerned about"; it may not be the case that they are using new inventions to mask their worries about something else.[27]

The term *panic* implies hysteria or a disproportionate reaction to something. To borrow from Hall et al., "when the official reaction to a person, groups of persons, or series of events is out of all proportion to the actual threat offered," we would call this a moral panic.[28] But I wonder, can researchers accurately measure the proportionality of the fears and lived realities of all social phenomena?[29] And further, aren't we justified in being worried about certain things (like, say, how private companies are setting their own parameters of participation in social media)? I worry that, in framing some or all of my case studies—mental health and social media, online anonymity and safety, digital photo editing and body image—as moral panics, the book would be read as a dismissal of legitimate concerns about social media and young people. I am fully aware (and heavily critical) of some recurrent narratives about the link between society and technology, particularly within the British news media, and do not deny the existence of what might be described as proper moral panics. But I have also been guilty of over-using the phrase in the past. Over time, I have grown far less comfortable labeling something as a moral panic and so I do not equate all instances of deterministic framing in, say, journalistic practice—asking how x impacts y—with a genuine moral panic in the way Cohen, Hall et al., Goode and Ben-Yehuda, and other authors have described.[30] My reluctance to use this phrase to describe certain discourses about young people and social media stems from a desire to instead embrace the tensions, contradictions, nuances, and paradoxes in how these technologies are actually experienced; I take seriously social worries while also embracing lessons learned to avoid a fetishization of their supposed "newness."

In 2012, Buckingham and Jensen asked, "Where do we draw the line between a proportionate, objective response and an irrational panic?"[31] This is a crucial question for me and one that I continue to struggle with in my work. While genuine moral panics do exist, and we can of course spot the evocation of "certain kinds of language" in discourses about new technologies, I would hesitate to label my case studies as such.[32] The complex picture I paint of each phenomenon throughout this book tells us that worries about these matters are sometimes warranted but are not necessarily panics.

Toward Platform Paradoxes

Buckingham and Jensen closed their 2012 article by confessing to having differing opinions on whether the phrase 'moral panic' should be retired, and I am equally uncertain. This is partly because we have seen some newer interpretations on the theory. Marwick, for example, updated the notions of media and moral panics by describing a "'technopanic," which for her was similar to a media panic but distinct in its focus on "computer-mediated technologies" and in its pathologization of young people's uses of these technologies.[33] Is there, I wonder, something unique about social media that warrants an extension or reconceptualization of moral panic theory? One of the many things I have learned from early internet researchers like Nancy Baym over the years has been to think twice before I call something "new," because most things in networked media have an analogue predecessor. You could probably unpack each supposedly new anxiety about social media and find an analogue antecedent, which means an exhaustive definition of a social media–specific sub-division of moral panic theory—a *platform panic*, perhaps—would probably be difficult to achieve.

Through this book, I therefore propose a conceptual shift toward *platform paradoxes*. Taking this approach means recognizing that people's uses and experiences of platforms can be positive while acknowledging the harms they often simultaneously enact. As Mick and Fournier explained in 1998, such an approach rejects either-or outcomes of technological use—"desirable vs. undesirable, anticipated vs. unanticipated, direct vs. indirect"—as "these categories are overly broad and do not adequately reflect the specific content and pressures of the cultural contradictions of technology."[34] A paradox is understood in this book to mean "the idea that polar opposite conditions can simultaneously exist, or at least can be potentiated, in the same thing," though the concept of paradoxes has, of course, been discussed in different ways over the years.[35] For young people specifically, it is sometimes only by accepting and facing risks on social media platforms that they can reap pleasures and rewards. To phrase this as my research participants might: I can feel connected to my peers through anonymous apps while also being bullied by them; editing pictures of myself can bring me self-confidence while also making me feel bad about myself; posting content that includes mental health–related hashtags can make me feel like I'm not alone, even though it means I will be shown recommended content that makes me feel worse. Truly paying attention to platform paradoxes means acknowledging how specific uses and experiences of social media can be *both* good and bad, not strictly either/or. The approach therefore demands a move away from binary ways of thinking as the benefits and harms of platforms will rarely, if ever, be equally weighted and one may not be experienced independently of the other. As Mick and Fournier put it, "When something is paradoxical, the saliences of the antithetical conditions are likely to constantly shift, probably due to situational factors, evoking the sensation of a teeter-totter, bobbing up and down between contrary feelings or opinions."[36]

I am not the first person to talk about the paradoxical nature of social media. Lots of this research, like my own, focuses on those with stigmatized identities or those who belong to marginalized social groups. For example, Haimson et al. interviewed 28 social media users who had recently experienced major life transitions.[37] The authors identified an "online authenticity paradox" in that the people in their study strived to achieve online authenticity and yet, "because doing so requires sharing negative experiences on social media," authenticity was only possible to them "at great personal cost."[38] Similarly, Yeshua-Katz and Martins conducted 33 interviews with bloggers from seven different countries, who blog about their experiences of living with anorexia.[39] While the sites they maintain are self-described as places for "anas" to receive support and share creative content like poems and song lyrics, they are also spaces for providing "specific instruction for initiating and maintaining anorexia nervosa," which explains why such spaces are publicly vilified (despite their deep complexity).[40] The authors' main finding was that, paradoxically, "blogging about anorexia serves to both alleviate *and* trigger anxiety about living with this stigmatized illness."[41]

In a different study, Yeshua-Katz and Hård af Segerstad researched boundary work among stigmatized communities online, interviewing 66 members and administrators from the following four groups: pro-ana blogs, an infertility discussion board, a Facebook group for bereaved parents, and two WhatsApp groups for war veterans with post-traumatic stress disorder.[42] The authors found that, "to offer safe and functioning environments of support, the communities must guard against impostors whose presence threatens their safe havens."[43] Paradoxically, however, the protective restrictions such groups impose may make them "inaccessible to those who truly need support and remove such groups from the public eye."[44]

In my research with young people, I have found plenty of paradoxical experiences like those described above. Building on this work, I offer an additional interpretation of the paradoxical nature of social media for today's young people. In thinking about platforms—understood as the non-neutral curators of our digital sociality—as and through paradoxes, I emphasize how rules and policies are inseparable from young people's experiences of social media. In this context, rules emerge via their enforcement, which is omnipresent and famously problematic. Alongside these rules, widespread social perceptions (not always panics, sometimes just perceptions) form about the benefits and consequences of those interventions, as do debates about what those rules should and should not be. I am also attentive to young people's knowledge of how their digital behaviors are perceived. They are acutely aware of what other people, usually adults, think they should and should not be doing on and with social media.

A platform paradox also considers how concerns about young people's safety can push them into activities that are themselves the objects of fear. Take the content of chapter 2 as an example: here, I note how some platforms are considered to be dangerous because of the presence of "harmful" content, like visual depictions of acts of self-harm. These fears have given rise to debates about what measures should be taken to address such activities, and by which groups. But the participants in my research (and in many others') tell me it is difficult to talk about mental health with people they know in face-to-face settings, and so they want to turn to social media to find support and like-minded individuals. Paradoxically, to exist as helpful spaces for those with mental health conditions, perhaps social media platforms have to be harmful, or at the very least risky, because engaging with mental health-related content is itself a risky endeavor.

Stigma, Secrecy, Safety, and Social Comparison: Conceptual Frameworks

Underpinning the notion of a platform paradox are several concepts, each with its own rich, pre-digital history. These concepts—stigma, secrecy, safety, and social comparison—emerged through the empirical research on which this book is based, sometimes intersecting and sometimes independently of each other. They have been pivotal in helping me to make sense of young people's digital lives, and understanding why their experiences are what they are. These four concepts are also tied up with the paradoxical experiences I discuss throughout this book—for example, when platforms help young people to evade stigma but are also stigmatizing. The concepts I explore here and throughout help us connect contemporary, acute debates to age-old concerns in academic fields like media and communication and sociology. In my geographical context, I hear concerns about the effects of, say, recommendation systems on our abilities to be informed citizens or that they lure us down a rabbit hole toward ill mental health or radicalization. I also hear worries about how digital photo editing might cause young people, particularly teenage girls, to develop unhealthy and unrealistic relationships with their bodies. This book is partly dedicated to asking what lessons we may learn from the past to approach these new technologies with the critical eye they and their users deserve. As Livingstone and Das put it, just because the way people engage with media and with each other via media has changed, "this does not mean that the conceptual repertoire best able to analyze them must be entirely new."[45]

The remainder of this chapter therefore privileges the historical treatment of current debates, locating topics like body image and platform technologies, or mental health and recommendation algorithms in a broader history of societal hope, euphoria, hype, anxiety, and panic around media and technologies. It is a happy accident that the four theoretical concepts underpinning this book—stigma, secrecy, safety, and social comparison—each starts with the letter *s*. While each is explored and critiqued at great length within my empirically based chapters (2 through 5), I write a short summary of them below, explaining how they apply to the cases I discuss in this book. These four concepts are deeply interwoven and are fundamental for working toward a more nuanced understanding of young, networked lives.

Stigma

The Kids Are Online partly deals with aspects of people's identities that are socially stigmatized. *Stigma* is a Greek word originally used to refer to a marking imprinted into people's skin, but it has taken on a different meaning over time.[46] Nowadays, not all stigmas can be seen; some come to be learned through social interaction. A stigma, Goffman explains, occurs when somebody possesses an attribute that makes them "different from others in the category of persons available for . . . [them] to be."[47] Stigmas are not inherent attributes and are instead learned through time and differ contextually; for example, levels of mental health stigma vary geographically, as I explain in chapter 2. Although "an attribute that stigmatizes one type of possessor can confirm the usualness of another," there are of course attributes "that almost everywhere in our society are discrediting."[48] Stigmatization therefore occurs when "an individual who might have been received easily in ordinary social intercourse possesses a trait that can obtrude itself upon attention and turn those of us whom he meets away from him, breaking the claim that his other attributes have on us. He possesses a stigma, an undesired differentness from what we had anticipated."[49]

According to Goffman, there are three types of stigma: first, "abominations of the body" (physical things that you can see); second, "blemishes of individual character" (things you do and feel); and third, "tribal stigma of race, nation, and religion."[50] The main consequence for those with a stigma, in their mind, is that they are reduced from being "a whole and usual person to a tainted, discounted one."[51] This means those with stigmatized identities do not feel wholly comfortable or welcome in certain places, and that's where social media comes in.

Because you can engage in identity play on some social media platforms, they can offer people places to escape stigma or help them find "like-others" to talk about their shared experiences.[52] Goffman's theory of "back places", which far pre-dates the internet and social media, can help us to understand this. Back places are "where persons of the individual's kind stand exposed and find they need not try to conceal their stigma, nor be overly concerned with cooperatively trying to disattend it."[53] Goffman makes a crucial distinction between two routes into back places: in some cases, people choose the company of those with the same or similar stigmas (for example, when you join a certain sub on Reddit). Back places can be positive spaces for those experiencing stigma, since in them "the individual will be able to be at ease" among those who are like them.[54] However, they "also run the risk of being easily discredited should a normal person known from elsewhere enter the place," which is precisely why certain functions within platforms— like the ability to create multiple accounts or use a platform pseudonymously—have so much social value.[55]

In other cases, people may find themselves involuntarily in a back place—for example, when such a place is "created as a result of individuals being herded together administratively against their will on the basis of a common stigma."[56] While Goffman wasn't writing about social media in his work, we might consider recommendation systems as examples of this "herding together."

Recommendation systems, which use data mining tools to collect information about their users to predict what else they might want to see, are an effective way for social media platforms to deal with the huge amounts of content they hold.[57] I expand on this concept much more in chapter 2, but this effectively means social media users are presumed to have certain identities based on their data trails, which means they are *herded together* and shown content from other users they are presumed to be similar to.

The stigmatized attributes I explore in this book aren't strictly things that place a person in a minority or necessarily marginalize them. Some do, of course, but when you are a young person—especially an adolescent—research tells us that questions about identity loom large in your life. This means much of adolescence is dedicated to figuring out which of the attributes you possess are stigmatized and to seeking out spaces where you can ask questions or be with people you feel are similar to you. While there have always been places in societies where stigmatized people feel safe, it is worth updating (and critiquing) Goffman's work to gauge its enduring relevance to digital societies. In this book, I explore Goffman's concept of stigma through discussions of the following: the creation of pseudonymous accounts dedicated to talking about mental health and other topics (chapters 2 and 4), practices of careful identity concealment among stigmatized individuals in forbidden places (chapter 2), and the risks and rewards of using anonymous apps to ask tricky identity-related questions (chapter 3).

Secrecy

As Young and Quan-Haase note, "by their very nature and design," social media platforms "encourage users to disclose substantial

amounts of personal information," and so it should come as no surprise that they are often used by young people for secret-sharing,
the consumption of secretive information, or for exploring secretive aspects of the self.[58] In 1977, Watson and Valtin defined a secret
as "knowledge which is intentionally concealed but which may be
shared with a restricted audience," and this book partly focuses on
two aspects of secrecy in young, digital lives.[59] It explores the secret
things young people do and say via social media and the secretive
things that are done *to* them in terms of, say, the hidden technical
functions that shape their digital experiences.

Readers may be wondering why I foreground secrecy in this
book more so than privacy, a similar concept that is widely taken
up by digital media researchers. There is a wealth of evidence telling us that young people take great care to negotiate their privacy
in digital spaces, contrary to popular rhetoric (largely expressed in
Western societies) that they don't care about their privacy. In a
2007 *New York Magazine* article, Emily Nussbaum labeled young
people as the "Say Everything" generation because they seemed to
be redefining privacy through their openness to sharing their lives
on sites like Myspace and LiveJournal.[60] Three years later, Meta
founder and CEO Mark Zuckerberg claimed during an award cer-
emony speech that privacy is no longer a "social norm," a view that
no doubt had an economic imperative (more sharing = more
money) but that certainly echoed a sentiment expressed in the
mid-to-late 2000s by many.[61] While it has clearly been important
to understand privacy-seeking behaviors in the face of such rhetorics, secrecy gets comparatively scarce attention in digital media
research. Indeed, secrecy emerged across all projects on which this
book is based, and far more so than privacy.

In 1977, Warren and Laslett made a conceptual distinction between privacy and secrecy which, in my view, still holds true today. They explained that secrecy "implies the concealment of something which is negatively valued by the excluded audience and, in some instances, by the perpetrator as well."[62] This means secrecy is "not only a strategy for hiding acts or attributes which others hold in moral disrepute, but it is also a means to escape being stigmatized for them."[63] Privacy and secrecy are differentiated "by the moral dimension of the behaviors to which they refer."[64] In Simmel's words, having a secret infers "moral badness," whereas privacy-seeking behaviors protect aspects of your life that are understood to be more morally neutral (think, for example, of a private conversation you have with nurses and doctors in medical settings or your expectation that conversations with a bank worker about your finances will remain private).[65] This means the justification to keep a secret is "less an independent ideological one than a response to ideology: a desire to avert the full wrath of whatever powerful groups are in control of the definition of 'undesirable elements.'"[66] Secrecy, as Finkenauer et al. explain, is "commonly associated with 'having something to hide': something shameful, furtive, or bad."[67] Whereas privacy "protects behavior which is either morally neutral or valued by society as well as by the perpetrators."[68]

The concept of secrecy emerges through *The Kids Are Online* in several ways. The book shows how young people create secret social media accounts dedicated to exploring their mental health—but also the secret platform processes that capitalize on their vulnerable identities by showing them potentially harmful content via recommendation algorithms (chapter 2). This book also explores how young people share secret thoughts about their peers and themselves through anonymous apps and how they grapple with the realities of knowing their own secrets may be revealed (chapter 3). It asks how and why young people explore secret parts of their identities in networked spaces where they can go un-named, simultaneously juggling both risks and rewards (chapter 4). And finally, this book examines the secretive practice of editing self-images before they are posted to social media (chapter 5).

Safety

In this book—particularly in chapter 4—I conceptualize young people's efforts to ensure their safety on social media: I explore their *personal safety*, which echoes more traditional understandings of what safety means for them and includes protection from things like threats, grooming, identity theft, and catfishing. And I also discuss their *social safety* concerns, which are understood here to mean protection from the risks associated with embarrassing identity disclosures among a young person's peers. Today's young people achieve safety on social media in various ways, one of which is through identity concealment: the practice of hiding certain things about themselves—like their legal name, age, school, and so on—to keep certain people from figuring out who they are. Through my research, I identified a range of concerns young people have about their safety, from unknown pedophiles and groomers coming to find them at school to seemingly more mundane (yet still important) worries about their peers finding out about an embarrassing hobby. Livingstone and Third explain that, while many social media platforms operate on a near-global scale, the environments accessible to my young participants "are heavily shaped by differences in language, geography, culture and power—as defined by the state, commerce or, most locally, family and community."[69] This means young people's worries about their safety are contextual, and they play out most vividly in terms of age and gender among those in my research.

Some of these behaviors—particularly those intended to ensure social safety—have also been understood through the lens of "privacy." For example, in 2010, Raynes-Goldie explained that Facebook users in their twenties often engage in "subversive practices" to protect their privacy online.[70] Some people used aliases instead of their real names, some managed multiple accounts on the platform, and others deleted posts and removed image tags.[71] While my younger participants still engage in behaviors that mirror the behaviors of Raynes-Goldie's participants, I would no longer describe these tactics as subversive. Using a pseudonym, maintaining multiple accounts on a platform, and curating your social media presence to limit unwanted associations are, in the mid-2020s, commonplace and perhaps even default behaviors. But my participants also take actions like these to be protected from the harms they fear may befall them.

There are various academic definitions of privacy, to the point where it has become somewhat of a cliché to say its definition is tough to pin down. In 1967, Westin defined privacy as "the claim of individuals, groups or institutions to determine for themselves when, how, and to what extent information about them is communicated to others."[72] In 1983, Parent argued that "a person's privacy is diminished exactly to the degree" that others possess "undocumented personal knowledge" about them.[73] In these well-cited pre-internet definitions of privacy, we can see a clear focus on a person's agency and control over information about themselves.

Later, in 2017, Trepte et al. defined privacy as "a process of boundary management and the strategies used by individuals to regulate access to the self."[74] This definition, written in relation to social media, nods to the intricate things people do to obtain such control. This means there are some clear overlaps between personal and social safety and privacy—most crucially, that privacy protection behaviors like those described by Raynes-Goldie (and mirrored by my participants) can *enable* both personal and social safety.

While privacy evidently plays into young, networked lives, I foreground the concept of "safety" in this book because it forces us to understand the end goal of my participants' behavior, which is often to evade what might be described as "real world" dangers or to escape embarrassing encounters with their peers. We need to understand why young people do what they do and where their concerns about their own and each other's safety come from. Safety is understood differently by different influences—their educators, parents and families, peers, among others—in their lives. In the minds of parents and carers, for example, "protection tends to trump participation,"[75] meaning young people in risk-averse cultures have "'inherited a popular discourse that is characterized primarily by fear,'" potentially minimizing their abilities to "'imagine and articulate the opportunities digital media affords them.'"[76] For my participants, the behaviors that are imagined by their parents and educators to ensure their safety are the very same ones they crave for their own protection: a paradoxical issue I describe in depth in chapter 4. Safety fears also, of course, differ dramatically between contexts. I therefore provide lots of information throughout this book about who my participants are to help readers understand where their fears come from.

Social Comparison

Part of everyday life for people of all ages involves comparing ourselves—our physical appearances, sure, but also our lifestyles and other parts of our identities—to other people's. It is feared that social media platforms make this process worse, as they "enable the making of frequent, multiple, and rapid comparisons 24/7 at any time of a user's choosing."[77] While social comparisons of course existed long before the internet did, the story goes that the availability of information about other people's lives facilitates a greater volume of comparisons, fundamentally making us feel worse about ourselves. Further, "unlike traditional media, social media provide the opportunity for comparisons with similar others, i.e., peers, who are particularly relevant comparison targets."[78] Concerns like these, especially when articulated by academics, tend to be influenced by Festinger's theory of social comparison, which considers how people's self-evaluations partly rest on comparisons to other people.[79] Festinger outlines two forms of social comparison: *upward comparisons* where people compare themselves to others they view as superior to them in some way, which motivates them to achieve similar results, and *downward comparisons* in which, for a person to feel better about themselves, they compare themselves to those they consider to be worse off. In chapter 5, Festinger's theory of social comparison underpins an analysis of teens' views on, and experiences of, digital photo editing. This term is defined here and throughout as the editing—not via pre-made filters—of images of the face and body, which are usually then posted to image-centric social media platforms.

Chapter 5 outlines several manifestations of social comparison, including a divergence between teens' comparisons of themselves to their peers (who they see in face-to-face settings) and of themselves to celebrities and influencers (who they view exclusively via screens). I noticed that teens found it difficult to compare their bodies to those of celebrities and influencers, in part because they assumed these images were highly edited (in a way that distorts the face and body beyond what could reasonably be considered realistic). But digital photo editing profoundly alters the process of social comparison, as what I call "transformational" editing in chapter 5 involves editing a photo to the point where an aspect of a person becomes borderline unrecognizable, leading people to compare themselves to images that are not real. Festinger explained that people are less likely to compare themselves to those with abilities "too far" from their own, from "either above or below."[80] This has an extent of applicability to the teens in my research, who recognized that celebrities and influencers were not, in their words, "real," as their self-images were perceived as likelier to be edited than their peers' images were and that their appearance may have been modified via cosmetic surgery. While all of my research participants in some way compared themselves to others when we spoke, the research underpinning chapter 5 is less concerned with such comparisons ("upwards," "downwards," and their so-called effects on a person) and is more focused on what those comparisons are; where they come from; what they tell us about things like gender, race, and beauty; and what they tell us about modern teenage life.

I now move to the first of my four case study chapters, on moderating the mental health crisis.

2 Moderating the Mental Health Crisis

Molly Russell was a 14-year-old White English girl who lived what her dad called a "future-looking" and "ordinary" life.[1] She was a keen horse rider in her younger years and juggled teenage pursuits like homework, the leading role in an upcoming school play, and relationships with friends and family.[2] Her dad described her as "someone full of love and hope and happiness, a young person full of promise and opportunity and potential."[3] But in a devastating turn of events, Molly died from an act of self-harm in 2017, following a period of becoming "more withdrawn" in the final year of her life.[4] After Molly passed, her dad gained access to her social media accounts. What he discovered triggered a wave of changes at some of the world's most powerful tech companies: not only had Molly sought out and saved thousands of posts about suicide and self-harm, her favorite platforms were sending her personalized recommendations for them.[5] Molly's dad accused social media giants of "helping to kill" his 14-year-old daughter.[6] Like many people her age, Molly was an avid social media user and her story is one of many to trigger fierce public debate about the extent of responsibility tech companies should have for their young users' well-being.

Research paints a complex picture of the link between social media and young people's mental health, as scholars across different disciplines—and sometimes those within the same discipline—are not in consensus. Some, for example, don't frame this as a relationship and instead try to demonstrate causation, asking how x unilaterally affects y. This approach is then critiqued by researchers like myself, who take different epistemological approaches and try to show how tricky it is to isolate social media as a causal factor in a person's declining mental health. While social media may be part of the equation for many young people who are struggling, it must be situated alongside other contextual factors that shape their lives:

The onset and development of mental disorders, such as anxiety and depression, are driven by a complex set of genetic and environmental factors. Suicide rates among people in most age groups have been increasing steadily for the past 20 years in the United States. Researchers cite access to guns, exposure to violence, structural discrimination and racism, sexism and sexual abuse, the opioid epidemic, economic hardship and social isolation as leading contributors.[7]

Büchi and Hargittai similarly explain that "people's unequal societal positions" are woven into their relationships with social media, by which they mean the "systematic differences between individuals of different socioeconomic backgrounds concerning their access to, skills in, uses of and outcomes derived from engagement with digital media."[8] The authors say this unevenness makes it unwise to generalize across populations, and yet we so often see this in blanket claims about social media's so-called effects on young people's mental health. Put differently, no two people will experience the same impacts on their mental health from social media use. But the diversities of young people's experiences and identities make it tricky for social media companies—especially those with near-global penetration—to decide which kinds of content they should and should not allow.

Most, if not all, social media companies have rules about what their users can do and say in relation to mental health. These rules are usually outlined in a platform's community guidelines: public-facing documents written in "plainspoken" language and intended to be read by users.[9] But these rules are sometimes broken, a reality that has led to widespread social concerns that platforms aren't safe enough for young people to use. And there are ongoing, substantive debates about what the rules should and should not be. This process is called *social media content moderation*, defined here and throughout as "the detection of, assessment of, and interventions taken on content or behaviour deemed unacceptable by platforms or other information intermediaries, including the rules they impose, the human labour and technologies required, and the institutional mechanisms of adjudication, enforcement, and appeal that support it."[10]

In response to heightened public pressure following tragedies like Molly's, social media companies often implement new content moderation policies. In an article titled "How a British Teen's Death Changed Social Media," *WIRED* reporter Meaker lists some of the changes prompted by Molly's case.[11] Pinterest, for example, switched off personalized recommendation emails—like the ones Molly received, which depicted "Depression Pins" she "may like"—for its underage users.[12] In 2019, Instagram changed its guidelines to prohibit graphic images of self-harm, which it later extended to drawings. Instagram also began to place sensitivity screens over posts that do not break its rules but that might be triggering to some users or that are otherwise difficult for people to see.[13] The screens blur visual posts and mark them as "sensitive," giving users the chance to either scroll past or click to view them. As Milosevic explains, it simply isn't good business to run a platform riddled with harmful content.[14] And so what matters to companies in terms of their business success is "the performative act of demonstrating to the public" that it cares about—and is "actively taking measures against"—a range of online harms, which explains why policy updates often follow public pressures.[15] But there is not, and will never be, clear consensus on what counts as a "harmful" form of content, and so tech companies are often accused of making the wrong choices.

For the past few years, I have researched, publicly commented on and even been involved in some controversial choices. This is partly because I sit on Meta's Suicide and Self-Injury (SSI) Advisory Board—an unpaid role that I have held for several years. We meet quarterly and our job is to advise Meta, predominantly the Facebook and Instagram platforms, on how to handle certain kinds of content relating to suicide, self-harm, and eating disorders. The board is made up of people from lots of different backgrounds (like academics, healthcare workers, and representatives from third-sector organizations) who live and work in different parts of the world, and I have learned so much from these meetings. I don't contribute to all the discussions, especially those where I don't have research-informed expertise. For example, I would not advise on the actions Facebook should take if, say, a person posted their own suicide note to their account. We are often asked to give our views on scenarios and presented with several options from which to choose, though some questions are more open-ended than others. One of the most contentious decisions I've been involved in was the moderation of healed self-harm scars in 2019.

Following the death of Molly Russell, one of Instagram's reactive content policies included placing sensitivity screens over images of healed self-harm scars, a decision that triggered conversations through hashtags like #YouCantCensorMySkin.[16] This action continues to be controversial and I'm still not sure it was the right call, but what would've been the right one? There are many outcomes of content moderation for social media users, of which a sensitivity screen is one.[17] So how should Instagram moderate an image of a healed self-harm scar?

1. Do nothing.
2. Send resources to the user who posted the image (for example, links to local charities).
3. Blur out the post using a sensitivity screen.
4. Remove the post entirely.
5. Reduce the circulation of the post and/or the visibility of the user who shared it.
6. Suspend the user's account.
7. Something else.

These are real world questions platforms like Instagram are grappling with, and they are connected to larger debates about deciding what counts as harmful content and in whose interests these classifications are made. While one person's self-expressions may function as therapeutic for them, they may be felt as harmful by others. The list above is not the one I was presented with during an SSI Advisory Board meeting, but it hopefully gives readers a sense of the range of options available and depth of conversation that followed among board members.

This chapter asks why young people turn to social media to engage with content about mental health and shows readers how platforms react when they do—reactions that cover the range of options listed above, from (1) do nothing to (6) suspend the user's account. I therefore begin this chapter by contextualizing current debates about the link between social media and mental health within a broader sociology of stigma: the meaning and experience of difference between members of a society. I then tell readers how and why people try to evade content moderation mechanisms like those described above to talk about their mental health. But the policies and their enforcement aren't the only issues I address in this chapter: I also lay out a sort of tug of war currently taking place between content moderation and platforms' governance of their own recommendation systems. Put differently, this chapter shows how social media platforms often work against themselves by recommending the very same content they purport to ban, which is precisely what happened to Molly Russell. Her Instagram Feed was packed full of posts about suicide and self-harm, and she received automated emails from Pinterest recommending her an image of a slashed thigh and a cartoon of a young girl hanging.[18]

I used digital methods to gather empirical data for the research underpinning some aspects of this chapter and therefore cannot claim with certainty that my participants were "young" in a strictly age-based sense. As Livingstone et al. note, "on the Internet no one knows who is an adult and who is a child, and SNSs rely heavily on users' professed ages or dates of birth."[19] However, the phenomena I discuss in this chapter are associated with *youthfulness*. I measure youthfulness here by the kinds of memes that are posted, by a post's aesthetics—in particular, when it demonstrates deep knowledge of internet trends and cultures—and by the demographics of the platforms I researched (which skewed young at the time of data collection). Today's young people find themselves at the center of fierce public debates about content moderation, and this chapter offers a step toward a greater understanding of—and potential intervention into—moderation in relation to mental health. It broadly argues that social media is neither straightforwardly good nor straightforwardly bad for our mental health. Taking a platform paradox approach to this relationship means recognizing that social media can be at once helpful *and* harmful to an individual and that it can be tricky, perhaps even impossible, to disentangle these experiences.

Stigma and Solace on Social Media

Mental health conditions have long and complex histories of being stigmatized in different ways, across different societies. Attitudes toward mental health differ dramatically across the globe, and different conditions face differing levels of stigma. In 2022, the World Health Organization (WHO) reported that "one of the biggest barriers to demand for mental health care is the stigma associated with mental health conditions."[20] And while levels of mental health stigma are high in all countries, they may be higher in many low- and middle-income countries, "which [can] lead to underreporting."[21] For many people, social media platforms are demonstrably positive spaces in which to have conversations and learn about mental health.[22] As far back as 2009, just as SNSs were taking off around the world, researchers in Taiwan spoke of the benefits of the internet for adolescents experiencing depression to "establish new relationships, find people who care about them and express feelings that they cannot express otherwise (or are even forbidden to express)."[23] The authors reminded readers that the adolescents in their study were situated in a Taiwanese context wherein little was known about depression at the time of writing. And while perceptions may have changed in some places around the world since 2009, others have not.

Stigma is a Greek word originally used to refer to a marking imprinted into people's skin, but it has taken on a different meaning over time.[24] Nowadays, not all stigmas can be seen but come to be learned through social interaction. A stigma, Goffman explains, occurs when somebody possesses an attribute that makes them "different from others in the category of persons available for . . . [them] to be."[25] A stigma is therefore not an inherent attribute and is instead the experience and meaning of difference. This means stigmatization occurs when "an individual who might have been received easily in ordinary social intercourse possesses a trait that can obtrude itself upon attention and turn those of us whom he meets away from him, breaking the claim that his other attributes have on us. He possesses a stigma, an undesired differentness from what we had anticipated."[26] According to Goffman, there are three types of stigma, one of which is "blemishes of individual character . . . inferred from a known record of, for example . . . mental disorder."[27] While it is beyond the scope of this chapter to fully explain why mental health conditions are stigmatized, I will share some standout historical explanations.

In some societies, mental health stigma is linked to the belief that those with such conditions are "victims of witchcraft" and thought to be contagious.[28] From the Middle Ages all the way through to the seventeenth century, the role of the Devil in what used to be called "mental disorder" was firmly entrenched in the Christian world.[29] Ill mental health has also historically been linked to criminality, like in ancient Roman times, when those deemed "mentally ill" were given a custodian who was responsible for their "control, safety, and well-being," and laws prevented them from marrying, divorcing, testifying in court and writing a will.[30] In eighteenth century London, it was reported that the Bethlehem Hospital took in around £400 in admission fees for people to "peer at the insane": "At a penny per visitor, this suggests that over 90,000 people visited the hospital that year during its Sunday open houses."[31]

We are two decades into the twenty-first century and there are questions—particularly in my geographical context, in England— asking if we are moving toward the *destigmatization* of mental health. From my standpoint, I witness more conversations about mental health than literature from decades (and centuries) past suggests was happening at the time. In the Covid-19 pandemic, for example, mental health became the driving force for arguments against England's nation-wide lockdowns, with calls for gyms and leisure centers to stay open for the sake of people's mental—not just physical—well-being.[32] Would this have happened 20 years ago? Perhaps not.

Conversations about mental health, productive or otherwise, popularly take place across social media platforms, one of which has a unique reputation in this space: tumblr. Indeed, in tumblr's 2019 *Year in Review* report, the platform positioned mental health as "the most important issue" for its community.[33] In their book on tumblr, Tiidenberg et al. introduce the concept of "silosociality" to describe the way people experience the platform; "silos" are defined by their "shared interests, but sustained through inward-facing shared vernacular and sensibility."[34] Silosociality is a unique condition only made possible by tumblr's specific features, functions, and rules: the platform quickly figures out who you are and what you want to see and reflects that as it guides you through your online journey.[35] Tiidenberg et al. make a distinction between what Goffman calls "back places" and the silos characterizing tumblr use. While Goffman describes back places as "spaces of ease" where people can escape their stigma, silos—though they may offer "reprieve or escape from everyday and mediated stressors"—are "not necessarily always spaces of ease or freedom."[36] Silos do not strictly form in direct response to stigma and, while they "may hold back places," they "are not back places in themselves."[37] Put differently, occupants of silos aren't necessarily there because they feel a part of their identity is stigmatized: they are placed there by tumblr, based on its judgements about their identity and presumed motivations behind their use of the platform. But lots of silos have stigma-evading functions; for example, people within silos run a "lesser risk of context collapse" (where people from distinct social groups are "collapsed" into one online space).[38] This can make tumblr feel safer and more pleasant for its users. In fact, in their research with Australian schools, Tiidenberg et al. found that, of more than thirty tumblr users in their sample, "none had more than one tumblr follower whom they knew personally beyond the platform."[39]

For those who want to engage with content about mental health, tumblr silos can clearly offer an escape from "vulnerability, shame, and stigma."[40] Aligned with the theme of this book, though, the situation is not that straightforward. Tiidenberg et al. also note how silos can quickly become toxic spaces, leading knowledgeable insiders to encourage distressing practices.[41] This means silos— and also back places—"do not straightforwardly help or harm" people.[42] They can in fact be paradoxical, as tumblr use necessitates that people are split into silos, which evidently has many benefits but also carries the risk of toxicity. For tumblr users whose silos orient them toward content relating to mental health, the platform can only be experienced as beneficial if they accept its risks and, sometimes, experience harms.

When someone carries a stigma, they become adept at managing their social situations, and this chapter explores some of the ways people use social media to seek solace from mental health stigma.[43] It argues that platforms are certainly tools for managing and circumventing stigma and yet can paradoxically function as stigmatizing spaces. I now turn to an exploration of how and why people try to evade content moderation mechanisms like those described above in order to talk about their mental health across various social media platforms.

"PLEASE be careful": Circumventing Content Moderation

Social media content sits in three realms of acceptability: permitted, prohibited, and reduced. These distinctions apply to hashtags: a string of alphanumeric characters preceded by the hash (#) symbol—for example, #kittens. Hashtags have become a crucial method of contextualization and meaning making for many social media users around the world. Some are niche and have fewer than 100 uses, but others have been used millions, sometimes billions of times. Hashtags are either unproblematically *permitted* by platforms or entirely *prohibited* (that is, they do not return any results when searched for). Some hashtags may also be *reduced* by a platform, which can mean several things, but in this instance refers to the reduction of their presence in various ways that does not amount to an outright ban or removal (for example, when a platform issues a support notification to its users when they search for certain terms). In a study conducted in 2016, Suzor found that hashtag moderation changed rapidly on Instagram: in the space of two weeks, hashtags like #anorexicnervosa, #thinnn, and #thynsperation went from being blocked to having "no posts" associated with them to then not being blocked at all.[44] Why are hashtags like this being moderated so inconsistently? And perhaps most crucially, what are the social ramifications of problematizing tags like these via content moderation?

Stigmatized individuals look for spaces where they can communicate with others on more equal footing, which is why social media—particularly platforms that allow pseudonymity—have become so popular with certain people. In their content analysis of thinspiration images shared on Instagram (those intended to promote thinness as a body ideal), Ging and Garvey found a dominance of similarly aestheticized posts: either text-heavy memes or black and white images of White girls and young women.[45] While these posts are visually dark and may therefore seem worrying to outsiders, dark aesthetics should not too hastily be equated with danger. The use of a particular visual aesthetic within a social group is a common method of signaling to other users that they "belong"; in short, certain people will take one look at an image and know it is for them. Ging and Garvey make a similar point: because the sad aesthetic has become so recognizable within certain mental health circles, it might contribute to relationship formation and inclusivity, particularly when contrasted with pro-ana forums, which the authors say are notorious for boundary policing.[46] Defining "pro-ana" internet content, Boero and Pasco explain that it is, in general, "non-recovery oriented" and "offers weight-loss tips, generates support, and provides non-judgmental community that does not take a negative attitude toward eating disorders."[47] Indeed, Zappavigna argues that internet memes tend to be "deployed for social bonding rather than for sharing information."[48] Social bonding of this kind is crucial for people experiencing stigma, who often need someone to provide them with "instruction in the tricks of the trade" and "for the comfort of feeling at home, at ease, accepted as a person who really is like any other normal person."[49]

There are lots of ways to find your people on social media; in fact, sometimes simply being on a platform, or a space within that platform, implies you belong to a certain group. But on platforms that operate on a more mass scale—like Instagram, which boasts over two billion users across all continents and across most countries around the world—it is trickier to find where you belong.[50] A common way to find your people on megaplatforms like Instagram is by using hashtags. Hashtags have three innate qualities: First, they are perhaps the most *visible* form of social media communication; they are used on post captions across various platforms and often end up at the center of global debates. Second, because not all hashtags are safe to use, their visibility makes them *vulnerable* to platforms' interventions. Finally, hashtags are *versatile*; they are ready to be re-shaped or even abandoned by users in response to platforms' rules. In 2016, Chancellor et al. published a paper about what they called "lexical variation" among eating disorder-related hashtags on Instagram.[51] From posts collected between January 2011 and November 2014, the researchers showed that people posting to eating disorder-related hashtags were slightly misspelling words and phrases to evade platform detection. For example, #bonespo, a portmanteau term to denote "bone inspiration" (the inspiration one gets from looking at images of protruding bones, like collarbones or ribcages) returned nine lexical variants, including these:

Bonespoo
Bonespoooo
Bonespooo
Bonesspo
Bonesporation
Bonessspo[52]

Chancellor et al.'s dataset also exposed phrases that, on the surface, have nothing to do with eating disorders and thereby enable users posting in this space to evade detection (for example, #secretsociety123). This more extreme form of circumvention is called *social steganography*, "a Greek word that means 'covered writing.'"[53] "To cryptographers and spies," social steganography is a method of "hiding information that conceals the very existence of a message."[54] Chancellor et al.'s paper drew a lot of press attention and, whether or not the authors intended for this to happen, Instagram subsequently banned many of the hashtags they found in a bid to minimize the circulation of potentially problematic content. While this might seem like a positive change, banning hashtags—especially when they are associated with mental health conditions—is a risky though easy move for platforms to make. This is largely because the use of a mental health–related hashtag like #anorexia or #depressed does not in itself indicate a user's desire to share harmful content. And what is harmful to one person may not be to another.

A recent example of the contextual complexities of mental health content comes from Reddit, which decided to ban the

30,000 strong r/ProED (shorthand for pro-eating disorder) sub-reddit in November 2018. This ban—which received surprisingly little press coverage—rattled many users of the sub, with one carefully explaining that, although the sub was named pro-ED, it was not, for them, a dangerous space:

> This morning, my only mental health resource was banned from Reddit. . . . r/ProED was the only support system I had for my disorder. In the country I live in, seeking mental health resources is grounds for termination of employment. I am not free to discuss my disorder or seek treatment. I suffer alone and there are times when I thought I wouldn't make it. r/ProED was my only outlet. It was my only safe place. And I am not the only one for whom this was the case. . . . r/ProED was a place of love and 100% against causing harm. At r/ProED we had no patience for "teaching" disordered behavior (primarily because like all mental disorders, eating disorders can't just be "picked up" or taught). Anyone who mistook r/ProED for a harmful sub had done nothing to educate themselves on the reality of the tone of discussion there. . . . To any Reddit powers-that-be who may be reading this: PLEASE educate yourselves before enabling quarantines or bans on mental health-related subs. PLEASE be more considerate before you destroy what many consider to be their only resource. People's lives are literally at stake here. PLEASE be careful.[55]—u/linedryonly

There is so much to unpack in this quote, and one especially important part is that those who belonged to r/ProED were accustomed to "a very candid and specific sense of humor." For u/linedryonly, part of the draw of r/ProED is that its users shared a language that would've been difficult for a non-member to decipher.

In my research, which I conducted in 2017 and published in 2018, I found that social media users posting about eating disorders often use code words to signal to others who are in the know.[56] They do this in various ways—like using workaround hashtags, as we already know—but I also found that code sharing occurs in people's social media profile biographies. Not all platforms ask their users to write a biographical note (or "bio"), but many do. The bio, where people can write around one hundred words about themselves, usually sits alongside a person's profile picture and username. For people with stigmas—especially the kinds of stigma that attract their own content moderation policies, like eating disorders—profile biographies are a core space to talk back to those who are watching them, both literally and figuratively. People in problematized social media contexts often know they are being watched, suggesting content moderation policies are experienced by many as a form of surveillance. Indeed, stringent moderation measures like those described in this chapter prompted Hendry's research participants—who were young women between the ages of 14 and 17—to further make their social media participation invisible: "They rework mental illness through ambiguous, supportive, or humorous practices or, through *imagined intimacy*, engage with images that feel relatable to them even if the images do not depict recognizable mental illness content or employ recognizable hashtags or titles."[57]

In my research on Instagram and tumblr, I found that people posting about eating disorders—regardless of whether their content outwardly "promoted" the worsening of a person's condition or not—used their profile biographies to talk back to imagined moderators.[58] I am not sure who the imagined moderator is: perhaps they are a platform worker or policymaker, a concerned bystander who may report their posts, a troll, or someone else. There are serious ethical considerations when repeating codewords from protected communities, and so I am not going to give lots of examples from my dataset here. But I will say that Instagram and tumblr users' bios included phrases like "not pro anything" to indicate their distance from a pro-eating disorder identity, "don't report just block" to discourage people from bringing their account to the attention of the company via reporting mechanisms, and "for myself" to distance themselves from behaviors that might be considered promotional, which goes against Instagram and tumblr's content policies.[59] Some users also share the name of a backup account in case theirs is removed. Similar themes also emerged in Cobb's work: "Users create a distinction between pro-ana and thinspo, suggesting that pro-ana is pathological but thinspo is acceptable. . . . For instance, one blogger describes herself as 'Ana [anorexic] Mia [bulimic] and addicted to thinspiration,' yet adds immediately after, 'This is *not* pro-ana' (Thinspo3), presumably in an attempt to distance herself from what has been decreed a contentious phenomenon."[60]

Cobb's findings remind me of the "imagined audience" theory, proposed in 1991 by Ang. In *Desperately Seeking the Audience*, Ang offered a novel exploration of television's role in its viewers' everyday lives, explaining why media industries often struggle to match their products with audience needs.[61] The rise of social media in the mid-2000s introduced new dimensions to this classic media theory. In a 2021 article, for example, Maris presented the "imagined industry" framework to show how, just as media industries have historically sought to "define, attract, and keep" their audience, those audience members also "desperately seek (new) media industries, looking for ways to make their identities and demands visible to the producers of culture."[62] Imagined industry theory holds true for those with identities deemed problematic by social media companies; these people are aware they are being watched by platforms. They have understandings of "how and why social media platforms moderate content," which offers "imaginaries of industrial motivations and practices."[63] The method of talking back to platforms via profile biographies therefore gives us a sense of the powerlessness people often feel on social media where one of your only meaningful methods of evading content moderation is to justify the purpose of your account in your profile bio, hopefully enabling you to retain your presence on what is, for many, a digital lifeline.

u/linedryonly's post also encourages readers to focus on the implications of blocking entire subreddits (or hashtags and similar communication techniques) in one swift and unexpected move. The Reddit user quoted above rightly notes that mental health issues, particularly eating disorders, are characterized by acts of *secrecy:* secret eating and purging, secret food restriction, secret exercise regimes, secret digital networks. But platforms like Reddit, which enable—indeed, celebrate—the use of pseudonyms give people a place to maintain secret identities to talk about their experiences. While I am not denying the presence of dangerous behaviors in these spaces, certain groups are excellent at self-moderation, as u/linedryonly notes above. Indeed, they say r/ProED members had "no patience" for those who joined to teach harmful behaviors.[64] The redditor also correctly points out that anorexia has the highest mortality rate of any mental health condition, which means removing anything like a subreddit, user account, post, or similar ED-related content overnight is an extremely dangerous act.[65] We still do not know why r/ProED was removed, and it would not be wise to speculate. But what we can say with near certainty is that the act removed a core support network for—and therefore endangered—upwards of 30,000 people.

The harmfulness of content moderation like that described above also points toward a paradox, and I return to an earlier-cited study by Yeshua-Katz and Hård af Segerstad to make this point.[66] In their research on boundary work in stigmatized communities online, the authors argued that the restrictions in place to guard against "imposters" who threaten "safe havens" may paradoxically make these havens "inaccessible to those who truly need support and remove such groups from the public eye."[67] Though content moderation is conceptualized as necessary in harm reduction, particularly for young people, it can paradoxically be experienced as a force full of harm, lessening the accessibility and visibility of key spaces to those who truly need them. This is precisely why people try to circumvent content moderation mechanisms—efforts that aren't always successful. In their two-year digital ethnography, Feuston et al. explored the consequences of banning social media content and accounts for those with eating disorders, unearthing "instances in which the experience of moderation led to dangerous offline behaviors, including purging."[68] As u/linedryonly explains above, the loss of support that results from moderation—particularly the removal of a person's account—can "create a downward stream of negative consequences" which includes amplifying their illness and making them feel socially isolated.[69]

For people with eating disorders, social media can function as a kind of diary. Aggregated content in particular, like posts or images that have been grouped together into albums or similar, becomes a "resource for reflection in the short and longer term," interwoven with a person's identity formation and therefore experience of their eating disorder.[70] Examples like this remind us why social media content moderation is so difficult: not only is it hard to define what counts as a "harm" beyond the highly obvious examples, but there are health-related, sometimes life-altering, consequences to punishing people for what they say online, even if their posts harm others. As Feuston et al. put it, "although content moderation is typically conceptualized as necessary for the greater good of online communities (e.g., preventing harassment, protecting individuals from graphic or triggering content), its potential harms are not well-understood or documented."[71] Indeed, for people with mental health conditions, content moderation might *itself* be experienced as an online harm. As Scott et al. note, design affordances like content moderation, which perpetuate social control structures, have a documented history of causing harm, including trauma.[72]

Relevance, Recommendation, and Reduction on Social Media

I have so far focused on instances where young people *seek out* risky social media content relating to mental health (for example, by searching for content via coded language). But in what follows, I shift readers' attention to occasions where something harmful happens *to* young people on social media without their full control and in a way they may find difficult to understand. Specifically, I am talking about instances where they are shown distressing content via social media's recommendation systems. This is partly what happened to Molly Russell.

Social platforms do not always present their users' content in a chronological list, instead showing people what they likely want to see in what may feel like (but is not) a random order. Because Molly Russell sought out posts about suicide and self-harm on her Instagram and Pinterest accounts, those platforms then directed seemingly relevant content back to her, sending her personalized recommendations via email and other digital means: "As Molly's father found, these recommendation systems don't discriminate. Social media shows you what you 'might love,' whether you like it or not—even if it violates the platform's own community guidelines."[73]

In a horrifying sense, this is evidence of a platform working exactly as it should. Instagram and Pinterest identified what Molly had engaged with because she searched for or interacted with it in some way, for example by liking it, commenting on it, or sharing it. The platforms then showed her more posts they deemed to be similar to the ones she was already engaging with and that, they presumed, she would've wanted to see. But platforms like Instagram and Pinterest were not initially designed to discriminate between harmful and harmless recommendations: if a piece of content is on a platform and makes it through all the guardrails, the logic goes that it can then be freely recommended. Naturally, this discovery led Molly's dad to accuse social media giants of "helping to kill" his 14-year-old daughter.[74] Both Instagram and Pinterest then met this accusation with new content policies designed to limit the recommendation and circulation of posts that might be harmful.[75] We are therefore left with new questions, ones that are highly unique to the social media landscape: Should platforms avoid recommending posts to users that are tagged with #anorexia or similar, non-promotional mental health-related phrases? If so, should posts that are explicitly about recovery be treated differently? And is recommendation moderation the right move, ethically, when we bring longer-standing social stigmatization into the conversation? Platforms must take care to avoid counterproductively—and paradoxically—stigmatizing the same people they are trying to reduce harms against and cutting off support systems for those who need them the most. After all, and as Tyler and Slater note, "negative attitudes around mental health problems are not only damaging and discriminatory but often exacerbate mental distress."[76]

Once a social media user is embedded in a particular network—through their followers; the content they share, like, save, and comment on; their clickstreams; and other forms of mined social media data—they do not need to rely on hashtags or other search mechanisms to find new content. Instead, platforms begin to recommend it to them. Recommendation systems are essentially information-filtering systems that use data mining techniques to predict users' interests and preferences, and they are an effective way for social media companies to deal with information overload.[77] The main type of recommendation system is called collaborative filtering. Collaborative filtering uses the tastes of other people who are like you to decide what else you might like: "In brief, consider the product recommendations one sees on Amazon. These, says the retailer, are the result of one's browsing and purchasing histories, which are correlated with those of Amazon's millions of other customers—a crowd—to determine whose buying patterns are similar to one's own. You, too, might like what this select group has bought, and vice-versa—a process Amazon calls, 'collaborative filtering.'"[78]

Recommendation systems work differently on different platforms. On Pinterest, for example, content curation is prioritized over creation and communication, as users are expected to scroll through the platform to find images to add to their Pin Boards. This means Pinterest's recommendation systems play a central role in how users discover new content. In my research—which involved creating brand new dummy accounts for research purposes, a method discussed in a peer reviewed journal article—I began to receive content recommendations, just as Molly Russell did.[79] Pinterest sent me one of many automated emails over the course of my research—conducted in mid-2017, before Molly's death hit the headlines—to show me things I might want to see. In one instance, I received an automated marketing email from Pinterest to match me with a user who was, apparently, also "interested in anorexia."[80] The word "anorexia" was presented in bold and the use of such typography told me this was an automated email, using a standardized template but tailored to individuals' interests. While this information might be helpful for some, for others it could make something like an eating disorder feel inescapable. This is a big problem, and I call it the *Funhouse Mirror Phenomenon*— that is, recommendation systems are not simply mirrors as they do not just reflect your preferences back at you: they also distort them, like a funhouse mirror, sending you recommendations for things you might not want to see in that moment or that you might not have sought out independently.[81] While Pinterest may have altered this specific feature since I conducted my research in 2017, these systems aren't going anywhere any time soon.

At the time of writing, the four most popular social media platforms among 13- to 17-year-olds in the UK are YouTube, TikTok, Instagram, and Snapchat, all of which are centrally organized via recommendations.[82] For example, when a TikTok user opens their app, they are shown a video from their For You page: videos the platform thinks they will want to see above all others. In late 2021, TikTok committed to improving its recommendation systems to avoid sequentially over-saturating people with content that might be harmful:

As we continue to develop new strategies to interrupt repetitive patterns, we're looking at how our system can better vary the kinds of content that may be recommended in a sequence. That's why we're testing ways to avoid recommending a series of similar content—such as around extreme dieting or fitness, sadness, or breakups—to protect against viewing too much of a content category that may be fine as a single video but problematic if viewed in clusters. We're also working to recognize if our system may inadvertently be recommending only very limited types of content that, though not violative of our policies, could have a negative effect if that's the majority of what someone watches, such as content about loneliness or weight loss. Our goal is for each person's For You feed to feature a breadth of content, creators, and topics. This work is being informed by ongoing conversations with experts across medicine, clinical psychology, and AI ethics, members of our Content Advisory Council, and our community.[83]

TikTok's prioritization of what it describes as a "breadth of content" is, to me, a welcome move and echoes decisions other platforms have made. For example, as I finalize this manuscript in January 2024, Meta has announced that it will not recommend content about "self-harm, graphic violence and eating disorders" to its teenage users.[84] While Instagram and Facebook users of all ages are still permitted to use these platforms to *share* their experiences relating to mental health (unless they are explicitly promotional or encouraging of harmful behaviors, of course), Meta's policy is to not recommend such posts to teenagers and to therefore make them "harder to find."[85]

These examples from TikTok and Meta are forms of *content reduction*, wherein content that is not quite bad enough to remove entirely will remain on a platform but will not circulate as freely as permitted content: "The offending content remains on the site, still available if a user can find it directly. However, the platform limits the conditions under which it circulates: whether or how it is offered up as a recommendation or search result, in an algorithmically generated feed, or 'up next' in users' queues."[86] The exact content reduction tactics used by each social media platform are somewhat opaque, in that some "have not acknowledged them publicly at all," while those that have are "circumspect" about them.[87] As Gillespie explains, although content reduction techniques are no longer hidden entirely from public view, platforms have thus far allowed them to "linger quietly in the shadow of removal policies."[88] This is because

> reducing without removing allows platforms the flexibility to intervene around quickly emerging phenomena, to go after content designed to elude prohibitions, and to curtail content they 'know' is bad but have a hard time articulating why. Seen in the best light, this flexibility makes it easier to respond quickly to changing problems—from the unpredictable outbursts of White nationalism, to the evasive tactics of pro-ana groups, to the constantly evolving QAnon conspiracy. In a less flattering light, reduction also avoids public accountability, as the interventions themselves are hard to spot, and are not—yet—reported as part of the platform's transparency obligations.[89]

Content reduction is by no means a new phenomenon, but it has garnered far less attention and debate than outright removal. Reduction also remains largely absent from "policymaking, and even much of the scholarly conversations about content moderation and platform governance."[90] But platforms are talking about reduction more and more, and we need to pay very close attention moving forwards.

Meta itself notes that not all content relating to mental health is harmful. The company says: "Take the example of someone posting about their ongoing struggle with thoughts of self-harm. This is an important story, and can help destigmatize these issues, but it's a complex topic and isn't necessarily suitable for all young people."[91] But content reduction strategies of this kind open up lots of tricky questions about young people and mental health—some of which we, rather frustratingly, may never have an answer to or be able to fully resolve. For example, do we trust social media companies to make ethical, responsible decisions about content reduction, if indeed it continues to garner less public scrutiny than other forms of moderation? What support mechanisms might content reduction policies like Meta's cut off from vulnerable young people? Readers should also be asking how we, as Instagram and TikTok users or as concerned bystanders, will know if these new strategies are working. Who is measuring their effectiveness and according to which benchmark(s)? As Horwitz notes, "Meta defines what constitutes harmful content, so it shapes the discussion of how successful it is at dealing with it."[92] And this, as former Meta employee Krieger says, is sort of like grading your own homework.[93]

To return to TikTok's new recommendation policy, how will the platform distinguish between "extreme" dieting and fitness content versus other, more "acceptable" forms? And in relation to Instagram's new policy, what counts as content relating to self-harm or eating disorders? Those whose content is deemed to fit the bill—and is subsequently reduced—may find themselves wondering why, say, the reach of their posts has diminished or why their formerly steady new follower count has stagnated. These might feel like pretty mundane questions to some readers, but they are important questions forming in the minds of young people who are already feeling vulnerable. And so we reach what is perhaps the most crucial question about content reduction policies: By reducing the circulation of content relating to mental health, are social media platforms perhaps tampering *with* people's mental health? Blanket banning all posts relating to self-harm and eating disorders to teens feels justifiable, of course, when considered in light of what happened to Molly Russell. But the question for me isn't really about whether they should or shouldn't reduce such content: it's more about how these classifications are being made and how transparently they are being conveyed to their users. Reduction tactics are, to some extent, paradoxical; they are intended to protect people from seeing harmful things, but they are potentially being experienced as a form of online harm by vulnerable individuals.

The Politics of Doing Enough

To close this chapter, I return to a statement I made earlier on, which referenced claims that mental health conditions are becoming destigmatized in certain contexts. Some researchers argue that "recent broad-based social and structural changes have combined to increase the level of sophistication with which the public views mental illness, creating a liberalizing attitudinal trend."[94] In England at least, I think I speak for most of us when I say we would be horrified if hospitals continued to take in admission fees for people to "peer at the insane," as they did in the eighteenth century.[95] There are concerted efforts to destigmatize mental health in different parts of the world by researchers, charities, advocacy groups, writers, and other social actors. Commenting on such initiatives, though, Tyler speaks of being "tired of hearing the claim—frequently made in charitable anti-stigma campaigns—that challenging the stigma associated with particular conditions—from poverty to mental ill health—can overcome 'barriers to help-seeking', without an acknowledgement of the ways in which stigma is deliberately designed into systems of social provision in ways that make help-seeking a desperate task."[96]

This statement is a crucial and powerful one on which to end this chapter. First, it is worth noting here that Goffman's work on stigma has been critiqued within academic circles for obscuring broader systems and perpetrators of power and for overly individualizing those experiencing stigma. And second, not only do Tyler's words remind us that calls for destigmatization are worrisome when infrastructures are not there to support them, but, in relation to social media, they highlight the limitations of policymaking in relation to mental health. I am frequently asked—usually by very good-natured people and organizations—to come up with solutions to make social media "safer" for their vulnerable users. And I tend to find myself giving in, largely because I am a deeply pragmatic person and because I worry that standing on the sidelines and shouting about these issues without getting my hands dirty contradicts my politics. But part of my answer to this question is that we cannot ignore wider social issues when we proclaim that social media is making people unwell, like the cost-of-living crisis, unemployment, discrimination, under-funding, and the inaccessibility of mental health services—nor can we ignore identity factors like social class, among many other structural constraints. Life is unbearably hard for so many people around the world, which means individuals' relationships with social apps will drastically differ between them. I am not saying this to let platforms off the hook entirely. Instead, I am trying to suggest that every time we accuse tech companies of not doing enough to protect their young users, I think we should ask ourselves what doing more would look like, and where the limits of current content moderation models may be.

Take TikTok as an example: the platform has near-global penetration, which makes it difficult, perhaps impossible, for the company to develop blanket policies around mental health–related content. As I explained earlier in this chapter, mental health stigma differs geographically, meaning TikTok's content policies will inevitably suit some contexts while alienating others. As an example, in June 2023, Kenya captured 54 percent of TikTok's global activity with Thailand claiming the second spot, and these countries will have mental health trends that differ from each other's and from Western nations'.[97] The push for platforms to make more and more rules is therefore not innately beneficial to the people they aim to protect. By calling for more or different or improved content moderation, we must acknowledge that *more* moderation is not always synonymous with *better* moderation. In this chapter, I have noted several reactive content policies in the wake of a social media–related tragedy, often a suicide, which typically take the form of easy technical tweaks like hashtag bans. Platforms will always need to work to mitigate against potential harms, and it is unreasonable to assume harmless social media participation is achievable, just as it would be unreasonable to suggest people will always behave perfectly in face-to-face settings. But, one day, and probably one day soon, platforms will run out of tweaks. They will run out of search terms to ban, and they will enforce so many content reduction rules that their infrastructures will become overly frustrating to their users. As Livingstone and Blum-Ross suggest, industry providers should therefore avoid "oversell[ing] technological 'solutions' for deep-seated problems" like the ones I've described in this chapter.[98] There is only so much platforms can do, which does not mean that they should abandon their efforts. But many of the world's most popular platforms are built on moderation models that simply do not work, and so the work will never be done, no matter how loudly we cry. And where children and young people are concerned, many of the current content moderation efforts are repairing the damages caused by a "largely age-blind (or implicitly adult)" internet, which has clearly become "starkly problematic" for young lives.[99]

For vulnerable people, participation in social media involves an intricate balance between "opportunities (for identity, intimacy, sociability) and risks (regarding privacy, misunderstanding, abuse)."[100] But the tricky thing about social media is that this careful negotiation often entails paradoxical experiences, both helpful and harmful at the same time. For example, in the context from which I write, there are longstanding social concerns around "stranger danger" on the internet, especially for young people, who are feared to fall prey to nefarious "faceless" individuals or groups. But this chapter has shown how, paradoxically, the same behavior that is said to be concerning can enhance feelings of safety for stigmatized individuals and strengthen bonds, even if those ties connect from one "faceless" account to the other. While I do not deny the presence of dangerous individuals across social media platforms, we must remember that, sometimes, the same young people we are trying to protect are the faceless ones, and for very good reasons. As Livingstone puts it, "While online risk carries a probability of harm to a child, this is not inevitable. Many factors can make a child more resilient or vulnerable to the consequences of exposure to risk. . . . Complicating matters further . . . the same activity can have positive consequences for one child and negative for another."[101]

This chapter has also shown how the restrictions social media companies put in place to guard against online harms may paradoxically bury certain controversial practices and spaces further underground, thus making them "inaccessible to those who truly need support" and "remov[ing] such groups from the public eye."[102] Though content moderation is taken for granted as a necessary force in harm reduction, for vulnerable social media users these systems can be experienced as harmful forces. Further, this chapter has shown how social media platforms often undermine their own efforts by recommending content they purport to ban, which is precisely what happened to Molly Russell. For platforms to be helpful to vulnerable users—for example, by showing you other like-minded people with whom you share a stigmatized attribute—they also have to risk harming such users by showing them more and more of something that may be distressing to them, even if that content does not explicitly break any rules. But what would it mean—ethically and in terms of health—if the circulation of such content were to be reduced?

The phenomena described in this chapter point toward a sobering conclusion: perhaps those who use social media to engage with content relating to mental health are, to a large extent, forced to accept a series of risks—along with any resultant harms—to be able to feel the benefits I have described. Engaging with mental health-related content across the range of social media platforms is thus an experience fraught with paradoxes. This does not mean we should do nothing or that we should simply give up. Readers of this chapter likely share a drive to protect those with vulnerabilities, particularly young people, and I appreciate that attending to paradoxes may be a difficult task in their line of work. But rather than viewing these paradoxes as an undefeatable battle, perhaps we can view them as opportunities to ask different kinds of questions from those popularly asked. For example, the infamous yet ultimately unanswerable question—Is social media good or bad for our mental health?—is far too broad "to merit robust conclusions," given the diversity of social media in the 2020s and likely beyond.[103] This question and many more like it dangerously tend to lead to either-or outcomes, which "do not adequately reflect the specific content and pressures of the cultural contradictions of technology."[104] Perhaps the paradoxes described in this chapter will provide the foundations to help push back against questions like these, to demand greater nuance and, crucially, to respect the realities of contemporary young lives.

3 *Amuse Me or Abuse Me* on Anonymous Apps

On Tuesday, March 3, 2020, I ran my final research workshop before a one-year hiatus triggered by, you guessed it, the global Covid-19 pandemic. The workshop was administered by my university's Widening Participation team, whose aim is to provide avenues into higher education for those with identities it considers to be underrepresented.[1] I ran these workshops about anonymous apps at my own institution before going into the field to visit schools beyond my city (Sheffield, England) to interview teens about their relationships with these apps. But the timing of this workshop—one of my final face-to-face work commitments before we went into a nationwide Covid-19 lockdown—isn't the only reason I remember it so vividly. I also remember it because I met Elsa.

During the workshop, I asked my 15- to 16-year-old participants to raise their hands if they used certain then popular social apps, along with ones I knew they would avoid. The results were predictable: most used Instagram, Snapchat, and YOLO; most laughed out loud when I asked if they used Facebook. But to my surprise, one student, Elsa, raised her hand to ask if I remembered an anonymous app called Sarahah, which she and her peers had used when they were younger. Globally popular anonymous apps allow their

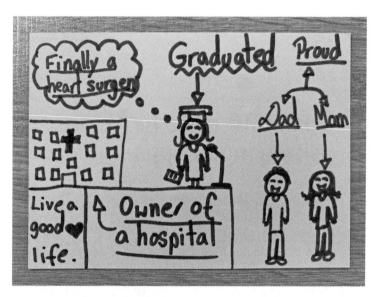

FIGURE 1. A photograph of the front of a postcard drawn by English teenager Elsa, depicting her goals for her future: becoming a heart surgeon and making her parents proud.

users to send messages to others without revealing information that might identify them, like their legal name. Anonymous apps are very popular among children and young people and often become "popular by surprise," rising to the top of app charts at breakneck speed, garnering millions of downloads and outpacing their mainstream rivals before being pulled for safety concerns, or being taken down by their own founders.[2] But I hadn't heard of this one. I felt both embarrassed and grateful: embarrassed that I was there to talk to them about anonymous apps while Sarahah's popularity had passed me by but grateful that Elsa had taught *me* about it.

For one of the workshop activities, I asked participants to create a postcard in the style of a PostSecret submission. PostSecret is

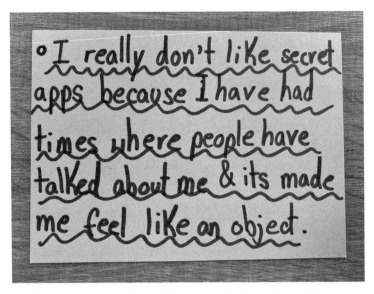

○ I really don't like secret apps because I have had times where people have talked about me & its made me feel like an object.

FIGURE 2. A photograph of the back of a postcard drawn by English teenager Elsa, revealing her views on anonymous apps.

an ongoing community art project founded by Frank Warren in 2004. It began when Warren "handed out 3,000 self-addressed postcards in Washington DC with instructions to share a secret and anonymously return it to him."[3] Warren then launched a website to exhibit the postcards he received and, with growing popularity, people began to design and submit their own postcards.[4] I asked participants to use their postcards to secretly tell me how they felt about anonymous apps and to decorate them however they saw fit. Elsa's postcard is pictured in Figures 1 and 2.

When the workshop ended, I spent the rest of the day learning everything I could about Sarahah, and one of my most fascinating discoveries was that the app was never supposed to be used by teenagers like Elsa. Sarahah, "which means 'frankness' or 'honesty' in Arabic," was designed to be used in Saudi Arabian corporate settings for employees to leave constructive feedback for their bosses.[5] But Sarahah's founder, Zain-Alabdin Tawfiq, soon realized the concept could be useful beyond the workplace, and in 2016 he launched Sarahah as a website, with an initial goal of attracting 1000 messages between users.[6] Despite spending no money on marketing, the site spread across several Arab countries and, in June 2016, Tawfiq hired a third-party company to launch Sarahah as an English-speaking app.[7] And that's when the Sarahah Saga began.

To Tawfiq's shock, Sarahah was hijacked by teens from all around the world, at one point attracting a staggering 300 million users from over 30 countries, including Egypt, India, Japan, the UK, and the US.[8] When people call Sarahah an overnight success, they mean it: the app jumped from #104 to #1 in the Apple App Store charts in only three days.[9] Sarahah's story is eerily similar to YOLO's, an app I discussed in the introduction. As YOLO founder Gregoire Henrion told a *TechCrunch* reporter: "It was not supposed to be a success. It was just for us to learn." He continued to explain their attitude to the launch, "Let's just put it on the App Store and see how people behave. It went 100% viral. It's crazy. Even we didn't believe our eyes when we saw that [it went to #1]."[10]

Sarahah was repurposed by teens as a Q&A app; a user could create an account, ask people a question, and receive anonymized responses from just about anyone. Although researchers don't know much about the kinds of questions teens asked on Sarahah, we know respondents weren't always on their best behavior. Anyone with or without a Sarahah account could reply to people's questions and so, naturally, the app was plagued with more complaints of bullying than its three (yes, three) staff members could safely handle.[11] Predictably, Sarahah was removed from app stores in 2018.[12]

. . .

There is so much to say about this story. We could talk about Sarahah's sudden popularity: Why was *this* app, above all others, plucked from obscurity and thrust into the social media spotlight? What made it so attractive to teens, specifically? And why did Sarahah—and many other apps of the same genre—ultimately fail? These questions have largely escaped academic attention, despite anonymous apps attracting millions of users worldwide. To get a sense of how popular the apps are, at one point, 20,000 questions were asked on Ask.fm—an anonymous website and app whose users can ask questions either privately to individual users or publicly via their profile—per *minute*.[13] It wouldn't surprise me if readers, even those who write about social media for a living, don't recognize some of the apps I mention in this chapter, and there's a very interesting reason for this: as a general rule of thumb, anonymous apps have a short shelf life, especially when compared with some of the current big players on the social media scene. While individual anonymous apps might have fleeting social popularity, this chapter argues that the genre has had just as much cultural impact on the lives of today's networked teens in England—and likely other places around the world—as the current big players have.

Although there are well-documented difficulties in reaching true anonymity in contemporary digital spaces, Bachmann et al.

crucially remind us that "diagnoses claiming the nearing end of anonymity are oversimplified."[14] The authors argue instead that "regimes of anonymity" are being reconfigured—and one way, especially for today's teens, is through the popularity of anonymous apps.[15] Despite their namesake, anonymous apps don't actually offer true anonymity. This is partly because the apps enable a form of networked anonymity, wherein message recipients understand that they are somehow networked with the sender (that they are "anonymous among friends").[16] Anonymous apps that were popular during my fieldwork included YOLO, LMK, and Tellonym, all of which are "tie-based" and therefore connect their users with the people they know on other apps or to the contacts list on their smartphone.[17] As Sharon and John explain, tie-based apps uniquely "give the feeling of a room full of friends, but where everybody is blindfolded."[18] This familiarity contributes to the pleasures and pitfalls of anonymous apps, as users participate in an exhilarating yet frustrating game of deanonymization, trying to work out who sent them certain messages.[19] This experience—distinct to tie-based anonymous apps—is precisely why Bachmann et al. call for a better understanding of how "regimes of anonymity are getting reconfigured" and how phenomena like anonymous apps are at once shaping and being shaped by our social practices.[20]

But this constant game of cat-and-mouse—trying to figure out which person from your school sent you an anonymous message—is making a significant mark on contemporary adolescence, not just in England but in other places around the world as well. The data I present in this chapter derives from qualitative interviews I conducted with 16- to 18-year-olds at Jaynes Sixth Form College, a research site, as mentioned in the introduction, educating students after high school between the ages of 16–18, before they attend university or enter the working world. Jaynes is located in a tradition-ally working-class and predominantly White city.[21] I interviewed a total of 21 students from Jaynes between June 2021 and April 2022, of which one identified as Black British, two as Asian British, and 18 as White British. Fourteen participants used she/her pronouns, six used he/him, and one used they/them.[22] For the teens at Jaynes, anonymous apps have played a substantial role in their friendships and identity development—particularly in terms of gender, sex, and sexuality—among many other facets of their complex lives. More than this, the apps play a *paradoxical* role: to be pleasurable to teens, anonymous apps necessitate displeasure, typically felt as surveillance among young women and those whose identities mark them as "others." For example, in a mostly White school, being a student of color might make you feel more at risk when a new anonymous app hits the scene. The same is true for those out-side of the "popular" social circles. Anonymity, at least in a more conceptual sense, is therefore very much alive, and it plays an exceptionally complex role in young, modern lives.

A Typology of Anonymous Apps

Although anonymous apps don't really enable true anonymity, this is the phrase people use to describe them and, crucially, it's how people *feel* while using them. This term is therefore the one I will use throughout this book. Anonymous apps are relation based, allowing users to "anonymously share content with people related to them" either by social affinity (tie based) or physical location (proximity based).[23] The premise of tie-based apps is that you con-nect them to other apps or to your contacts list on your smartphone. Secret, for example—launched in 2014 and shut down by its founder in 2015—allowed users to anonymously share secrets with their Facebook friends or phone contacts.[24] People's secrets appeared in a feed displayed on the Secret app and users were told only that a secret had been posted by a "friend" or "friend of a friend."[25] Proximity-based apps work a bit differently. Born-again anonymous app Yik Yak, for example, works by displaying a feed of "Yaks" (posts, basically) from unnamed users within a five-mile radius. This means apps like Yik Yak work especially well in campus settings, like universities. Not all proximity-based anonymous apps use geo-locative data, though (in fact, this is quite rare). Most apps in this category instead offer *localized* anonymity: where users are linked together by their affiliation, usually a school or university, and are verified by signing up with their institutional email address.

To make things even more complicated, there are several subgenres of anonymous apps, defined as such not necessarily by their technical functionality (as delineated by the proximity/tie-based model) but rather by how they are marketed. While this list is not intended to be exhaustive and may well have changed by the time the reader finds this book, it aims to give a sense of the diversity of communication available within the anonymous app genre. *Secret-telling apps* like Whisper (2012-present) emphasize telling secrets or confessing to something, usually to an audience of known individuals but sometimes to total strangers. These apps want people to reveal hidden things about themselves or the people they know. People use *feedback or Q&A apps* like Tellonym (2016–present) to ask a question to a known audience and receive anonymized answers. Some apps frame this as asking for "feedback" on, say, a user's personality or appearance. They are usually connected to mainstream social apps, meaning people receive anonymized responses from people they know. *Gossip apps* like Yik Yak (2013–

2017; 2021–present) typically offer something called localized anonymity. This means users are linked together by their affiliation, usually a school or university, and are verified by signing up with their institutional email address. Apps like this often display a feed of posts from anonymized people within a user's network, meaning they are often used for spreading gossip about known individuals. Finally, *social apps* like Fling (2014–2016) connect you to complete strangers, enabling you to expand your social network. These apps often allow video and image sharing and work by connecting you to a specific person in a randomized way.

The apps I list above can be further categorized as follows: in *standalone* apps anonymous communication takes place only within the app; in *embedded* apps, functionalities from anonymous apps are merged with mainstream apps—for example, using YOLO to ask your Snapchat friends for anonymized feedback; *hybrid* can do both of the above (exist either in a standalone way or be embedded into other apps if a user so chooses). By the time this book comes out, the currently trending anonymous apps will almost certainly have tombstones in the social media graveyard. But one reason I have crafted the typology above is because the sub-genres I list will likely still be popular, and so, in their efforts to learn about anonymous apps, I encourage readers to think beyond individual apps and consider the sub-genre to which they belong.

Introducing Jaynes Confessionals

Crucial context for this chapter is an incident that occurred at Jaynes Sixth Form College in the months preceding my very first research visit, in June 2021. This incident led their then head of safeguarding, Dave, who later became the college's deputy headteacher and one of my interviewees, to invite me to speak to their students about social media safety. The college later welcomed me to conduct my fieldwork. At Jaynes, a still unidentified student—let's called them Anon—set up an account on the anonymous app Tellonym and asked college students to submit gossip about their peers and staff at the school. Founded in 2016, Tellonym is a Q&A app "that lets you ask and answer questions about each other anonymously and non-anonymously."[26] As the Internet Matters organization tells us, Tellonym is highly popular among teens and has proven to be very controversial. Two schools in the Greater Manchester area in England have issued warnings to parents about the app, claiming it allows "inappropriate postings, comments and photographs which have caused upset and distress to young people," and two other schools have experienced incidents that led to police involvement.[27] Messages sent and received through Tellonym are called tells, and every tell "is sent and received to the recipient's private inbox, which no one else can see."[28] If a person decides to respond to a tell, the original question (but not the identity of the sender) will become visible to all other users who are following the tell recipient. The person who initiated the gossip account on Tellonym, Anon, used their smartphone to take screenshots of the tells they received and then re-shared them to a separate Instagram account. This Instagram account became highly followed among students at Jaynes and even by non-students from the surrounding area. The account was called Jaynes Confessionals and the point of it was to spread unsubstantiated gossip about the college's students and staff. None of the staff ever found out who Anon was, but I suspect some of the students knew.

Each school I've worked with since 2020 has experienced an incident with either anonymous apps or school-based meme accounts, but this phenomenon—truly widespread across English schools and, I suspect, others around the world—isn't widely discussed academically. This baffles me, because it's no exaggeration to say that Jaynes Confessionals touched the lives of every student at the college, even if they were never featured on it. It affected the staff who worked at the college and even those who simply worked nearby. Maddie and Alisha, both 17, told me that even the woman who ran the local sandwich shop was the focus of "creepy" and "sexual" comments shared through the app.

By the time I took my final research visits to Jaynes Sixth Form College in April 2022, some of the students I interviewed had joined the college *after* Jaynes Confessionals was shut down by its founder. This is an important point to note early on. I interviewed students from two different academic year groups, meaning the anonymous apps they used—and the associated school-wide app dramas they described—were different for each. The themes and experiences, however, had striking similarities, which is why I have grouped them together in my analysis. Newer iterations of Jaynes Confessionals were on the rise, making all students' experiences and views of anonymous apps strikingly similar, once again reminding us that it almost doesn't matter what the name of the app is or what's in vogue now. What matters is what the apps essentially do and how they tap into longer-standing aspects of teenage life, like bullying, surveillance, sexualization, gender norms, and popularity. I now turn to a discussion of the findings from this research, grouping them into two broad categories. I first discuss why anonymous apps are so globally popular among teens, before explaining why individual apps so often fail. Crucial to note before we get into these sections is that, although I have separated these explanations largely for ease of reading, one cannot exist without the other—that is, the reasons anonymous apps become so popular among teens are precisely the ones that contribute to their downfall.

Why Are Anonymous Apps So Popular?

1. They enable identity exploration.

Anonymous apps are popular because their users don't have to put their names or faces to what they say. This means the apps' popularity among young people, particularly teens, makes perfect sense. As Davis puts it, "Questions of identity—the sense of who one is and in what one believes—loom large for adolescents in Western societies. It is during this stage of development that individuals contemplate for the first time such questions as 'Who am I? How do I fit into the world around me?'"[29] During adolescence, you decide which parts of your evolving identity you want to share with others—a process called *self-disclosure*. There's lots of evidence to suggest that people disclose different things according to the stage of adolescence they are in (early, middle, or late), and there are significant gender differences in self-disclosure behaviors. Adolescents also tend to lean more toward friends for self-disclosure than toward their parents or families as they grow up. Talking about mother-child relationships, Watson and Valtin note that the ages 5 through 12 "witness a shift from a seeming willingness to tell mother everything—even incriminating information confided by a friend—to an unwillingness to tell her many things," a shift that is then amplified during teenage years.[30] Though secret sharing is a known form of relationship building between teens, there are still things they wouldn't want their friends to know. For example, Solís et al. explain that teens tend to tell their friends about "bad" behaviors like staying out late rather than more personal secrets.[31] And there are some things teens don't want to tell *anyone* known to them in a face-to-face setting (or, at least, things they don't want to be traced back to them). Enter: anonymous apps.

Even the few teens I spoke to who don't use anonymous apps, like 17-year-old Monica, clearly recognized their place in young lives:

> MONICA: There are a lot of people in homes where they can't speak to anyone, or schools that are just lacking in mental health [guidance], and just society in general. Even though it's definitely getting better with mental health, there are definitely some societies that are very rigid and don't talk about mental health. And it's a sort of like . . . it's a safe . . . well mostly safe for someone to be able to tell someone if they can't also like expose who they are because of maybe reputation or . . .

Monica is a White British pupil at Jaynes Sixth Form College and was one of my most empathetic research participants, telling me much more about her concerns regarding *other* people's lives, particularly her worries about their mental health, than she did about her own. She loves music, telling me she "couldn't live without" it, and enjoys reading fiction in her spare time. Monica spoke at length about the systems shaping her and her peers' experiences, particularly of school and technology (and the relationship between those two things). It therefore came as no surprise that, though she had never used anonymous apps herself, she could empathize with their users and recognized their social value. Teens who do use anonymous apps use them to talk about things like bodily functions, gender identity, home life dynamics, mental health issues, and romantic relationships. They also sought compliments about their personality or appearance.

Seventeen-year-old Asian-British Lyrica, for example, told me that she uses the anonymous chat section of the Flo app—a women's health app offering insights into menstrual health—to ask questions about her period and discharge patterns, because there's "no way in hell" she could ask those questions at home. Lyrica told me that, much against her parents' intentions for her, she would describe herself as "quite a stereotypical creative person" who, just like Monica, loves music and music production along with acting and theater. Warren and Laslett explain that those most likely to benefit from secrecy include those who have "inadequate financial or other resources to provide themselves with privacy," like children and "the morally stigmatized."[32] Because Monica feels people her age have been failed institutionally—because they don't feel able to speak to their teachers or other authority figures in their lives and because mental health provision isn't up to scratch—they receive substantial benefits from anonymous apps. Anonymity afforded Lyrica the opportunity to gain vital insight into her menstrual health, something she felt unable to obtain in face-to-face settings due to stigma and other cultural constraints.

2. They are useful mechanisms to evade stigma.

The topics listed above—bodily functions, gender identity, home-life dynamics, mental health issues, and romantic relationships—are difficult for some teens to discuss with people they know. A secret is defined as "'knowledge which is intentionally concealed but which may be shared with a restricted audience."[33] In a social media age, this audience is often found through anonymous apps.

As I explained in chapter 1, Warren and Laslett made a conceptual distinction between privacy and secrecy in 1977 which, in my view, still holds true today. They explained that secrecy "implies the concealment of something which is negatively valued by the excluded audience and, in some instances, by the perpetrator as well."[34] This means secrecy is "not only a strategy for hiding acts or attributes which others hold in moral disrepute, but it is also a means to escape being stigmatized for them."[35] Privacy, on the other hand, "protects behavior which is either morally neutral or valued by society as well as by the perpetrators."[36] But everyone has secrets, and a person's desire to conceal aspects of their identity on social media should not readily be conflated with wrongdoing. Like 17-year-old Molly said:

> MOLLY: I think that's why anonymous apps have become so popular: because people don't have to expose themselves, and people won't think you're a bad person or a good person because no one knows who you are.

Molly—one of my White British participants—fell into the non-anonymous-app-user group and had strong opinions on the apps' dangers, which she had held since she was around 12 or 13 years old, long before the Jaynes Confessionals incident. She, like Monica, was an extremely empathetic person, able to put her own fears of the apps aside to recognize why they were appealing to her peers. Molly was another music lover in the group. But she focused more on discovering new music and taking inspiration from her different emotions during the day to seek out something to match her mood to specific songs. She was also learning Spanish at the time we spoke and, though I didn't directly ask her which universities she was applying to, Molly told me she was "definitely not"—with crystal-clear emphasis—applying to study at Oxbridge (the universities of Oxford or Cambridge), unlike her older brother.

There's plenty of academic research about disclosing secrets. Watson and Valtin explain that children tell different kinds of secrets—which they classify as guilty, innocent, dangerous, and embarrassing—according to their age.[37] For children and young people, one of the benefits of disclosing secrets is to build trust with their peers.[38] Anonymous apps have, of course, changed the nature of such disclosures: maybe you use a tie-based app to tell a school friend a secret but they don't know who sent it, or you might use a more general confessional-style app to get something off your chest and see if it resonates with anyone. But we've been sharing our secrets in this way for decades, even centuries. Remember when you used to scribble your secrets on the bathroom wall at school? There's a name for it: latrinalia.[39] So while anonymous apps might feel new and scary, they have an analogue precedent and might be considered "the bathroom stall for a younger generation."[40]

3. They aren't as public facing as other social apps.
Crucial to the appeal of anonymous apps—particularly among my research participants—is that many of their users have grown up on social media. Mainstream, older platforms like Instagram thus hold an enormous backlog of content about teens, giving rise to reasonable concerns about what their digital archive will mean for them as they grow up. I am a millennial and I grew up on MSN Messenger, Habbo Hotel, Neopets, and Myspace. Facebook made its way into my friendship groups when I was about 17 and formed a core part of my undergraduate university experience. Then, in my early twenties, I moved on to Instagram, where I rewarded my

earliest followers with highly artistic, heavily filtered photos of trees, something 17-year-old Alisha, one of my research participants, certainly didn't approve of:

> ALISHA: Sorry if anyone still does this, but I used to take a picture of my food and stuff way back when I first started Instagram. It's just . . . no one cares.

While I would certainly say I grew up online, the technologies I used as a teen didn't reach nearly as far into my everyday life as today's top platforms. Stories, Snaps, Reels, Shorts: features found across social apps like these encourage people to capture their lives spontaneously using handheld, all-encompassing devices that may rarely leave their owners' side. But when I was a teen, I would upload pictures from my digital camera to a Facebook album at some point after a big night out or a holiday: certainly not the style of communication today's teens engage in.

An attitude among the educators I spoke to—and one that had been internalized by many of the teens at Jaynes Sixth Form College—was that once it's on social media, it's there forever. This is a concept I discuss in depth in chapter 4, but I mention it here because it forms a core part of anonymous apps' enduring popularity. This discourse has created a sense of fear among teens that saying the "wrong" thing on more public social media fora might come back to ruin the rest of their lives. Anonymous apps, however, don't hold information in a profile. You don't upload albums of images or categorize or archive posts in any way, and you're certainly not encouraged to use your legal name or real images of yourself. In their definition of social media platforms, Burgess et al. rightly center "content sharing, public communication, and interpersonal connection" instead of the profile and its showcasing of friends and networks, as we typically saw in earlier definitions of social networks.[41] That said, the apps aren't *actually* anonymous. In 2013, Hannah Smith, a 14-year-old English girl, died by suicide "after what her family described as 'months of torment'" on the anonymous app Ask.fm, wherein Hannah received devastating messages criticizing her appearance and urging her to kill herself.[42] As Milosevic explains, "Ask.fm agreed to cooperate with the police in determining the cause behind the girl's death and in revealing the identities behind the usernames, which the coroner had obtained from Hannah's computer and mobile phone."[43]

Let's take anonymous app Yik Yak as another example. While marketing itself as an anonymous app, Yik Yak's privacy and legal policies state that users' anonymity could be breached by providing information like IP addresses, date and time stamps, GPS coordinates, and Yik Yak handles or usernames to "'comply with the law, a judicial proceeding, court order, subpoena or other legal process.'"[44] For reference, Yik Yak was initially launched in 2013 but, after significant controversies (like bomb threats at US universities), the app was "sold for scrap" in 2017.[45] In 2021, however, the app returned from the dead, accompanied by an annoyingly good catchphrase: *the yak is back*.[46] Yik Yak's policies remind us that online anonymity is not an "absolute condition."[47] It should instead be understood as a *spectrum*, ranging "from the totally anonymous to the thoroughly named."[48] Although anonymous apps can therefore be deanonymized in rare instances like the one described above, the *discourse* of anonymity was, for the teens in my research, a far more powerful force than the apps' technical actualities.

Some concerns about the longevity of digital data can be amusing. When Molly, whom I introduced earlier, first went to download the TikTok app, she realized she already had an account from when the app was previously called Musical.ly. Molly logged back into her account and found some videos she uploaded when she was 12 years old, laughing her head off and telling me: "I really wanted to die [when I saw them]. I did not know this was on the internet." But there are many instances where people's old social media posts have come back to haunt them, especially ones expressing racist, sexist, homophobic, or similar sentiments. These anecdotes—which are then relayed back to teens by adults and educators—lead teens to value spaces where they can say things they fear they may be judged for in the future. What is so ironic about this formulation is that teens are warned about posting the "wrong" things on social media and are told to worry about what might come back to haunt them in the future. But at the same time, and quite paradoxically, they feel they are berated by some people in their lives—sometimes their peers, sometimes by adults—for using anonymous apps and for valuing anonymity in general. And while anonymous apps are clearly valuable spaces that allow teens to evade social stigma, they can also be experienced as places where those same stigmas are perpetuated, making their usage at once risky and rewarding.

Why Do Anonymous Apps Fail?

1. They attract bullying behaviors.
If you search for "anonymous apps" on Google News or a similar search engine, I am willing to bet the first few results will be about bullying. This is for good reason. Although the purpose of this chapter is to make a nuanced, evidence-based contribution to heated debates about anonymous apps, I know full well they are

used for bullying. The apps have factored into several teens' suicides, and they can be the reason many kids hate going to school. These facts are even well known among anonymous app founders: speaking to the founder of Lipsi—designed for young people to receive anonymous feedback from their peers—Matthew Segal in 2018, *Refinery29* writer Madeline Buxton writes, "Segal is well of aware of the bad precedent of the business he's in. 'Anonymous messaging is a very tarnished and stigmatized field—I knew that from the get-go,' Segal told *Refinery29* over email."[49] I conducted my research because few academics had directly asked teens below university age about their views and experiences of anonymous apps, and I wanted to put their voices at the forefront of public debates about the apps' places in our digital society. As someone who effectively grew up online and who teaches about the complexities of human-technology relations, I went into my research with an open mind, welcome to the possibility of finding wholesome stories about anonymous apps. And while I certainly heard those stories, I also found real problems.

. . .

The main reason anonymous apps fail is because they attract bullying behaviors. Anonymous apps, which typically become very popular very quickly, are often not adequately staffed or technically designed to cope with bad behavior, and so they are removed from app stores after a run of bad press, earning their rightful place in the social media Hall of Shame.[50] While bullying can take place on any social app, the argument goes that people are likelier to bully others when their own identity is unknown. This is because of something called the *online disinhibition effect:* when people say and do things online "that they wouldn't ordinarily say and do in the face-to-face world. They loosen up, feel less restrained, and express themselves more openly."[51] But there's a real chicken-and-egg formulation to understanding bullying on anonymous apps: Do the apps attract bullying behaviors because communication is anonymized, or do app users—exposed to bad press about the apps' dangers—behave badly because that's what they think the app is for?

According to Englander et al., bullying has three characteristics: an *intent* to hurt and a *repetition* of hurtful behavior, both of which are enabled by a *power imbalance* between a bully and their recipient(s).[52] The Anti-Bullying Alliance similarly defines bullying as "the repetitive, intentional hurting of one person or group by another person or group, where the relationship involves an imbalance of power. It can happen face to face or online."[53] This online-offline distinction led to the emergence of a new term in academic and other literature in the mid-2000s: cyberbullying. Cyberbullying is said to differ from what might be termed *traditional* or *face-to-face* bullying for three key reasons: (1) bullies can be anonymous (in other words, they can conceal parts of their identity), (2) online spaces offer different levels of publicness from other bullying fora, and (3) there is—especially among children and young people—a sense that bullying does not stop when you get home from school or other social occasions.[54]

Cyberbullying "is not easily defined and operationalized."[55] Indeed, academic consensus seems to be that there is no consensus, given the term's famed difficulties to be defined. As Sheanoda et al. noted in 2021, confusion about the definition of cyberbullying among academics is also shared by young people.[56] Borrowing from Miller and Slater's exploration of internet use in Trinidad,

Hine's work on embeddedness can help us understand this tension.[57] Hine rejects a distinction between digital and non-digital lives, arguing that digital technologies have become so deeply "entwined with multiple forms of context and frames of meaning-making" that it's no longer wise to separate them out.[58] Livingstone and Third make a similar point: "We need to move beyond the idea that children's digital practices constitute a specialized set of activities cleaved off from the so-called 'real world'. We must concern ourselves not only with 'what happens online' but also with how what happens online is entwined with the conditions and possibilities of children's everyday lives."[59]

An embedded approach to internet research represents one of many moves away from scholarly and other constructions of the internet as a cyberspace, a term popularized during the first wave of internet research in the late 1980s and early 1990s. It captured dominant discourses of the internet at the time, in which it was imagined to be a domain set "apart from everyday life," in part because of the non-portability of desktop computers and because anonymity was celebrated, not stigmatized.[60] The so-called online disinhibition effect is said to occur when a person *disassociates* what they say or do online from the rest of their lives: "They don't have to own their behavior by acknowledging it within the full context of an integrated online/offline identity. The online self becomes a compartmentalized self."[61] But Hine's embedded approach embraces the many ways (materially, technically, psychologically) technologies like social media get wrapped up in our lives and are tough to fully disentangle from. It alludes to the fact that it is very difficult to be truly anonymous online, and our compartmentalized identities and identity trails are linked together in ways we cannot imagine. Using an online-offline justification for separating bullying from cyberbullying therefore risks minimizing the intricate overlap between these two phenomena.

Anonymity is emphasized in academic literature as a central, defining feature of cyberbullying, but anonymity is not a necessity for this kind of behavior. Some research "suggests that children know who the so-called perpetrators are, and cyberbullying can happen within close relationships between one-time friends."[62] Statistics paint a similar picture: in the 2014 Pew Internet Report, of those adults who experienced online harassment, only 38 percent said a stranger was responsible for their most recent incident.[63] Not all my participants had ever used an anonymous app: as 17-year-old Molly said, "I just don't like the idea of using [them], not even to say anything positive." Smith, also 17, said something similar as he emphasized his lack of need for the apps in contrast to "certain types of people":

> SMITH: I feel like these apps are for certain types of people, like people who are, I don't know, depressed and they want to talk about something, or I don't know, there's a certain type of people. I'm not that type of person.

Asian-British Smith was one of my quieter participants. He took part in a paired interview with Alexandra and was fairly closed off in the first half of our conversation, perhaps because his first introduction to anonymous apps was through my workshop. Smith didn't use social media very often, telling me he uses "WhatsApp for family, [and] Instagram and Snapchat for friends," and only uses the latter two platforms to talk to people he knows through in-person settings. Smith was an admirably hard worker, pursuing a degree in medicine at either the University of Leeds or the

University of Sheffield. He told me he didn't have much free time to use social media:

> SMITH: I'm trying to get into medicine, so I think the other day I deleted Snapchat. I was like, "I can't be on this, I need to work hard." So I feel like being in college has taken me away from social media.

When asked to tell me a little about himself as we sat down for our interview, Smith shrugged and said there was "nothing interesting" to know, other than his favorite color ("dark red"). But as the interview progressed, the balance of speaking time shifted from Alexandra to Smith, which I was very pleased with, as I felt it reflected his growing comfort in the interview space. He spoke extensively about the rules he feels social apps, not just anonymous apps, should have and particularly the guardrails he would like to see in relation to bullying. While he echoed some social stereotypes of anonymous apps during the interview, perhaps due to his non-use, his views on the social media platforms he had directly experienced were incredibly nuanced.

My participants who had used anonymous apps, however, told me detailed stories of the bullying behaviors they personally experienced or witnessed, which included appearance-based insults, encouragement to self-harm (e.g., KYS (kill yourself)), threats to their own or others' lives, fake compliments, gossip about sex or relationships, homophobia, photo manipulation (with intent to harm), and sexist name-calling (e.g., slag, bitch). There was an especially interesting gender dynamic in discussions of bullying among my participants. I noticed that my male participants usually talked about things that happened to other people, mainly girls, whereas my female and non-binary participants talked about problems *they* had faced. But this finding may itself be gendered: in Ofcom's 2022 Media Use and Attitudes Report, the organization reported that "girls were significantly more likely than boys to say that they would always tell someone about something worrying or nasty that they had seen."[64] This finding isn't new: one of the first academic discussions of cyberbullying (as a distinct phenomenon from bullying) reported that most victims and witnesses did not report the incident to adults.[65] It's hard to know whether boys do genuinely experience fewer instances of bullying than girls and non-binary teens or if they just talk about it less, for reasons that are deeply ingrained into our social fabric.

Two of my female participants—17-year-olds Charlie and Chloe, who I say more about later—also wondered about male perspectives on the apps. They assumed girls would have a "worse" (Charlie) opinion of anonymous apps, whereas "guys would be like, 'it was just a laugh'" (Chloe). Here, Charlie and Chloe are referring to the kinds of banter often articulated by (and associated with) groups of young men, especially in a British context, through which sexist comments can be passed off as just "having a laugh."[66] Declaring something as banter provides "a way for men to convey discourses of gender relations and sexist ideas" in a way that diminishes the "implications and effects" of the comments.[67] Charlie and Chloe imagine that, when boys do experience online harms, they are better equipped than other genders to pass them off as harmless remarks. While male participants told me they try to shrug off bullying on anonymous apps, my female and non-binary participants were likelier to link their app usage to a loss of control and agency—a sentiment captured by 17-year-old Bella, who readers first met in the introduction: "It's like getting a phone call and no caller ID; you're like, 'Who is this?' Like, 'What do you want?' You're just a bit powerless."

Anonymous apps did not only make female and non-binary teens feel powerless; participants of all genders noted the deep paranoia they felt, not only while using the apps but at other times as well. Just knowing the apps exist and that someone might be talking about them was a source of anxiety, an issue I discuss in the next section. As Lyrica explained, "the bad things weren't really horrendous from my perspective, it was just more of a building of what it could be. It was more of a 'What if?' than an 'It's happening.'" White-British Arthur, 17 years old, said something very similar. For him, there are "aspects of, like, paranoia" that accompany anonymous app use. While you could receive a comment that says: "Oh, I think blah de blah looks really nice today, I wish I was dating them or something," there's "another side of it, where someone could say something personal, and then you didn't know where to place it." Arthur and Lyrica were interviewed together and were clearly very close friends, making the interview a real pleasure to conduct. Arthur described himself as an "all-rounder" in terms of interests and hobbies, which included musical theater ("and theater in general") and sport, and he floated between different social groups within and beyond his college with ease. Arthur disliked anonymous apps, telling me that he went against the grain when he was a high school student by trying to get his school confessions page shut down, because "people were really upset about it." Like Lyrica, Arthur didn't get many "horrendous" comments about himself through the apps, as the comments he received were thankfully mainly focused on "really small things." He gives examples like, "Oh, is your hair different." But for both Lyrica and Arthur, the issue wasn't so much with the comments themselves but with the climate of distrust the looming presence of the apps created among their friendship groups:

> LYRICA: It became like a trust issue with your friends. 'Cause if something personal's mentioned, then you kind of over-think everyone you've ever talked to. Like, did I say that to someone? Did someone say that about me? Have they said something? . . . And it's like, when it goes from being funny to, like, you turning on your own friends—so it's like, "I said that to you, now that's out, why did you say that, was that you?"

For many teens, the pleasures and perils of anonymous apps come from their *anticipatory* nature. Lyrica puts it powerfully when she says "I think this entire platform is just built on the fear of teenagers." Perceptions among my participants were that anonymous apps are, like many social phenomena, worse for girls and nonbinary people, along with those who are of color and not heterosexual. Like 17-year-old Jess said, for girls, "mean" comments and appearance-based insults—as I discuss later—are par for the course on anonymous apps:

> JESS: I received just like, some straight up mean comments, like, "You're annoying," "You're ugly," things like that. *Just the basics.*

It became clear to me early on in our interview that Jess—who was interviewed alongside her friend Claire—had been bullied in her younger years. White-British Jess absolutely loves her dogs and going for long walks and has a personal style that wasn't mirrored by any of the other teens I interviewed, which reflected her statement that she'd made a conscious effort to become more comfortable in her own skin throughout her adolescence. During the workshop, Jess looked back on some of the comments she had previously received on an anonymous app connected to Instagram. While some people "would genuinely be nice, being kind and making inside jokes" to Jess, she ultimately felt the app's "negatives probably do outweigh the positives." When I asked Jess if her peers had similar experiences with anonymous apps, she only ever told me stories about girls, as she "didn't know many boys who actually used them." According to Jess, one of the girls in her year group "got hate so bad" through anonymous apps that "they went and spoke to teachers about it, and then the teachers had to do a whole assembly on it all." Sharing gendered experiences like Jess' is not, of course, intended to diminish the experiences of the boys, some of whom told me that they received comments encouraging them to take their own lives, among other incredibly harmful things. While the nature of this experience varied across genders, all active and previous users of anonymous apps spoke of their general feelings of paranoia when one is trending at a school. Clearly, then, young people's experiences of anonymous apps are deeply contextual, especially varying by gender identity.

2. They are used for gossip and rumor spreading.
Anonymous apps offer the perfect breeding ground for spreading gossip and rumors about known individuals; Jaynes Confessionals provides a good example of this. To my surprise, a couple of my participants admitted to using anonymous apps to bully their peers. I didn't expect this to happen and later wondered if my own identity had helped me here: I was in my very late twenties when I conducted my interviews, but I wore the kinds of clothes they might wear and looked a bit younger than my age (or so I was told).

On one of my visits, for example, I wore an Urban Outfitters blue corduroy zip-up jacket, a plain white T-shirt tucked into navy blue tailored trousers, along with white Nike Air Force Ones and a black Kånken backpack. To be clear, I didn't strategically wear these clothes to make me look younger: I wore them because they reflected my personal style at the time, and I felt I owed it to my participants—who told me so much about their lives and gave up their time to speak to me—to be as much *myself* as I appropriately could. After admitting she had made a few comments about her peers on anonymous apps, Bella said:

> BELLA: I'm so embarrassed I did that, like I don't even remember doing it. I was young, but I think it's just one of them things like . . . I think when you're young, you're bored, and I guess when you are younger . . . Like probably people have certain things going on at home and when you can anonymously bully someone, it's pretty easy, like, you can get whatever stress or tension you've got out on just these apps.

Very early on in our interview, after we'd spent some time together in the pre-interview workshop, Bonnie and Clyde likewise admitted to bullying their peers on Jaynes Confessionals. Bonnie and Clyde—who participated in a paired interview—were, like the aliases they chose for themselves, an exceptionally memorable duo. They were the very best of friends and perfectly matched each other's energy. After I had hit the record button and asked them to tell me a little about themselves, Bonnie insisted that "age [goes] before beauty" and shifted the spotlight to Clyde, who rolled his eyes and told me he was 18 years old, White British, and gay, with interests in philosophy, politics, and dance. Seventeen-year-old,

White British, and bisexual Bonnie told me she "constantly, a bit obsessively" reads feminist literature and was described by Clyde as a "horse girl" (as am I, and I told her that). Theirs was the only interview in which I nearly abandoned my semi-structured guide only one question in:

> YSABEL: Okay, so I did have this list of questions, but I just want to be like, "No, tell me about Jaynes Confessionals. Tell me how you felt."
> CLYDE: I really liked it.
> BONNIE: I loved it.
> CLYDE: I proper rinsed people on it though, which I don't know if I should admit to.

As our interview progressed, the pair's conversation took a more serious turn. I noticed that both Bonnie and Clyde—Bonnie in particular—had troubling experiences on the app, making me wonder if their bold and unabashed statements at the start of our interview were masking deeper feelings about Jaynes Confessionals. While I don't doubt that the duo made harsh comments about their peers, their overall experience of Jaynes Confessionals was far more complex. Clyde, for example, exposed a peer, Jake, for cheating on Bonnie:

> CLYDE: Jake got quite a lot [of hate], but he had it coming.
> BONNIE: Oh yeah, he had it coming.
> YSABEL: Why did he have it coming?
> CLYDE: He had sex with Bonnie and then straight afterwards he was making moves on other girls like "Oh yeah, she was a good shag though she's proper ugly. I was just trying to get my numbers up."

Jaynes Confessionals wasn't Bonnie's first experience with an anonymous app-related drama. Bonnie wasn't as local to Jaynes as some of the other students were and she travelled further than others to reach the campus. She chose Jaynes because it was a mixed-gender sixth form college, in contrast to her all-girls private (paid-for) high school (which, to put it bluntly, she hated). Bonnie spent most of her time at high school being bullied by other girls and found solace in horse riding. At one point, her mood became so low that she developed an eating disorder and tried to take her own life: something she and Clyde have in-jokes about, demonstrating the depth of their friendship and, hopefully, comfort during their paired interview. Clyde shared a similar story about his own journey through adolescence:

> CLYDE: I was a dickhead at high school. I'll put it out there. I got bullied at the first high school I went to and then just did the complete opposite and was a bully at the second one. So I knew for a fact . . . and I was gay as well back then, raging neon pink hair, back then living in the most conservative town.

While Bonnie and Clyde both admitted (with varying levels of directness) to being bullies, their decision to post gossip about their peers to anonymous apps must be read within this broader social context.

For Jaynes students, *especially* for girls, the confessionals account heightened their feelings of peer and sexual surveillance. Maddie, for example, said that, when the account was just starting out and still in a "jokey" phase, she didn't necessarily mind if she was mentioned. But "as it got bigger, I was reading through the posts and I was like, 'Oh god, what if I'm mentioned?' I was actually kind of scared that everyone in the college would see." Alisha, 17, who was interviewed alongside Maddie, her friend, said something very similar: because Jaynes Confessionals began when students returned from a pandemic-related nationwide lockdown, and therefore didn't really know each other's names, descriptions of students were vague. Alisha said she'd likely be described as "just like 'Oh, that blond girl in my class,'" instead of by her name. But:

> ALISHA: Every time it would start off like that, I thought, "Oh my god, what if it's me?" But it never was. I don't know if that's good or bad, but you were always just scared you were going to be on it.

Alisha and Maddie—two friends who chose to take part in a paired interview—gave me by far the most descriptive details about Jaynes Confessionals. While this meant they said a little less about themselves and their experiences with anonymous apps than my other participants, they took a lot of pleasure in teaching me everything I needed to know about the incident. Maddie told me that she was keen to pursue a career in psychology, specifically criminal psychology, and enjoys following sports on social media. Like Arthur, Alisha was aiming to pursue a career in medicine after sixth form, though she did not articulate quite the same restrictive relationship with social media that he did.

Charlie and Chloe articulated particularly intense feelings of surveillance in relation to anonymous apps. They recognized their experience as being tied to gendered norms around appearance and sexuality, which I say more about in the next section. Crucial to note here, though, is that Jaynes Confessionals didn't exist solely through an anonymous app (Tellonym, in this case). It was brought to life by *screenshots* of messages sent into Tellonym by Jaynes students, which were then shared to a dedicated Instagram account. Screenshots—the act of taking an exact image of the data you can see on a smartphone, tablet, or other digital screen (e.g., a WhatsApp conversation or an email)—have a social life beyond their immediate technical functions.[68] Jaynes explains that, within teen friendship groups, screenshots play an integral role in group members' negotiations of "hierarchies of friendship, power, and for establishing peer trust."[69]

Those rare students who were never featured on Jaynes Confessionals, either because they simply did not or because they were in the younger year group, seemed to have a more neutral—indeed, sometimes celebratory—opinion of it, often seeing the humorous side. Some students claimed their peers' experiences of Jaynes Confessionals were tied to their social status. For example, I was told multiple times that the "Emos" who socialized in an area called Virgin Alley at break times didn't fare so well on the apps (Dave, the sixth form's deputy headteacher, was mortified I had learned of this anecdote). But then again, neither did the "popular" kids, as Chloe explained:

> CHLOE: I remember one girl, she was on there so many times, there was one post on her each time it posted.
>
> YSABEL: Why her?
>
> CHLOE: Because she's a confident lass and she goes round talking to everyone, so she's quite popular and stuff like that and she's deemed as fit and stuff like that. There were so many posts about it because I've spoken to her about it as well and she just felt really awkward and didn't particularly

want to come into college because of it. Because I know it's
not a bad comment, but you don't know who's been saying it,
[and] people are going to be staring at you and judging
whether you are fit or not.

It was clear from my interactions with Chloe and the other students, mainly the girls, that Chloe fell into the "popular" group.
But 17-year-olds Claire and Jess, who both told me they fell into the
"middle" of the popularity spectrum felt that popular girls primarily received compliments. They told me the lesser-popular social
groups received the harshest bullying, not necessarily through blatantly mean comments but through "fake compliments":

CLAIRE: I don't think they always realized, and a lot of the time I
felt really bad, because I just knew that, at a girls' sleepover,
they were all there like having a laugh at that, and being like
"Ha, ha, nobody actually likes you" kind of thing, by saying
like, "Oh my God, I really like you" and stuff like that. And I
feel like that was quite prominent in my school, rather than
like, people actually insulting people. It was a lot of like
taking the mick of people by fake compliments.

Although Claire's comment referred to her use of anonymous
apps at a younger age, what became clear during my research was
that teens who stand out in a given social spectrum in any way—
including because of their identity—have a disproportionately bad
time during school-based incidents like Jaynes Confessionals. For
example, some students—along with the college's deputy
headteacher, Dave—told me that there were a few homophobic
posts on Jaynes Confessionals. Chloe also linked her racial

identity—being one of the few Black girls at a predominantly White college—to her experiences of Jaynes Confessionals. During our interview, Chloe described her passion for wearing bright clothing and for weaving vivid colors into her braids. Chloe told me these choices were pivotal for embracing her racial identity and heritage, but her fears of being featured in Jaynes Confessionals led her to dramatically change her appearance:

> CHLOE: I just didn't want to get included in it, I didn't want to be written about. I just wore . . . you know how sometimes I will wear different clothing?
>
> CHARLIE: Yeah, you just wore plain clothing so no one could slate you.
>
> CHLOE: Yeah, I just wore plain clothing and I blended in. . . . It was really anxiety inducing because it made you feel like everybody's eyes were on you, everybody was watching. . . . I'm constantly looking around to see if anyone is staring at me. . . . I come to college wearing baggy clothes now, so nobody can see. It's like . . . I don't come to college to be sexualized, I come to college to learn. I shouldn't have to worry about being sexualized.

Charlie then went on to say that she remembers "being so aware of myself that I could see myself in the third person" and linked this to her lived experience of Mulvey's "male gaze" theory, something she learned about at college. Indeed, Chloe's experiences of Jaynes Confessionals inspired her Extended Project Qualification (EPQ). An EPQ allows students to lead their own projects and is undertaken alongside A-Levels (a qualification English students can take for admission into university).[70] Chloe's EPQ focused on the representation of women in advertisements across different periods, using the male gaze and other feminist theories to understand the historical over-sexualization of women. I say more about appearance-related concerns in what follows, but for now I want to note that, for these reasons and more, it frankly amazes me that, while school meme and gossip accounts have been at the heart of so many teens' lives, it is still the big players—the Instagrams, the Snapchats, the TikToks—that seem to receive most public and academic attention.

3. They are used to make appearance-based insults.

One Friday evening, Amara, a teenager from an all-girls' high school in the Midlands, England, used YOLO to rank the attractiveness of her female peers. Using the YOLO add-on, Amara asked her Instagram followers to choose who they felt were the most and least attractive girls at the school. Her game spread across the school and, by the end of the weekend, Amara had arrived at what she called The Definitive List of the School's Ugliest Girls. On the following Monday morning, the school's deputy headteacher, Akshay—who knew nothing about the list or what YOLO was—had a queue of angry parents at his office door demanding repercussions for this blatant act of bullying—not for Amara alone but also for everyone who responded to her YOLO question. Akshay described this incident to me as "the modern day *Mean Girls*," referencing the film's infamous Burn Book, which the "Plastics" clique created to list a salacious piece of gossip about each of their female and gay male peers. The disclosure of a secret has historically been known for helping children to build trust with their peers.[71] But anonymous apps, especially feedback/Q&A apps, are interesting exceptions because young people often share "nice" secrets and yet they do not know who sent them. And so, while the apps offer the capacity for sharing pleasant secret thoughts and confessions, they are not useful for trust-building in the way in-person secret-telling has historically been understood. What they do offer is respite from *stigma*—but without the extra positives other forms of secret disclosure famously bring.

Stories like this came out of every school I visited and from every educator I spoke to during the course of my research. They highlight many complex facets of teen relationships with technology, like the struggles educators face to know when and how to intervene when this behavior occurs beyond the school gates. Talking about Jaynes Confessionals, Jess said: "I think the teachers didn't really know how to address it because it's a thing that's out of school, and then online" (something I say more about in chapter 4). But from teens' perspectives, The Definitive List of the School's Ugliest Girls and similar initiatives highlight a pervasive feeling of *surveillance* underpinning their experiences of anonymous apps, particularly for older female teens (16–18). Bella summarized this age-specific experience:

> BELLA: I'm 17, do you know what I mean? Like . . . things are more serious now, like relationships, friendships, home life. People go out on a weekend and do things, like, 'cause we're older. When you're like 13, 14, the only things you've really got to say are petty little comments.

Interestingly, some of the 13- and 14-year-old boys I spoke to from Mason-Oakes Academy said exactly the same thing about people younger than themselves. Fourteen-year-old Samuel, for example, said of younger kids using anonymous apps, "they're probably going to have a problem that isn't really that serious compared to a high school student in their teenage years." Samuel, whose pronouns are they/them, was a student from Mason-Oakes Academy and whose interview—and their peers' interviews—I discuss in chapter 4.

The Definitive List of the School's Ugliest Girls was far from the only appearance-based initiative circulating on anonymous apps. In the introduction, I introduced *Amuse Me or Abuse Me*, a game played by Bella in her younger years where the aim was to ask your Snapchat network to send you, again via the anonymous app YOLO, either a funny, light-hearted message or an abusive one. For Bella, there was something engaging about these games, which she continued to play despite the barrage of hateful messages she received. I am not sure I would call this "pleasure" or "enjoyment," but for Bella, the risks involved in playing games like *Amuse Me or Abuse Me* were worth taking: "I was clearly looking for people's opinions. I'm not sure why, like, I think it was just something you do when you're young." This meant Bella experienced anonymous apps as *paradoxical*: to be pleasurable to her, YOLO necessitated displeasure, like abuse. Jess made a similar point: in her younger years, she said she would use anonymous apps to ask people questions like, "What's something you couldn't live without?" But the experience of posting, tainted with the fear that she wouldn't get enough replies, led Jess to reply to her own questions (something another participant said was "cringey," so kudos to Jess for admitting this to me):

> JESS: If you don't get enough comments, [that means] nobody likes you; you're not popular. And it's a bit embarrassing if you post like: "Guys, ask me a question!" and then nobody asks you anything.

Over on Jaynes Confessionals, the founder, Anon, played a game with their followers called "Hot or Dog," in which they used Instagram to name female classmates and then ask people to anonymously say whether they were "hot" or "a dog" via Tellonym (eerily similar to how Facebook first started out). As Alexandra recalls, Anon would then count up the replies and publish them to the Jaynes Confessionals Instagram account:

> ALEXANDRA: They did polls, and it would be, like, this person ended up with 60, that one 40 and it's just sad for that person who's maybe lower. Like the other person, their self-esteem gets boosted but theirs [the first person] doesn't, and it can perhaps be bad for their mental health.

When describing Hot or Dog (and Jaynes Confessionals in general), most of my male participants, my one non-binary participant, and the teachers used "they" or no pronouns at all when describing Anon, as the person behind the account (and therefore their gender) were unknown. But I found it very interesting that pretty much all the girls said "he" when describing Anon. This could mean two things: they maybe think (or know) that this person uses he/him pronouns, or, more likely, it is because their dominant experiences of the app are gendered. As I noted earlier, the Jaynes Confessionals account was set up just as sixth formers returned to the classroom after a Covid-19 national lockdown, which happened to coincide with a new academic year. This meant pupils weren't usually described by their name on the account (unless they were prolific, like Chloe explained in the previous section) and were instead described by what they wore:

CHLOE: So, it's like, they would describe you as a person, what you were wearing and then say, "They're proper fit or they're an absolute dog," because they didn't know anyone's names. So it wasn't specific, but you would be thinking, "What am I going to wear?" I made sure they could only ever get a proper bland description of me, so nobody would know.

Here, Chloe describes how she changed her appearance when Jaynes Confessionals was an active presence at her sixth form. She would wear "bland" clothes so that, if she did feature on the app, she might not be recognizable from the description. Although Jaynes has a majority-White student population, Chloe was not the only Black girl and so she still clearly felt that changing her appearance would afford her a level of protection not just from being identified but also from being *objectified*.

My female participants across the board expressed "a clear idea of the criteria for judgement and sought to align themselves with what is deemed 'appropriate' femininity."[72] As Chloe explains below, this meant not wearing tight clothes (and therefore "revealing" her body shape); not wearing shorter length clothes, like skirts or crop tops; and not wearing overly unique clothing:

CHLOE: When we had the heatwave, oh my gosh, I was like, "I can't go to college in jeans and a jumper anymore, that's my comfort and I cannot go to college looking like that. I'm going to have to wear shorts and a T-shirt." And I was so self-conscious that entire week of people judging me and how they're seeing me.

Reflecting on Jaynes Confessionals, Bonnie similarly explained: "I have a really bad problem when it comes to image and just people looking at me, and that's when I struggle to come into College." Not all Jaynes students I spoke to felt that the Confessionals page should've been taken down (they told me that the founder took it down when it started to attract too much negative attention, like police involvement). But the overwhelming majority argued that their teachers only sought to remove the account when reputational damage had occurred to the institution. They felt the college should have instead acted when their pupils—the girls in particular—were having a difficult time. With regard to this point, I close this section with a statement made by Chloe, which was echoed by several of her peers:

> CHLOE: The college thought it was like, they're saying bad things about the college, let's take that page down. But the students were thinking, they're sexualizing teenage girls online for anyone to see, this page should be taken down.

Beyond Risk and Reward on Anonymous Apps

Dividing this chapter into a critical analysis explaining why anonymous apps are so popular and then why they so often fail does not at first seem to lend itself well to attending to the phenomenon as and through paradoxes, since it might seem to necessitate a separation between good and bad, positive and negative, helpful and harmful, which I have consciously sought to avoid throughout this book. But I organized the chapter this way deliberately, as it enabled me to show readers how and why it is that the same reasons anonymous

apps become so popular among teens—they enable identity exploration, are useful mechanisms to evade stigma, and are less public-
facing than other social apps—are precisely what contribute to their
undoing: the presence of bullying behaviors, gossip and rumor
spreading, and appearance-based insults. Clearly, anonymous apps
cannot be easily labelled as either risky or rewarding. They are, like
so many youthful technological phenomena, experienced in both
these ways, and sometimes one cannot exist without the other. We
also need to know significantly more about them before drawing
such firm, either-or conclusions. I say this in chapter 6 but also note
here that there are, of course, limitations to the knowledge I have
produced. While anonymous apps are a truly global phenomenon, I
would be keen to know if users' experiences change geographically.
Regardless, I feel confident in saying that anonymous apps are experienced by Jaynes Sixth Form College students as *paradoxical*. To be
pleasurable to teens, anonymous apps necessitate displeasures.
Participation in anonymous apps is a notoriously risky endeavor, but
only by experiencing the displeasures that accompany anonymous
app use can their users hope to achieve some pleasures or rewards
from them. Anonymous apps are risky not only in the sense that the
content might be harmful but also in the sense that their users never
quite know if their participation is going to pay off. In short, because
anonymous apps are *so* notoriously problematic, teens know their
users have to take the risk before they get the rewards. As 14-year-
old Jack said about Tellonym (a teen I introduce you to in the next
chapter), "it's so stereotyped to be an app that you're not nice to people on, so that's what it is now." Indeed, perhaps this displeasure and
the game-playing is part of the pleasure itself.

I am often asked if I think anonymous apps have a place in society, and after reading stories like Chloe's and many other teens',

it's tough to straightforwardly say yes. I also have lots of residual questions, not yet answered by my research; for example, as anonymous apps capitalize on authenticity, they become privy to teens' innermost thoughts, so what happens to their data when an app company dies, as they do so frequently? But then you read what people like 16-year-old White-British Victoria have to say: "You only really hear about an anonymous app when something goes wrong, . . . so that's what they're associated with . . . but you don't learn that you can actually get help from there." Victoria's interview was especially powerful, as she used it to tell me about a severe trauma she had experienced on anonymous apps. As a younger teen, Victoria opened a private Instagram account and only accepted follower requests from a small number of known friends. Her private Instagram was a space for Victoria to represent herself and her interests in a way she felt she couldn't on a more public account, though she didn't tell me specifically what kinds of things she posted. My assumption, based on what follows, is that she posted content she feared may be stigmatized by people beyond her close friend group. One of her "friends" then took those pictures and edited them to "make me look like, completely weird" and shared them on the "it" anonymous app her peers used at the time. The edited photos were then screenshot and widely circulated across her high school. Victoria told her mum what had happened and, while the school had formal conversations with those who shared the edited images to their real-name social media accounts (e.g., their Snapchats), no one ever found out who stole and edited the pictures in the first place.

Despite Victoria's traumatic experience, she couldn't quite decide if anonymous apps had a place in the world or not. She spoke of the value—both for herself and her peers—of using anonymous apps to escape feelings of shame and judgement: "With anonymous apps . . . if you're worried about something, you can ask it and it gives you just this sense of freedom that you're okay. 'Cause if you put your name to it, you might get judged for asking it." The contradictions littered through my interview with Victoria are, for me, precisely what make her story so striking. Victoria wasn't the only participant to whom this applied: sometimes, in the space of one sentence, teens would make contradictory statements about anonymous apps. The ones who had faced the most harm—usually people at either end of the popularity spectrum—quite understandably held the most negative views of the apps. But the people somewhere in the middle tended to see it from both sides. While ridding the world of anonymous apps felt quite extreme to most participants, they had at least witnessed, if not experienced, the harms that befall many app users.

"It's complicated" is not a great conclusion to this chapter. But, as with so many tensions in the tech-teen debate, it's all contextual, all situational. There are of course spaces away from anonymous apps teens *could* go to ask certain questions (Reddit, for example, though the site is not without its own faults), but many of these apps nudge you to upload pictures of yourself, create a profile, curate a feed, and so on, making these more mainstream platforms less conducive to secret-keeping and escapes from stigma. Social media do not have to be social in the sense that you put more and more of yourself out there for the world to see. Sometimes, as van der Nagel tells us, you want to compartmentalize aspects of your identity across platforms and, sadly for their critics, anonymous apps are ideal places for teens to ask questions about topics they feel are stigmatized.[73] I couldn't conclude this chapter any better than with the words of 17-year-old Monica:

I think the world would be a better place without anonymous apps, but that's . . . that means the world would change because people are seeking what the world doesn't have on anonymous apps . . . if the world offered it, offered this safe space to talk about something and you . . . like you can identify yourself with that—but society doesn't allow that. If the world offered this, I don't think anonymous apps would be necessary.

4 *Personal and Social Safety in Anonymous Communication*

Today's teens feel they are relentlessly warned of the dangers of social media and too often told that the online world is unsafe for them. Elements of this are unfortunately true: as Livingstone and Third note, the internet was invented by and for adults and thus inherited by children and young people.[1] This means contemporary measures taken in the name of internet safety are effectively undoing the decisions previously made by private companies with only adults and non-vulnerable populations in mind. But English teens tell me these known safety issues have resulted in precious few opportunities—both within schools and at home—for them to discuss the *benefits* of digital communication alongside the potential harms. Social anxieties around internet safety have also created an understandable situation in which teens want to use "nicknames," a word I have borrowed from my interviewees and one I use throughout this chapter, on social media and other digital spaces like gaming platforms. But today's networked teens face a conundrum: although social media participation feels much safer when they can use a nickname, opportunities for identity concealment are said to be shrinking. Anonymity is currently described as being "under attack" from technical forces, including communication infrastructures, storage and processing capabilities, sensory devices, and low-cost ways of analyzing digital data.[2] These influences are making it harder to engage in digital communication without somehow revealing who you are: where you are physically located, identity markers like your age, and other information that is increasingly easy to obtain or at the very least infer. Opportunities for identity concealment also vary geographically, as different countries are more or less stringent when it comes to real-name registration. But today's teens don't all necessarily want true anonymity (which implies the total absence of personally identifying information)—many of them just want to use social platforms without having to reveal their legal name or a photograph of themselves.

The draw of a conscious separation between online and offline lives, spaces, and selves is enduringly relevant for many young people today, and so I open this chapter by telling readers a story from my interview with Ray, an Asian-British 40-something male who was a safeguarding lead for a school trust (a group of schools working in collaboration) in Northern England. The Trust serves over 4,000 pupils, and Ray's role is, to use his words, to ensure those with special educational needs (SEN) have "the best deal" and "make the best progress" they possibly can. During our conversation, which took place through Microsoft Teams in January 2021, Ray described an incident where a group of English teens had an argument over Facebook. A number of threats were made, and the argument led to a physical fight on the grounds of the high school where Ray previously worked. When we spoke, Ray recalled a conversation he had with one of the teens:

RAY: When I was talking to one of the victims, she used the phrase—and it sticks in my mind—I asked her what had happened and she said, "Oh no, that was in real life," and I said, "Oh, what's real life?" She said, "Oh, you know, that's face to face," and I said, "So what's the other?" She said, "Oh that's real life as well, it's just we do it online," and I said, "Oh right, is there any difference at all?" She said, "No, not really, *we're just a lot braver when we're online.*"

Clearly, a discursive separation between "online" and "offline" was crucial for the teen in Ray's story to understand why a falling out on Facebook led to such a violent outcome. She seemed to suggest that people said things during the Facebook argument they would not say in face-to-face settings, hence the vicious consequences. While the teens in Ray's story were not, in fact, concealing their identities in any way through Facebook and were thus wholly accountable for their words, a perceived distinction between the *behaviors* in different communication spaces—in-person settings versus an online platform like Facebook—is clearly an enduringly powerful way today's teens make sense of social media.

What we're seeing now, as I make the final edits to this chapter from my home in England in 2024, is a negative, somewhat fearful social mood toward identity concealment, including frequent calls to end online anonymity. Such calls often launch in the wake of a high-profile, trolling-related suicide and manifest as a petition or social media campaign.[3] Within this context, anonymity is understood as both under threat and threatening.[4] This trend marks a significant shift from celebratory discourses surrounding the rise of the internet in the 1990s, on which people excitedly greeted the chance to "play a role as close to or as far away from one's 'real self'" as one chose to.[5] This wouldn't be a chapter on anonymity if it didn't mention Peter Steiner's famous cartoon in a 1993 edition of the *New Yorker*, which read, "on the Internet, nobody knows you're a dog." This cartoon represented a then novel form of human communication, in which you could (supposedly) be anyone you wanted to be, freed from your "earthly" body, "allowing for pure communication unfettered from discrimination."[6] Over thirty years on, we're hearing concerns about social media companies' failures to keep platforms safe, and even the most optimistic tech user would struggle to deny that the goal of communicating without the risk of discrimination has not been realized. No longer are internet users assumed to be excited to go online and pretend to be someone else, not least because *going* online is a spatially oriented phrase that does not feel entirely accurate anymore, given the portability of networked devices versus older, static desktop computers. As Patelis puts it, "The virtual is no longer understood as something more than an extension of real social life. Actually, one could say that virtual identity and anonymity are stigmatized. . . . Role-playing, the virtual as distinct and different from the real, is understood as fake."[7]

However, online spaces explicitly allowing identity play remain crucial for young people today, particularly those with marginalized or stigmatized identities. And as my research shows, the idea that our identities can be fragmented and are never whole or complete helps today's teens to navigate their identities across different communicative spaces.

Drawing on empirical data from qualitative interviews with 15 teens and five adults working in the English education sector, this chapter explores the motivations behind and consequences of identity concealment for today's young people. The data I present in this chapter predominantly derives from qualitative interviews I conducted with students from Mason-Oakes Academy, a non-paid-for all-boys high school located in the North of England. I interviewed a total of 15 students from Mason-Oakes Academy over the course of two research visits in July 2021, of which one participant identified as Black British, one as mixed race, and 13 as White British. All participants were aged either 13 or 14. Of these 15 participants, only one, Samuel, used they/them pronouns, with the others selecting he/him.

This chapter argues that anonymity offers young people, especially adolescents, profound *social safety*, helping them to explore their identities away from their peers' prying eyes. Anonymity also provides them with *personal safety*, as they can conceal things like their age and the school they go to, protecting them from real-world dangers. While the teens in my study felt that hiding their names was a safe practice and could enable greater protection from malign actors, they worried about what might happen when other people were anonymous. For today's teens, anonymity is, paradoxically, experienced as both a method of protection and a threat, and this inevitably leads to complex perspectives on its social value. However, public discourses about the harms of online anonymity are at odds with the messages teens receive from adults, who encourage them to hide their names, the school they attend, their age, and other things that may put their personal safety at risk. Adults also emphasize the consequences of teens' social media engagement and how "bad" behaviors may affect their future prospects. This creates an extra level of surveillance from adults, who check in on teens' content to make sure it is palatable. Paradoxically, though, adults' behaviors enhance the draw of identity concealment, potentially pushing teens' social media use further underground. This leads us to a challenging question: How should online anonymity be governed when it is at once risky and safe? This chapter is not about offering easy solutions to this question; the situation is messy, and we have to be okay with that. But we can tease out some clarity about certain aspects, like the reasons why teens crave identity concealment, the techniques they use to achieve it, and their thoughts and experiences of online anonymity.

Being Who You Want to Be on the Real-Name Web

It's hard to miss ongoing, polarizing debates about the promises and perils of online anonymity. Does it embolden people to abuse others or allow truer self-expression? Does it encourage deception or make people feel safer? These are complex questions without clear answers. And anonymity is, as David Byttow—founder of the now defunct confessional app Secret—said, "the ultimate double-edged sword."[8] True anonymity, defined as the total absence of personally identifying information, is tough to achieve.[9] In 1999, Wallace told us that anonymity was "never perfectly complete," a sentiment that still rings true today and is precisely why van der Nagel dedicated a PhD thesis to a shift in terminology toward *pseudonymity*, which she and other authors describe as practices of identity concealment.[10] When I use the term *anonymity* in this chapter, be it my own phrasing or my participants', readers should note their and my own shared awareness that true anonymity is extremely difficult to achieve. But for today's teens, the underlying principle behind the phrase—namely, that you don't always have to reveal everything about yourself when you use social media or other internet spaces—is what makes it enduringly meaningful.

Today's teens are savvy at recognizing the vernacular of a given platform, figuring out whether pseudonymity is the norm and leveraging identity play to their advantage.[11] When a new user signs up to a social platform, they are asked to provide certain details, typically a username, date of birth, and email address. These three data points are usually required fields, with optional fields requesting things like a mobile telephone number and gender identity. As I explained in the introduction, not all currently popular platforms ask their users to create a profile featuring things like a profile photo and short biographical statement. Again, some platforms do, but I raise this point here to nod to the diversity of identity requirements across online social spaces. This alters the degree to which a person can falsify their identity markers or not provide them at all. As Gibbs et al. explain, these elements are then combined with the culture a given platform creates, both in its own marketing materials and policy statements and via bottom-up user cultures.[12] This concept can be represented by comparing two platforms with contrasting approaches to identity: some platforms, like Facebook, ideally want you to use your "real" (i.e., legal) name and want to tie you to a form of government-issued ID if possible. A person's "real" identity is of course tricky to pin down as, say, your legal name may feel less "real" to you than the pseudonym you use online, through which you maintain an identity closer to the person you would describe as the one you "really" are. Any uses of this phrase in this chapter and throughout should therefore be read with this argument in mind. But other platforms, like Reddit and 4chan, actively discourage the use of legal names. The founders of Facebook and 4chan famously went head-to-head with their contrasting views on identity, with Facebook's Mark Zuckerberg claiming "the default is now social" and asking users to bring their real identities to

Facebook and 4chan's Chris Poole conversely arguing "anonymity *is* authenticity."[13] These competing discourses remind us that social platforms only enable us to "be who we want to be . . . within the boundaries set and influenced by the system."[14] While top-down decisions to limit identity performativity on a social platform may masquerade as safety considerations, particularly where young people are involved, we must remember that it is highly profitable to tie internet and social media users to a singular identity (in the technical sense, of course). When you use the internet and social media, you generate an enormous amount of data about who you are. Most social apps want to figure out what you like, who you're connected with, your demographic details, and other information in order to tailor advertisements to you: a process called social media data mining.[15] Data spanning a single user's internet activity is very attractive to third-party advertisers and thus more profitable for platforms, reminding us that "real name" debates cannot be divorced from the political economy of the Internet."[16] In other words, we must not forget that online naming policies can have an underlying profit motive and aren't solely about user safety. As Bayne et al. argue, such profit logics have sadly diminished the values of anonymity, privacy, secrecy, and ephemerality: some of the things today's networked teens, a few of whom are introduced below, value the most.[17]

Personal and Social Safety in Anonymous Communication

This chapter introduces readers to students from Mason-Oakes Academy, a non-paid-for all-boys high school located in the North of England. The school accepts students who live within a particular catchment area (a geographic radius from the school) between the ages of 11 and 16. Mason-Oakes is located, like Jaynes Sixth Form College, in a Northern English city widely considered to be working class, with its roots in the Industrial Revolution. It has a majority-White population and in the 2019 General Election was a Labour Party stronghold. I interviewed a total of 15 students from Mason-Oakes Academy over the course of two research visits in July 2021. My research with Mason-Oakes students was part of the same project discussed in chapter 3, which explored teens' views of anonymous apps. But to my surprise, most of my participants from Mason-Oakes did not have direct experience with the apps. This, they told me, was because their cohorts had spent over a year in and out of Covid-related school closures and nationwide lockdowns. Many Mason-Oakes students explained that anonymous apps only work effectively when their users are physically visible to each another in a non-app capacity, like a school, seeing each other on most days, generating life stories and relationships to negotiate through the apps. I'm certain the teens from Mason-Oakes will use anonymous apps in the future; in fact, when I directly asked my participants if they would try a new anonymous app, the answer was a resounding yes. To borrow 14-year-old Darren's words: "I'd join it just to see what it's like. If I liked it, I'd probably just keep it installed, but if not, I'd probably delete it the next day."

Although the teens from Mason-Oakes Academy did not have much experience with anonymous apps, they spoke extensively about naming practices across a range of online spaces, from Instagram and Discord to Xbox Live. As with so many unexpected qualitative research scenarios, students' lack of anonymous app usage was itself a finding and helped to produce some fascinating insights into other parts of their digital lives. For example, during one of my research interviews—a group discussion with 14-year-olds Samuel, Tyrone, and Lamar (whom I discuss later), I learned that Mason-Oakes Academy once had its own dedicated "meme account" created by one of its students. Tyrone told me about this account, which was interesting as he was the only one of my research participants, across all interview-based projects discussed in this book, to say he didn't have a smartphone: "I don't really use the internet that much. I've got a Nokia brick." White-British Tyrone lives "in the middle of nowhere" and has a close-knit friend group in his village, with whom he loves riding his bike, especially in the warmer months. And yet, despite his smartphone resistance, Tyrone had impressive knowledge of the technologies and trends around him, including the Mason-Oakes Memes Instagram page. White-British Samuel—who uses they/them pronouns and was my only non-binary participant from Mason-Oakes Academy—enjoys gaming and art. One of Samuel's favorite things to do is to "just start drawing sketches of characters into my art-book or random pieces of paper that are around the house," and so I was pleased they felt comfortable enough to doodle on their participant consent form and information sheet while we spoke.

I barely found anything out about the Mason-Oakes Memes Instagram account because my participants' teacher was present in the room during our group interview: an ethical and methodological decision I explain in appendix C. But 14-year-old Samuel still felt comfortable enough to tell me that they were bullied on the meme account:

SAMUEL: I've been called Sid from *Toy Story* ever since year six.
LAMAR: Yeah. People are real mean to him about that.
SAMUEL: Yeah, but not anymore because I really don't care about it.

TYRONE: He embraces it now.

SAMUEL: Yeah, in the past, I used to bloody get into a massive tantrum about it. I'd start yelling at everyone.

YSABEL: Does it not bother you anymore?

SAMUEL: No, it's because ever since I took therapy last year, I've been a little different about handling situations.

The group also told me that the meme account had "homophobic language on it":

TYRONE: [Some of the posts] talk about how we're all gay because of our uniform and because it's an all-boys school.

Tyrone told me that his peers eventually figured out who made the account because the people who created it posted a picture of themselves (leading Tyrone to comment, "They're clearly not that smart"). The meme account is one of many fascinating, powerful, and surprising stories to emerge from my conversations with Mason-Oakes students. I learned something new about teens' experiences of—and views on—anonymized communication in every interview and, though qualitative researchers are usually cautioned to cease their work when they reach "data saturation," I am certain I could've interviewed every student at the school and still discovered something new in each conversation. While I'm therefore loath to compress their words into just one book chapter, I wish to show readers how our in-depth conversations lay bare the complexities of teens' opinion formation when it comes to naming on social media. In what follows, I explore how my interviews with students from Mason-Oakes Academy featured a complex mix of social safety concerns—the risks associated with embarrassing identity disclosures among peers—with personal safety concerns, which align more closely with traditional understandings of what safety means, including things like threats of physical violence, grooming, identity theft, and catfishing.

Social Safety: Protection from Peers

All my participants from Mason-Oakes Academy celebrated opportunities for identity concealment online because concealment enabled self-exploration, especially regarding things they feared their peers would mock. In 1968, Erikson argued that people's identities are developed across eight distinct stages over a person's life. One of these stages is "identity versus confusion" and it appears during adolescence.[18] Other theories on identity development have since emerged, many of them expanding on or critiquing Erikson's work, but they tend to share the view that one of the main developmental tasks for adolescents is to construct their own sense of identity.[19] And for adolescents, peer groups have a significant influence on identity development.[20] The resounding belief among the teens I spoke to was that online anonymity is beneficial because you can say things that may be shameful or embarrassing without anyone—particularly your peers—knowing who you are. During his interview with Joseph and Asher, 14-year-old White-British Lee spoke of age-based distinctions in teens' comfort using what he called "real names" on social media:

> LEE: You get a lot of 14- or 15-year-olds now using their real names, but when they were younger, a lot of people would go by a completely different name because of school, because they don't want anyone in school to find them.

In his free time, Lee enjoys playing golf and gaming. He told me he uses different names across platforms, a mixture of his real name and pseudonyms, depending on the account's purpose, and also has a spam email address for online shopping. One of Lee's motivations for using a pseudonym on some platforms was due to context collapse—when people from distinct social groups are "collapsed" into one online space—specifically relating to worries that older family members will discover things about him on his socials.[21] In other words, Lee feels like he can't be himself on social media when his older family members are watching.

An interesting methodological note about this research is that I interviewed Mason-Oakes students in peer groups of two or three, roughly of their choosing. When they entered the room for our pre-interview workshop, participants were asked by their teacher to choose their own seats. I then asked students to get into small groups to complete a series of tasks. When the workshop activities came to an end, their teacher asked if they would rather be interviewed in those groups or alone, and all students from Mason-Oakes opted to participate in group interviews. This meant I didn't create ideal conditions for people to say to me, privately, something like: "I have *this* specific interest/hobby, but I don't want anyone to know about it." But I didn't want to overrule their teacher or go against their wishes, and so we stuck with the groups. That said, several participants alluded to motivations for concealing their names on certain platforms. For example, when justifying his decision to use what he called a "nickname" on some of his social media accounts, 14-year-old mixed-race Lamar said:

LAMAR: I don't want many real people I know being able to trace back to my account. It's not that I'm doing anything really bad, but it's kind of embarrassing, so I don't want people in real life finding me out.

Here, Lamar explains that something he does on a particular social media account could be mocked by his peers. He denies that this activity is "bad," which I take here to mean something that goes beyond the realms of social acceptability and that might be mocked by his peers and lead to embarrassment, which is similar to what Lee told me. In 1956, Goffman explained that, while all social encounters have the potential to lead to embarrassment, people craft their self-presentations to avoid such an occurrence, which is precisely why Lamar benefits from platforms with looser restrictions around naming and identity verification.[22] Lamar may have also avoided sharing his embarrassing habits due to his relationships with the other members of his interview group: Samuel and Tyrone. Lamar was fairly new to Mason-Oakes Academy as his family had recently experienced some hardships, and so, while Samuel and Tyrone were very much his friends, he was clearly reticent to divulge too much about his life. This meant Lamar valued identity concealment online, having experienced its benefits profoundly:

> LAMAR: I think personally, yes, anonymity definitely deserves a place on the internet because . . . Because you're not going to have many people to talk to most of the time, especially if maybe there's troubles in your home. You're not going to complain to your parents about that, and a lot of people don't feel comfortable talking to teachers about stuff.

During our conversation, Lamar created a powerful distinction between two parts of his identity: what he called his real life versus his presence on social media and other online spaces, like Discord and Xbox Live, as Lamar is an avid gamer. As discussed earlier in this chapter, some of the first critiques of internet communication were heavily influenced by post-structuralist notions of identity. Such approaches imagined that people's fractured identities, to use Hall's term, were spread across online and offline spaces.[23] This was a simpler distinction in the early days of internet communication, as people accessed websites, forums, chat rooms, and so on through static desktop computers. To sit at your desk with the aim of *going* on the internet therefore made the online-offline distinction—and subsequent identity compartmentalizations—more rigid than it is today. The sense that you enter some kind of cyberspace when you use the internet has now fallen out of fashion somewhat as the internet has crept into so many parts of our lives, from household appliances to tracking devices on our pets. This means the concept of a distinct cyberspace has been replaced by a growing interest in the embeddedness, to borrow Hine's phrase, between digital and non-digital spaces—which includes the increasing reliance on digital media in many places around the world for completing everyday tasks.[24] Any yet the discursive distinction between online and offline spaces is clearly enduringly relevant to teens like Lamar, who feels his identity is fragmented across different spaces in his life.

A conscious separation of his online activities from his physical identity at school is crucial for Lamar's feelings of social safety: protection from the risks associated with embarrassing identity disclosures among peers. A teen's social safety is at risk when their peers discover things about them, including hobbies and other interests, personal experiences (for example, related to health), or perhaps romantic interests and sexual feelings, that could lead to feelings of embarrassment. What we see across my participants' articulations is, above all, a sense that the *notion* of anonymity, whether or not it is fully realized in practice, forms a core part of contemporary adolescence. This is partly because it helps with their identity explorations and, more specifically, affords them the chance to evade stigma while exploring secret parts of themselves, which offers substantial social safety. To remind readers, the distinction between *secrecy* and its close relative *privacy* is that the latter "protects behavior which is either morally neutral or valued by society,"[25] whereas the former is "commonly associated with 'having something to hide': something shameful, furtive, or bad."[26] Put differently, having a secret infers "moral badness," whereas privacy-seeking behaviors protect parts of your life that are understood to be more morally neutral.[27] For teens like Lamar, identity concealment across online spaces, particularly social media, helps him to secretly engage in behaviors that he feels would be considered shameful to his peers, which is why he values it so much.

Other teens cited similar reasons when praising online anonymity, telling me it helped shy people to feel brave, allowed them to confess sexual attraction without the fear of rejection, helped them to discuss mental health issues, and above all, protected them from shame—a concept that emerged in all our conversations but a word that only Harry used directly. Thirteen-year-old White-British Harry, who chose he/him pronouns, was interviewed alongside his friends Jeremy and Richard. Theirs was a very funny interview: the three boys clearly got on well and often finished each other's sentences, perhaps due to their similar demographics. Harry told me that he loves being outside and, while he finds things to do during the colder, darker months in England, like gaming, his favorite times are when the sun is shining, it's light outside, and he's playing football and riding his bike with his friends. Harry says he has a happy home life and that his parents are fine with him having a smartphone and a desktop computer, on which he "sometimes" uses Instagram, watches lots of videos on YouTube, Snapchats his friends, and uses Discord to talk to people—some of whom he knows and some he doesn't—while he plays games. Harry's parents bought him a smartphone when he was 12 and let him download Facebook and then, when he turned 13, he was trusted to download other apps by himself. Harry told me:

> HARRY: I mean my parents don't really mind what I download because they know I'm like smart enough not to do any dumb decisions on it that'll mean something happens to me. So, they don't really mind me doing stuff, like downloading social media, because they know I'm not going to, like, act dumb on it, or anything like that.

The only account where Harry uses his real name is on his private Instagram, and for the rest he uses what he calls a nickname. But some of his friends, like Jeremy, know to attribute this nickname to him when they see it on other platforms, like Discord. The reason Harry uses a nickname is because he thinks it's "dangerous" to use your real name on social media, though he feels safe enough to use it on his private Instagram account. But he particularly values nicknames because "no one will shame" him for the questions he asks: a useful tool to have at your disposal as an adolescent full of questions about your identity and the world around you. Although Harry never gave specifics about the questions he's asked online or would perhaps like to ask, it's clear that anonymity is crucial for him to achieve social safety.

During their interview, 13-year-olds James and Osas—who were interviewed alongside Tom—similarly spoke about the relief of making anonymized disclosures on social media:

> JAMES: Well, it could make some people feel, like, relieved.
> 'Cause, like, they're getting their secret off them that maybe they can't tell anybody.
> OSAS: If you have something really, like, stuck on your chest you just want to get out, you can just do that.

White-British James—who uses he/him pronouns—is an avid soccer and rugby player with lots of support from his dad. He told me his mum monitored his phone "until a certain age" but is now trusted to make his own decisions about which apps to download. James was quite resistant to identity concealment online: he seemed to recognize the benefits of anonymity for other people his age but not for himself, claiming he uses his real name across platforms because he "can't be bothered" to use a nickname. I'll admit I struggled to read James as easily as I did some of my other participants, which could have been because James, Osas, and Tom weren't close friends. Osas and Tom seemed to be fairly friendly with each other, but James didn't feel like a part of their group, perhaps leading to him being more closed off during our conversation.

Black-British Osas—who chose this name as a nod to his ancestry—was preparing to head to a summer basketball camp when we spoke and was clearly very excited about it. He uses Snapchat to talk to his friends and TikTok to "kill off time" (don't we all . . .) and told me that he first got a smartphone when he was 9 years old. By now, Osas's parents allowed him to download the apps he wanted to use without needing their prior consent:

"My mum knew I wouldn't do anything weird or bad. So, she trusted me." But the one rule his parents have is around swearing: "I have complete freedom of what to do on it but mostly, I'm not allowed to swear on it, which is understandable and for my own benefit." When Osas reached the last part of this sentence—"for my own benefit"—I distinctly remember him turning around to look at his teacher, who was sitting at the back of the room, again reminding us that the conditions in which a qualitative interview takes place can shape what participants say, especially when they are children. Osas uses various nicknames across platforms, unlike Harry, who has a pseudonym that people know to link directly to him.

The quotes from James and Osas around anonymity and getting something off your chest were fascinating to me, as they differed so much from what the older teens at Jaynes Sixth Form College said. While Jaynes students did of course talk about the benefits of anonymity for sharing things you might not in in-person settings, the feeling of relief, specifically, wasn't present during our conversations. As Finkenauer et al. explain, there is something quite distinct about the two stages of adolescence to which my participants belonged: ages 13–14 and ages 16–18.[28] Research suggests that the older adolescents from Jaynes Sixth Form College would be likelier than younger teens to demonstrate "increased independence from parental supervision and protection" and to lean more on their friends and even strategies of introspection to solve problems and disclose secrets.[29] On the other hand, the younger adolescents from Mason-Oakes Academy—who we would expect to be less likely to divulge to their peers—might struggle to know where to turn when they have a secret to disclose, hence the perceived value of identity concealment on social media, and of spaces like anonymous apps among others for secret disclosures.

A couple of minutes before Osas explained the one rule his parents imposed on his social media use, however, he told me:

> OSAS: If you have secrets, just keep them to yourself. [Or] if they're important or could change someone's life or something, then talk to an adult.

Taken together, these quotes from Osas—about the benefits of anonymity for getting things off your chest but also about *not* using digital media to disclose secrets—seem to reveal his inner conflict about the value of anonymized communication in his and his peers' lives. But this tension also potentially nods to the performative nature of the interview scenario. As I've previously explained, at Mason-Oakes Academy I was required to have a member of school staff in the room for the duration of my interviews, and Osas's framing in the quote above—"talk to an adult"—potentially suggests that he felt pressure to say what he perceived to be the right thing in front of his teacher, and the wording may echo things adults have said to him in the past. This tension might also reflect the life stage he is in: one in which you turn to your parents rather than your peers when things go wrong.[30] It was clear to me that Osas's complex views on anonymity were governed by a combination of factors, were influenced by the stage of adolescence he was at, and included his teachers' and parents'/carers' views.

While the teens at Mason-Oakes Academy highlighted the many reasons they valued identity concealment online, they were evidently aware that anonymity is risky business. Dichotomies like good/bad, positive/negative, and safe/risky were present in *all* Mason-Oakes students' articulations, sometimes in the same sentence. Richard, for example, said:

RICHARD: I see the benefits because, you know, quite a lot of people have things that maybe they don't want to say with their name on it. But if the other person answers in a negative way, that could put harm on the other person.

White-British, 13-year-old Richard enjoys drawing, gaming, and mountain biking and was interviewed alongside his two friends, Jeremy and Harry, who I introduced earlier. Just like his friend Harry, Richard uses what he described as his real name on his Instagram account but uses a nickname on Discord and YouTube. He does this due to each platform's vernacular: the unique culture of a given platform, which shapes how its users communicate therein.[31] For example, Richard (among most other participants) felt it wasn't the norm on Discord to use his real name, and so he didn't. But because he felt that, at his age, platforms like Instagram and Snapchat were for communicating with known individuals, he was more comfortable using his real name (or, at least, elements of his real name). Throughout our interview, Richard—along with all other teens I interviewed—frequently weighed up the value of anonymous disclosure against the costs of participation. For Richard, anonymity is only risky because of *other people's* behavior. He therefore feels that hiding his name is an act that poses little risk to him (i.e., it is "safe") and that risks lie in other people's unpredictable and potentially negative responses to his anonymized thoughts.

A core finding—and one that did not occur as frequently in my Jaynes Sixth Form College interviews—from my conversations with Mason-Oakes students was a near-constant wrestling between good and bad designations when critiquing online anonymity. Moreover, students attempted to force their views on naming practices into one of these two categories. This meant participants often went in circles and struggled to arrive at a firm conclusion. This finding has highly influenced this book's underpinning philosophy of avoiding either-or designations for examining the relationship between technologies and society. Such categories are, as Mick and Fournier note, "overly broad and do not adequately reflect the specific content and pressures of the cultural contradictions of technology."[32] There is a good reason the teens from Mason-Oakes Academy couldn't decide if anonymity was good or bad for them and that is because they experience anonymity and wider naming practices on social media as *paradoxical*: both good and bad at the same time. Dichotomies ultimately flatten paradoxes. Richard, for example, told me that people need to say things without their names in order to reap social benefits but that to achieve this means taking a risk that something bad might happen, like someone responding with a negative comment. For teens like Richard, only by taking a risk on social media can he hope to receive a reward, which means both states—good and bad, positive and negative, safe and risky—apply at once.

Social Safety: Protection from Adults

Today's teens aren't only interested in protecting their social safety in relation to their peers: they must also carefully manage their social media visibility with an eye to the adults in their lives. In their research, Duffy and Chan argue that today's young people, specifically those aged 18-24, are socialized to "anticipate the incessant monitoring" of their social media participation by "family, educators, and (above all) employers."[33] As the authors note, "With the astonishing uptake of social media platforms, anecdotes about digital faux pas—a thoughtless Tweet, brash Facebook update, or indiscrete Instagram post—circulate widely in popular culture. In a 2016 survey, more than 25% of companies admitted to reprimanding or terminating an employee for content posted online, with 60% using social media to vet candidates."[34]

The concept Duffy and Chan introduce through their work is *imagined surveillance,* which describes "how individuals conceive of the scrutiny that could take place across the social media ecology and, consequently, may engender future risks or opportunities."[35] With the word *imagined* they are not suggesting that such surveillance does not exist but that people have various *imaginings* of its sources and perpetuators.[36] In my research, the adults I interviewed warned me about the consequences of "bad" social media misuse among young people.

Adults' perspectives were not designed to be the focus of the research on which this chapter is based, as it aimed to explore young people's opinions of anonymous apps (and, as it turned out, anonymity in general). But there were occasions when I met an educator whose words I wanted to get on record, and these interviews were also crucial in ensuring my research continued during Covid-19-related school closures in England. By keeping up with my contacts, I ensured I was ready to return to my fieldwork when schools reopened. My adult participants all work in the Education sector in England, and readers are invited to consult the table in appendix C for a full list of their names and other crucial demographic details, but I summarize them here for the reader's convenience. Akshay is a 40-something, male, Asian-British deputy headteacher of an all-girls faith-based secondary school (ages 11–16), located in the Midlands area of England. Dave is a 40-something, male, White-British vice principal and designated safeguarding lead of Jaynes

Sixth Form College (ages 16–19). Kirstie, whose age is unknown to me, is a female White-British youth justice officer based in the North of England. Louise, whose age is also unknown to me, is a White-British assistant headteacher at a primary school (ages 4–11). She has responsibilities for safeguarding, special educational needs (SEN), attendance, pastoral links, and supporting families. My favorite story from my conversation with Louise was that, on learning that a company in her local area ran an after-school TikTok dance club that most of her pupils couldn't afford to attend, she set one up for free at her school instead. Her sign-up sheet was full only two days after launching the club. Finally, I interviewed Ray, whom I introduced at the start of this chapter.

While Duffy and Chan's concept of imagined surveillance is highly relevant to my research, it manifested in a different way due to the ages of our respective participants: mine were aged 13–18 and Duffy and Chan's were 18- to 24-year-olds. For example, in relation to Jaynes Confessionals (the anonymous app-based phenomenon described at length in chapter 3), the college's deputy headteacher and safeguarding lead, Dave, told me he faced several hurdles when he used official channels—like platforms' own reporting tools, and even the police—to try to take down the account. He said:

> DAVE: In the end, I resorted to maybe the old-fashioned way of doing it, which was monitoring it daily and anybody that liked or commented on it, I basically phoned the parents. I phoned about 70 sets of parents over the course of a week or two and just said to them, do you realize the content your sons or daughters are liking, and the fact that it's linked to the College, and that this could . . . compromise their place at the

College? . . . They were all horrified because I read some of the comments out and said, do you realize that your son or daughter has liked this post and this is what they're liking and it's linked almost to their profile and their reputation and this isn't going to go away in the future, this could be regurgitated and screenshotted? I didn't have one that challenged me back.

Especially interesting in the quote above is that Dave highlights the future consequences of harmful social media participation (in this case, liking content associated with bullying behaviors). He says social media content, even likes, aren't "going to go away in the future" and could harm teens' "reputation[s]." While Duffy and Chan's participants were concerned about the *possibility* that prospective employers might be monitoring their accounts, my younger participants were actively being monitored by their educators as they were posting. My teenage participants were all warned about the (unspecified) future consequences of their actions. Ray, for example, said:

RAY: If somebody wants to be harsh and be mean and target someone online, I think they know now the evidence will always be there. . . . We would always make the pupil know that what you did over that weekend, you know, will be there forever. You maybe didn't do it face to face, because you wouldn't; you'd never do that. You know, you tackle ten girls all at once? Of course, you wouldn't, because you would expect the response would be visceral and would be real and would be physical in reality, you know?

Here, Ray recalls how he tells younger children and adolescents that there is residual, consequential evidence of what they do on social media. This is something Kirstie also alluded to:

> KIRSTIE: I don't like talking about a whole demographic of people . . . but I think when you do look at brain development, they don't understand consequential thinking skills and things like that.

But a common theme among my interviews with adults was the lack of specificity around what counts as saying "the wrong thing" on social media. Dave and I spoke extensively about the politics of talking to young people about new technologies. He told me that he feels the shift from high school (ages 12–16) to sixth form or college (ages 16–19) in England is that, for younger teens, educators feel they need to focus on saying "these are the risks, these are the dangers, this is what you need to look out for," whereas older teens like those at Jaynes Sixth Form College are told:

> DAVE: You're a young adult, you're responsible for what you say, you're responsible for your post, you're responsible for your profile—I suppose both physically and digitally—and that you have to be responsible for what you post and what you put out there. So therefore, if you do x, y, and z, these are the consequence or potential consequences, this is what it could mean.

When I was a student at a British Sixth Form College and first downloaded Facebook, we were told by our teachers that photos of alcohol consumption and "risqué" images would be frowned upon by university admissions officers (a warning that evidently never materialized, three university degrees later). What counts as the wrong social media post for an 18- to 24-year-old is, as Duffy and Chan explain, something that might be deemed unprofessional.[37] But the criteria for a bad social media post is far less specific for adolescents. There's also less clarity on what the actual consequences are for younger teens: as an 18- to 24-year-old, the story goes that saying or doing bad things means you don't get a job or that you get fired from the job you have. But does the same theory apply to, say, a 14-year-old? Perhaps it does; Asher, for example, told me:

> ASHER: When people use their real name, they're a lot more
> wary of stuff. They don't say anything bad that might affect
> the future and stuff like that. If they ever want to get a job,
> they would backtrack stuff like that. They'll worry that
> someone will say, "Oh, you did this back then." It's just how
> you have to live your life.[38]

For younger teens like Asher, achieving social safety is tied up with anonymity, as it affords an additional layer of protection from adults' prying eyes and from potential punishment. Put differently, if teens are being told that what they say on social media will come back to haunt them (and if they are also directly being surveilled by adults in their lives), why *wouldn't* they value anonymity?

Personal Safety: Protection from the Unknown

Across my interviews with the 13- to 14-year-olds from Mason-Oakes Academy, all participants at some point mentioned that their main issue with anonymity is the lack of accountability for harmful behaviors and threats to their personal safety. This form of safety echoes more traditional understandings of what safety means and includes protection from things like threats, grooming, identity theft, and catfishing—all of which arose as examples during my interviews with Mason-Oakes Academy students. These personal safety issues are to be distinguished from social safety concerns, which are connected to the protection from risks associated with embarrassing identity disclosures among peers. My participants told me that, when people behave themselves, the benefits of identity concealment are crystal clear. But what bothers teens is that there seem to be no consequences for threats to, or violations of, their personal safety. This is not something they fear as such but something they have a strong sense of justice about. This sentiment is summarized by 14-year-old Jamal:

> JAMAL: [With anonymity] I believe there's a lot more bad than good. . . . You can say a lot more stuff without consequences than you would be able to say in real life.

Here, Jamal tells me the consequences of bad behavior differ on social media from those in real life (by which he means in-person situations). White-British Jamal—who chose he/him pronouns—enjoys painting and being outside in his free time. Jamal, who was interviewed alongside Darren and Jack, told me he uses an "online name" on Instagram and Discord but then uses his "real name" on Twitter and Snapchat. Like all Mason-Oakes interviewees, Jamal weighed up the pros and cons of anonymity, sometimes in the same sentence, but spoke extensively about his issues with accountability. When asked how he would feel if online anonymity was no longer a possibility, he said it would come as a welcome relief:

> JAMAL: It would give more room to actually do things about people saying stuff like that online or people thinking there'll be no consequences for talking to people the way they do on certain apps.

The teens in my study aren't necessarily afraid to participate in social media because people are "hiding" their identities, as the discourse about online anonymity so often goes; instead, they feel frustrated by the lack of punishment if things go wrong. They perceive apps offering anonymity—or instances where people don't attach their name to a profile—to be worse for their personal safety than other forms of social media. This is because, to borrow 14-year-old Jack's words:

> JACK: [People] just think they can say what they want and get away with it, which nine times out of ten, they do.

Jack's interview was a memorable one, largely because of his witty, confident demeanor. When I asked each member of the group to tell me a little about themselves, Jack replied:

> JACK: Right, me next, all right: I'm Jack, I play rugby, and I'm exceptionally tall for my age, which I love. It always gives me a boost. I'm beautiful. It sounds very vain, but honesty is the best policy.

But Jack's confidence and wit weren't the only things that made his words stand out: I remember them because of what they seemed to be masking. During our interview, Jack told me he feels that there are "no consequences" for anonymized bad behaviors. Jack was one of the few Mason-Oakes participants who had directly (and extensively) used anonymous apps, and so part of my conversation with him, Darren, and Jamal focused on these apps more than my other discussions did. Jack compared anonymous apps to Facebook, Twitter, Instagram, and Snapchat, which, he explained, have their own "dark sides" but aren't quite as bad as anonymous apps due to the lack of consequences "bad" users face on the latter. Here, he's not necessarily saying the app *companies* are either better or worse at controlling harmful behaviors via content moderation but that anonymous apps by their very nature bring out the worst in their users:

> JACK: It's the same with a lot of apps, like Facebook and like
> Twitter and Instagram and Snapchat, they're all good for
> their own parts. It's like they've all got their own dark sides to
> everything, haven't they? And I feel like the dark side comes
> out on these more because nobody knows who it is and
> there's no consequences for it, really, so they're all going to
> just think they can say what they want and get away with it,
> which nine times out of ten, they do.

Jack's words resonate with Suler's "online disinhibition effect," a theory of internet communication which posits that people's behavior worsens when they don't have to give their real (i.e., legal) name.[39] Jack's views on identity concealment are partly informed by a particularly bad experience on the anonymous app Tellonym:

> JACK: I got one message . . . when I was with this girl, and I split
> up with her and someone put on it that they were going to
> rape her and send me a video of it.

I then asked Jack if he told anyone about this experience, to which he replied:

> JACK: I just left it. I couldn't be bothered. I knew nowt was going
> to happen about it, so I just left it. Because they're obviously
> not going to get found out or anything—are they?—because
> it's anonymous and none of them can get back to it so you
> move on, you forget about it—don't you?—and I did. It hasn't
> really bothered me since.

Jack then had another bad experience:

> JACK: Pardon my French, but I was getting called a c**t and stuff
> on the apps. But I was like, alright, that's fine, I can deal with
> that.

During the course of my research, participants didn't usually tell me stories of threats to their own personal safety like Jack did, but several told me of other people whose personal safety had been threatened. For example, I asked 14-year-old Darren why he uses nicknames on his Twitter and TikTok accounts, and he said it was because they're not "personal app[s], like Instagram," which he views as safer spaces to include your "real" identity markers. But on Twitter and TikTok, he engages with more people he doesn't know in non-app settings. He therefore uses nicknames on Twitter: "I wouldn't want strangers knowing my name or anything." Crucial to note here is that I didn't get to know Darren as well as some of my other participants. He was a little more reserved at the start of our conversation and mainly relied on Jack and Jamal to answer questions, due in part to the fact that he was a bit nervous, but also perhaps because we discussed Jack's traumatic experiences early on in the conversation, which of course took a lot of time to unpack. But Darren opened up toward the end of our interview and I got to hear his views on his personal safety, particularly on Discord:

> DARREN: There's a bunch of groomers on Discord as well.
> JAMAL: Yeah, people lying about their ages.
> DARREN: It's awful.
> YSABEL: How do you know there are groomers on Discord?
> DARREN: There's been a lot of cases like all over, where it's been a bunch of . . . even big personalities within the internet space have been shown usually on Discord as a groomer or a pedophile through their messages they've sent to minors on there.

During some of my interviews, I asked Mason-Oakes students to tell me which platforms they used nicknames on, and Discord came out on top as the platform participants felt least comfortable using their real identity markers. But other platforms like Instagram and TikTok received mixed responses depending on the purpose of the teen's account. Although all Mason-Oakes teens I spoke to used nicknames on at least one social media account, some engaged in this practice on a wider scale than others. Tom and Osas, for example, used a range of nicknames across social media platforms to avoid their accounts being connected to one another:

TOM: I normally use, like, a nickname, just to be secure. . . . Just in case someone, like, bad sends stuff to me or stuff like that.

OSAS: Obviously, you'll be in more danger if you, like, put your name on it. It's pretty obvious to just put any nickname that you know of, or any nickname you use in games. . . . [But] if you have a lot of accounts, don't use, like, the same nickname, otherwise, like, if you get hacked and all that, they could get all those apps. So, I tweak some of my nicknames on other accounts.

The teens at Mason-Oakes Academy are highly aware of extreme personal safety risks like grooming and pedophilia, along with issues like hacking, and therefore feel safer on social media and similar apps (e.g., gaming) when using nicknames. Osas, for example, told me that he wouldn't use a fully verified and real name internet because of what he feels are a set of "obvious danger[s]." Lee echoes this rhetoric:

LEE: To be honest, about 99 percent of the people on the internet are not who they say they are. So, you're kind of like expecting to find some fake people on there.

But this finding wasn't surprising to me, partly because this discourse was perpetuated by some of the adults in their lives. In the quotes below, Louise and Dave both spoke of their worries of teens including real identifiers on social media:

LOUISE: I think the most important thing is, yes, make sure the apps are age appropriate what you're letting your child use, but they've got to learn to keep themselves safe. So, it's about teaching children to keep themselves safe online. So, if anybody asks you your name, your address, you know, your phone number, and all that, you report that to an adult straightaway. . . . . Just because the person says they're 7-year-old Ben, that that doesn't necessarily mean it's actually Ben behind that keyboard.

DAVE: We have small groups of students who are quite naïve around the types of things they post about themselves. So, they would put things out, just for example, they might give identifying facts, their [school] lanyard or something to identify the locality of where they're from and things like that and that will cause them potential problems.

As with so many facets of the Great Anonymity Debate, adults' and teens' fears seem to reside in what *other people* do when they are permitted to be anonymous. Messages like these from educators would surely push teens toward pseudonymity, not only for harm-aversion, as Louise and Dave explain above, but also so they don't feel surveilled by their educational institutions and other adults in their lives. For example, some of the teens from Mason-Oakes cited the risks of using their real names and posting pictures of themselves in their uniforms, which may have come directly from adults in their lives. While I am not suggesting there are no dangers in doing this or that this is bad advice, I am providing context for the teens' views on anonymity and its perceived benefits for their personal (as opposed to social) safety. To be clear: I am not trying to criticize adults for instilling fear in teens. I say more about this in my concluding chapter; I am sympathetic to English adults, particularly educators, because many struggle with finding the confidence necessary to talk to teens about social media.

The fast-paced nature of the evolution of digital technologies causes educators to feel under-confident, as they struggle to keep up with the latest trends and inventions, as Livingstone and Blum-Ross also found.[40]

The teens from Mason-Oakes—and also some of the influential adults in their lives—think anonymity writ large is scary because they don't know who other people are, what those people's intentions might be, and thus what the threats may be to teens' personal safety—but they also claim that it is important to *be* anonymous because those same scary, unknown people might be able to find you. I am therefore greatly indebted to the teens from Mason-Oakes Academy, who helped me to identify some profound contradictions in what seems to be pervasive social messaging about online anonymity in England and, most likely, beyond.

The Internet Is Forever

I close this chapter by sharing an anecdote from Louise, who told me of a severe case of bullying on a girls' WhatsApp group chat at the school at which she teaches:

> LOUISE: It was a WhatsApp chat, and the girls had joined this one group, and then obviously because they can, then add further girls to the group. It ended up being maybe . . . like a group of four girls, four friends, then it ended up being probably, I don't know, 20 girls who joined. And they'd got this photograph of this girl, a screenshot of her, and then they'd all annotated it, you know, with various—oh look at this, look at her glasses, you know, and that sort of thing. And then obviously the next one of them screenshotted it, added

their bit, and it was just constant, constant, constant attacks on this girl. . . . [At school,] we said the consequences of this could be . . . and I know it sounds really harsh, but actually she could have gone and jumped off a bridge because she could not get away from this nasty bullying. . . . And actually showing them that scale of what it could lead to and the consequences, and how you would live with yourself and things—they were quite shocked by that.

Fears and criticisms of online anonymity hinge on the notion that people behave differently when their in-person identity markers aren't attached to their communication. And yet, the girls in the group chat described above—who used WhatsApp to communicate and therefore knew exactly who was saying what—did not need to conceal their identities to engage in harmful bullying behaviors. Here and throughout, recognizing the difficulties of achieving of achieving "true" anonymity, I take this term to mean practices of identity concealment in online spaces. This could mean people use a pseudonym (or a nickname, as many of my participants call them); decline to include any identifying details at all, like a profile picture or their age; or entirely falsify their identity markers and adopt new ones. But clearly, harmful behaviors are rife in spaces where people are *exactly* who they say they are.

Anonymous communication does not exist in a vacuum. As I explained in the previous chapter, students at Jaynes Sixth Form College felt their educational environment was overly permissive toward sexual harassment and the over-sexualization of female and female-presenting students. These discourses then made their way over to anonymous apps like Tellonym, where students faced extensive sexual objectification to the point that they changed how they dressed and acted in their everyday lives. Bayne et al. explain that, on the university campus they researched, the dominant use of anonymous app Yik Yak was for "peer support, empathy and community building, with very limited evidence of toxicity."[41] Likewise, Black et al.'s research found that most exchanges on Yik Yak across the campuses they studied were "focused on commentary about campus life rather than victimization or hate" and that the research did not "reveal bullying or insulting posts so inflammatory as to call for the demonizing of the entire application."[42] These stories of anonymous app users having, put simply, just an average, fun experience need to be told alongside the bad. Anonymity itself (that is, the absence of identifying information) is not problematic or harmful by default, and yet it would be equally unwise to ignore the countless cases of harmful behaviors enacted via concealed identities.

A common theme across my interviews with teens and adults was that a key risk of online anonymity lies in what other people do: the groomers, the bullies, the catfish. These malign actors, as I explain above, present teens with *personal safety* concerns. While the teens in my study felt that hiding their names was a safe practice and indeed might enable greater protection from malign actors, teens worried about what might happen when other people were anonymous. For today's teens, anonymity is, paradoxically, both a threat and a method of protection, inevitably leading to complex perspectives on its social value. But the teens in my research identified another set of concerns that feature less heavily in debates around online anonymity; these concerns emphasize the value of identity concealment for them. Teens told me of the benefits of anonymized communication for exploring aspects of their identities that may be mocked by their peers. These, I argue, should be understood as *social safety* concerns and can be defined as the risks associated with embarrassing identity disclosures among peers. It's easy to forget what it felt like to be a teenager, but thankfully academics aplenty have written about the centrality of identity formation as a key "task" in adolescent life. Teens can use identity concealment tactics to explore many facets of their growing selves, including potential interests, current hobbies, and romantic or sexual interests. Identity concealment, however far along the spectrum of anonymity a teen may be, is essential for the maintenance of their social safety. This is precisely why I frame it as a paradox: identity concealment is socially stigmatized in many places around the world, perhaps even feared, and yet even with its risks it offers highly meaningful forms of safety for today's teens.

Teens also benefit from identity concealment to avoid adults' prying eyes. A standout theme from my interviews with adults was an emphasis on the *consequences* of teens' social media engagement and how those consequences affect other aspects of young, growing lives. I identified concerns that children and young people don't understand that what you do on social media impacts other parts of your life. This has potentially created an opportunity for children and young people to face an extra level of surveillance from adults, who check in on their content to make sure it's palatable. Paradoxically, though, this enhances the draw of identity concealment, potentially pushing teens' social media use further underground. Indeed, warning teens of the drawbacks of social media's permanence surely makes nicknames all the more alluring. Especially in a English context, there are frequent calls to "end" online anonymity, usually in the form of a petition or social media campaign that launches in the wake of a high-profile, trolling-related suicide.[43] But this discourse is at odds with the messages teens receive from adults, who encourage them to hide their name, school, age, and other things that may put their personal safety at risk. And teens themselves are keen to conceal their identities to enhance their safety on an even greater scale. So this leads us to a challenging question: How should online anonymity be governed when it is at once risky and safe?

These complex debates are emerging in many societies where, as Patelis crucially reminds us, identity concealment is being stigmatized.[44] While the teens in my research spoke extensively about the harms that have befallen themselves and their friends via anonymized communication, they saw anonymity itself as something that could help reduce the risk of such harms. Crucially, teens are willing to accept the costs of participation on social media and have devised sophisticated techniques—which typically center on identity concealment—for self-protection. Academic arguments about the benefits of anonymity largely focus on its usefulness for people with marginalized identities, along the lines of, for example, sexual orientation, gender identity, and race and ethnicity. And while this is of course true, the students I spoke to across both Mason-Oakes Academy and Jaynes Sixth Form College—whose identities are *not* necessarily considered (by themselves or society writ large) to be marginalized—find immense value in anonymity. This finding reminds me of rhetorics about internet privacy that suggest people should only worry about surveillance technologies and privacy violations if they've got "something to hide."[45] And yet, as Marwick and Hargittai remind us, such rhetorics can be leveraged as useful justifications for privacy violations.[46] Along similar lines, I would argue that anonymity for anonymity's sake is enduringly valuable to young people, regardless of their identity, though of course more so for those who are at risk.

Teens' views on anonymity also reveal the profound limitations in either-or judgements when it comes to their technology use. In each sentence, and especially in my interviews with the teens from Mason-Oakes Academy, I often saw both sides of the coin: the good and bad, the positives and negatives, the promises and pitfalls. While I find divisions like these to be frustrating and reductive, especially when used to describe social media, their presence in teens' own articulations is powerful and revealing, and certainly must not be dismissed. When presented with all the evidence, it's tough to see how anyone could have a clear, one-sided perspective on online anonymity. This shows readers, however frustratingly, that current debates around online anonymity are impossible to settle; that we must become far more comfortable admitting these conceptual and practical challenges and sitting in our discomfort, while making context-sensitive interventions for today's young people.

5   At-Home Photoshopping and the New War on Body Image

Skinny waist, big boobs, narrow shoulders, narrow ribcage. Slim-thick, as it was.

ROWAN, 17

Each new academic year, I have the good fortune of teaching final-year undergraduate social science students in a class called Digital Identities. The aim of the class is that students learn something new about their relationships with digital media, from the Instagram account they've made for their cat to their Spotify playlist for long drives. Students can also reflect on their attempts to eschew such technologies altogether. One of their assessments involves a weeklong diary-keeping exercise, in which students are asked to reflect on their interactions with digital media. They must then use academic literature we've discussed in class to make sense of their diary entries. In her essay, one of my students, let's call her Freya, wrote about her experience of being tagged in her friend Kait's Instagram post. The post was a full-length photo of Freya and Kait, taken at a "pre-drinks" event before a night out.[1] In her essay, Freya insightfully used Festinger's social comparison theory to critique her diary entries.[2] She wrote about why she thought her body looked worse than Kait's and reflected on her decision to only eat toast for three days in a bid to lose weight.[3]

I continued with my grading and, a few essays later, came across the exact same photo. But this time, the essay's author was Kait, who wrote an honest 2500-word critique of her digital photo editing habits. Yes, Kait had edited the photo of her and Freya but, as she explained in her essay, Kait only retouched her *own* body, making it thicker and thinner in what she perceived to be the "right" places. I was horrified, not at the act per se but by the special access the assignment gave me to the internal dynamics of their interaction. No amount of training had prepared me for the realization that one of my students had starved herself because she'd compared her body shape to one that literally wasn't real.

. . .

The type of editing Kait engaged in—using a smartphone app to change the shape of her body in a way she felt happier with and then uploading the edited image to Instagram—is rooted in a much longer history of what people call "photoshopping."[4] Older, one-to-many media texts like magazine advertisements have long faced academic and public scrutiny for using digital techniques to enhance images of people or products. This longstanding practice has led to the colloquialization of *photoshopping* as a catch-all term to refer to all photo editing, even if it doesn't use the official Adobe Photoshop software.[5] Criticisms of both traditional and social media photo editing partly arise from concerns about the authenticity of the products or objects being depicted, which when purchased, may not have the same results. On certain apps and in certain places around the world, social media influencers are required to declare when they have been paid to advertise or promote a product. In 2018, the UK's Advertising Standards Authority (ASA), Committee of Advertising Practice (CAP), and Competition and Markets Authority (CMA) compiled a guide for influencers on "making clear that ads are ads."[6] Some posts might be considered sponsored content rather than an advertisement, and slightly different rules apply in each of these cases. But their recommendations all point to the importance of content being clearly identifiable as affiliated with a product, service, or brand to avoid misleading consumers. The guidance recommends using approved words like "ad," "advert," "advertising," or "advertisement," and it says these words can be used in hashtag form but should not be buried within a sea of tags. Influencers are told to avoid using phrases like "spon" (shorthand for 'sponsored content') or saying things like "in association with," as this doesn't make brand affiliations sufficiently clear. Explaining why hidden ads are harmful, the CMA says, "they can persuade people to buy things they might not usually buy if they'd known that the content was not a non-biased opinion, review or recommendation."[7]

In addition to this issue, in England and other places around the world, we are currently hearing public concerns that highly edited photos of social media users' faces and bodies—not just influencers but ordinary people, too—could set impossible body image standards, contributing to low self-esteem among teens in particular. *Body image* is described by McGovern et al. as "the umbrella term used to describe perceptions, cognitions, affects, behaviors and subjective evaluations of one's body. Body dissatisfaction is a subcomponent of body image that occurs when an individual has negative views about their body image and perceives a discrepancy between their ideal and actual body image."[8]

Body dissatisfaction, as Warren et al. note, is "one of the most well-established, empirically supported risk factors for the development of eating disorders," which is why digital photo editing has received such intense public scrutiny in many places around the world.[9] While the same anxieties were of course shared about older media formats, the widespread availability of photo editing tools—at-home photoshopping—has sparked fresh debates and concerns. Whereas media imagery on television and in magazines used to be reserved for traditional celebrities, the story goes that anyone—ordinary, everyday social media users—can now edit their photos and present false realities. Within this context, digital photo editing should be understood as a distinct concept from *filters*, which refers to built-in technologies found on apps like Instagram Stories and Snapchat. Filters can adjust images in one click (for example, making an image black-and-white) and can also be used to quickly alter the dimensions of your face in humorous or serious ways. Digital photo editing therefore encompasses a range of techniques; however, this chapter uses the term in relation to the editing—not via pre-made filters—of images of the face and body. Digital photo editing can be undertaken through in-platform tools on visual social media like Instagram, which allow users to edit the brightness, contrast, and other elements of an image. Smartphone users can also download an external app like Facetune or FaceApp to engage in more sophisticated forms of editing that allow them to, say, smooth out their skin or change how their body looks.

It has therefore been claimed that digital photo editing is "changing the way we see ourselves," and some research paints a bleak picture of the link between teens' body image and social media.[10] For example, in 2014, Harrison and Hefner reported that exposure to retouched images led to a drop in self-esteem among adolescents of all genders, and research by Kleemans et al. in 2016 showed that adolescent girls were largely unable to distinguish edited from non-edited images of people's faces and bodies.[11] It is crucial, however, to note that these studies sought to examine the *effects* of social apps like Instagram on adolescents, and readers will know by now that human-technology relations are incredibly complex and cannot be adequately captured by simple cause-and-effect models of research, as this work typically cannot account for the wider range of social factors influencing a person's identity. This chapter therefore creates room for alternative narratives of photo editing by avoiding methods that measure causation. I instead seek to learn more about people's experiences and hear their open, honest thoughts, whatever they may be.

This chapter is based on a qualitative pilot study I conducted across June and July 2022. The research involved a group workshop and semi-structured interviews with eight teenagers at Willow Sixth Form, a private (paid-for) all-girls school in the North of England. In my dataset, I have one Congolese participant, one Indian British participant, and six who are White British. Seven participants use she/her pronouns and one uses they/them. All participants were aged 17 at the time we spoke. More details on the methods and ethics of this research are described in appendix D, and readers should note that workshop data is primarily used as supplementary descriptive data throughout this chapter and so, unlike my interview transcripts, it has not been subject to rigorous thematic (or other) modes of analysis. While I worked with a smaller group of students on this project than in the studies discussed in chapters 3 and 4, to borrow Chow's words, "I do not aim to arrive at any grand narratives or common patterns" about female and non-binary teens at large.[12] I instead wish to tell you about the lives and views of my research participants, which will, I hope, shed invaluable insight into digital photo editing and tell us where we ought to look next. Their experiences—as with most participants introduced through this book—indicate that, in order to be helpful, digital photo editing must also be harmful. That is, digital photo editing in what I describe below as a light-touch way can be helpful because it enables my participants and their peers to hide their insecurities. But, paradoxically, masking those so-called flaws with editing tools makes them less visible to other teens and contributes to upholding the same societal beauty standards that informed their insecurities to begin with.

From Representation to Self-Representation

Media representation can be understood as the process by which a media text conveys a particular identity, social issue, world event, or similar to its audience. Hall, for example, defined representation as "the process by which meaning is produced and exchanged between members of a culture."[13] He argued that things do not have a fixed or unchanging meaning and that we "in society, within human cultures," make things mean.[14] In the 1970s, Hall devised the encoding/decoding model to mark a shift away from the media effects theories I historicized in chapter 1.[15] This model of communication, which sought to synthesize both media power (which produces ideology) and audience power (which resists and negotiates those meanings), describes the process by which meaning is encoded into a particular text and then decoded by its audience.[16] This model, grouped within other active audience theories from the same era, marked an important academic shift beyond thinking about media effects (like changes in behaviors or beliefs) toward asking how people make meaning when they engage with texts like films, television programs, magazines, and newspapers. It is not the case, of course, that media audiences were once passive and later became active. Each of these is a *conceptualization* about audiences and each has its own explanatory strengths and weaknesses (as in, neither term alone can sufficiently capture audience engagement with a media text), which is leveraged by various parties including academia, industry, and the press. The terms are also used to represent generations of media research. Academics have explored representations of identity markers like gender and race in media texts; such studies often criticize how certain identities are misrepresented and therefore do not offer realistic depictions of our social world.

However, in more recent years, academics have shifted their attention to studies of self-representation: how ordinary people leverage digital technologies like social media to portray their own identities. Unlike in traditional media like television series or films, it's not wholly accurate to talk about how things like beauty norms "are portrayed" on platforms like Instagram. The platform itself does not *do* the portraying; people instead self-represent on social media. A decade or so ago, it therefore seemed "highly reasonable" to think that social media might be very beneficial for issues like body image: "Finally, women and girls (and men and boys) would no longer be exposed to and compare themselves with all those beautiful models in the magazines, but instead, would now be exposed to the diverse range of normal body sizes and shapes exhibited by their peers, i.e., ordinary people."[17]

But as is the case with so many innovations, things haven't quite turned out that way.[18] Contrary to older fantasies about the potential diversity of self-representations on social media, we're now hearing widespread concerns about the enhancement, adjustment, and at worst, outright fakery of some of the images we see on apps like Instagram. There are several dimensions to the body image–social media debate, but the concern underpinning this chapter is that self-images posted to platforms like Instagram are not "authentic." Lindholm defined authentic things as those that are "original, real, and pure. They are what they purport to be; their provenance and authorship are known and verified."[19] The authentic, then, "is understood to be the reverse of everything that is defined as 'pseudo-, sham-, make-believe, makeshift-, mock-, would-be-, fake-, phony-, semi-, near-, baloney-, synthetic-.'"[20] As Thumim notes, self-representations indeed "promise to deliver authentic accounts of individual 'ordinary people,'" but this is a promise we don't always keep.[21]

In response to these concerns, the Norwegian government recently introduced a new law requiring advertisers and influencers to declare when they have edited a photo on social media.[22] There's a Norwegian word for "what all of this falsified perfection might be doing to our psyches: *kroppspress*, which translates quite literally as 'body pressure.'"[23] Such laws have older precedents, of course: in 2012, Israel passed its Photoshop Law, requiring ad agencies to disclose if photos of models had been digitally manipulated to make them appear thinner, and also banned the use of models with a body mass index (BMI) of 18.5 or less (or who "appear to have such a low index").[24] The French government passed a similar law in 2017.[25] In 2021, in the US, Massachusetts state representative Kay Khan proposed a bill to provide tax credits to businesses that "pledge to not digitally alter models' natural body size or shape, and skin tone or texture, in advertisements."[26] And in 2022, UK conservative politician and medical general practitioner (GP)

Dr. Luke Evans introduced the Digitally Altered Body Images Bill.[27] This bill requires advertisers, broadcasters, and publishers to "display a logo in cases where an image of a human body or body part has been digitally altered in its proportions."[28]

The effectiveness of such efforts is still relatively unknown. Some studies indicate that disclaimers "do not appear to be a useful approach for reducing the impact of idealized social media images," though writers usually acknowledge that more research in this area is needed.[29] In their review and meta-analysis on the effectiveness of disclaimer labels pertaining to digital photo editing, Danthinne et al. outline some significant limitations. For example, they say extant research tends to have small sample sizes, meaning their findings aren't (yet) generalizable.[30] The authors also note that existing studies tend to focus on university-age and female participants from Western countries.[31] Alongside or instead of disclaimer labels, researchers have generated a number of recommendations, for example, "portraying a greater diversity of body shapes/sizes in the media (a recommendation favored by adolescent girls); learning about body image in schools (preferred among adolescent boys); and emphasizing more focus on function and health as well as seeing greater diversity of media images (preferred among adults)."[32] Some of these ideas were echoed in my conversations with teenagers at Willow Sixth Form, described in the remainder of this chapter.

Research on social media and body image often asks how photo-based platforms and associated practices like photo editing might impact people's body image and body satisfaction. White university-aged women are usually the focus of such studies. However, I did not frame my research questions in this way, not least because the qualitative methods I used cannot isolate social media as a causal factor in a person's body dissatisfaction—but also because I did not (morally or ethically) want to frame my participants as *affected* or *impacted* by technologies like social media, since it felt to me that doing so disempowered them. I do not deny that the act of seeing images has an emotive dimension (in other words, that people see images and feel something about them), but I'm less interested in attempting to prove cause and effect than I am in hearing teens' own thoughts about digital photo editing, whether or not they engage in such practices, and about whether they feel any level of governance is required.

A Typology of Acceptable Digital Photo Editing

The research on which this chapter is based asked how the eight 17-year-olds mentioned above feel about their own and other people's photo editing habits on social media, particularly on the visual platforms they favor, like Instagram and TikTok. My research was conducted at a private (fee-paying) sixth form, making it very different from the schools described in chapters 3 and 4. Fees sit at around £5,000 per academic term and there are three terms per school year. Willow primarily prepares its 16- to 18-year-old students to complete their A-Levels, which can be used for entry into universities. The sixth form is located in a city with a majority-White population and has a social stereotype of being one of the wealthier parts of Northern England, especially compared with the other Northern cities I've mentioned thus far, housing plenty of historical buildings and other tourist attractions. My pilot study used two qualitative research methods: an hour-long group workshop with all eight participants and semi-structured in-depth interviews with three participants. During the workshop, students were split into pairs or groups of three and asked to map out a framework for an article to be published in a magazine like *Teen Vogue*. They were told their article should respond to the new Norwegian photo editing law, discussed above. Students were given clear instructions about what to include (like a title, tagline, angle, sub-section headings, etc.), and later asked to feed their work back to the rest of the group. Workshop participants were then asked to follow up via email if they wished to participate in an interview to tell me more about their views on digital photo editing. I had a very short timeframe in which to conduct my workshop and interviews: I received my research funding in May 2022 and the term at Willow Sixth Form ended in early July 2022. As a result, I was only able to conduct follow-up interviews with three teens. This chapter therefore shares excerpts from my hour-long interviews with Kiana, Ria, and Rowan and includes supplementary workshop materials created by the five other students: Eadie, Emma, Frankie, Hannah, and Tilly.

. . .

I admit I was surprised to find some acceptance of digital photo editing across my eight research participants, even among those who didn't do it themselves or who didn't often post to social media. During the group workshop, I didn't outright ask my participants to say whether they edited their photos. I assumed this practice was socially stigmatized and, as such, that they wouldn't admit to doing it, especially not in front of their peers. But I was wrong about this. During the workshop, most participants admitted to editing *something* about their appearance in a photo and then uploading it to social media. And I was clearly mistaken to think this was a taboo topic. Of course, I recognize that I spoke to a very specific demographic: 17-year-olds who, barring one student, used she/her pronouns and whose families could afford to send them to a fee-paying school. But still, I admit that I was surprised and humbled by their candid conversations.

Ria, for example, said she feels digital photo editing is acceptable "to a degree," because she "get[s] that everyone has their own insecurities." She said that, among her friend group, it's not that controversial if someone gets caught editing their social media images: "People get over it. It's like gossip, it will die down in a couple of . . . however long." Ria—who uses she/her pronouns and is Indian-British—told me she doesn't post very much to social media and tends to edit her pictures in more of a "humorous" way, like editing someone's face on to an image. Instagram is Ria's go-to platform, on which she maintains a private account just for her friends. This, she says, helps her to feel she doesn't "have to look a certain way" because the people on her account "already know" what she looks like. Ria also has a TikTok account but doesn't post to it, and she uses Snapchat to directly contact people she knows. At the start of our interview, as we were getting to know each other, Ria would confidently tell me she didn't post much to social media and doesn't really care what people think about her online presence. But toward the end of our conversation, Ria insightfully reflected on this point and told me she doesn't know why she "feels so serious" about limiting her presence on platforms. When prompted to reflect on this, she told me she doesn't like the thought of prying, unknown eyes judging her posts and therefore struggles with the loss of control over who sees what. I remember feeling grateful that Ria became more comfortable with me as our conversation progressed; after all, an interview about digital photo editing can bring up lots of sensitive issues. She eventually became comfortable enough to retract her earlier points and—quite vulnerably, I think—tell me she actually thought and cared deeply about being perceived on social apps.

Kiana explained that she hasn't ever engaged in what she would describe as "major" editing (distorting her face or body) and has instead just altered the backgrounds of some social media posts to remove other people. That said, she wouldn't rule out face and body editing in the future: "Maybe I should adjust how I look a bit to make myself look a bit thinner." Kiana—who uses she/her pronouns and is Congolese—told me that her relationship with her body has changed over the last few years. Where she previously felt insecure about "naturally" having "the lips and the bum" derived from her Congolese heritage, she finds it "weird" that as a younger teen she was bullied for the very physical features that now seem to be desirable among girls her age. Quite early on in our interview, Kiana was keen to tell me that the digital photo editing techniques she sees often involve White girls essentially "trying to look like other ethnic groups," a powerful point and one that I reflect more on later. These trends, Kiana told me, have prompted much self-reflection over the last few years, and I wonder if her near-instant comfort in the interview scenario might've been because she'd been waiting for the chance to say these things to someone who would really listen. All the workshop participants from Willow Sixth Form were trying out the BeReal app at the time we spoke, which Kiana particularly enjoyed because she said it gave her much more "control" over who saw her posts. She felt happier to post something like "a picture of me looking tired or in bed" on her BeReal, whereas on Instagram she feels she has to "look a certain way to post," very much mirroring what Ria said. Kiana is working on her relationship with Instagram, though; she's trying to "become more chilled" and "fun with it," assuring herself that her pictures "don't have to be 100 percent perfect" all the time. She also posts to Snapchat and TikTok but mainly to individuals or via private accounts and remarked that her Snapchat usage has dwindled since she was around 13.

Rowan told me they have never edited a photo of themselves and uploaded it to social media, but empathized with people who do:

> ROWAN: I feel like, if you post a picture of yourself, and people have said that to you, or you've seen other people on social media who are also edited, then you think, well I should look like that. People have told me I should look like that, therefore I'm going to edit myself to look like that. I think it definitely does come from a place of insecurity, which is a bit sad.

Rowan—who uses they/them pronouns and told me they are "very White, and British"—mainly used Instagram and TikTok but set a 90-minute cap on TikTok per day because, during one particularly deep TikTok session, they had the realization that "three hours had passed, and I was like, what am I doing, what is the point?" Like Ria, Rowan only posted to Instagram, on which they maintained a small, private circle of known friends and contacts. Their pictures are mainly from scuba diving as they feel "insecure" about posting more ordinary photos of themselves; for Rowan, it's important to achieve harmony between their selfhood on social media and the person people will meet in real life. Rowan enjoys going to the gym and engaging with gym-related content on social media, remarking that beauty standards manifest differently within these communities. In the gym Instagram/#gymstagram space, Rowan told me that people edit their photos to accentuate certain parts of their bodies, like narrowing their waists or enlarging their thighs or biceps, despite them already "look[ing] amazing." This leads Rowan to feel that there is a "main set of rules" that are broadly known in relation to societal beauty standards but that these rules branch out into "sub-sections," each with its own norms and cultures. This was such a fascinating way of looking at beauty norms and one that I hadn't fully considered before I spoke to Rowan. Importantly, Rowan was also keen for me to know that they were speaking strictly from an English context and that beauty norms will likely vary geographically.

During our interview, Kiana distinguished between people who edit their self-images in a way that retains their *realisticness*, especially ordinary people (like her peers), versus influencers who lie about having edited their self-images or who edit them in a way that depicts an unrealistic appearance:

> KIANA: I don't think photoshopping is a bad thing necessarily, but if it goes to an extent where influencers are promoting this unrealistic body standard because they've edited, and they haven't claimed that they've edited—that this is their natural state or whatever—I think that could be quite harmful to people.

Rowan made a near-identical comment: "Removing like a spot or something is a bit different from physically changing the way your body is, if you know what I mean?" Ria, Kiana, and Rowan identify two important critiques of the practice of digital photo editing in the quotes above. First, they distinguish between the levels of editing people engage in and the degree to which society is permissive of each level. Second, they make distinctions about who engages in digital photo editing and the extent to which a person has the responsibility to set an example, particularly to younger or more vulnerable people. With regards to the second point, it was clear to me that Ria, Kiana, and Rowan—and, indeed, all eight participants across the workshop space—were far less forgiving of celebrities' and influencers' photo editing habits, because they perceive these famous people to have more sway over their peers than other people their own age. For example, Ria says:

RIA: I think it's just annoying when you see, like, especially the celebrities that claim that they don't, but it's just obvious that they do, and it just sets loads of unachievable standards for other people viewing them.

Present in my participants' words is a reminder that ordinary people don't often see celebrities and influencers in-person, and so we don't know what they actually look like. This, for my participants, is precisely why it can be irresponsible when celebrities and influencers edit their self-images: because we can't compare social media imagery to what we see in face-to-face settings, unrealistic beauty and body standards are set. For my participants, it's not quite so bad when ordinary people, like their peers, edit their self-images. This is because they interact in face-to-face settings and can therefore easily identify when social media images have been edited.

Part of everyday life for people of all ages involves comparing ourselves to others. As Festinger noted in his 1954 theory of social comparison, "there exists in the human organism, a drive to evaluate his opinions and his abilities."[33] It is feared that social media platforms make social comparisons worse, as they "enable the making of frequent, multiple, and rapid comparisons 24/7 at any time of a user's choosing."[34] While social comparisons of course existed long before the internet did, the story goes that the availability of information about other people's lives facilitates a greater volume of comparisons, fundamentally making us feel worse about ourselves. Furthermore, "unlike traditional media, social media provide the opportunity for comparisons with similar others, i.e., peers, who are particularly relevant comparison targets."[35] This phenomenon might partly explain why Rowan has a philosophy to maintain harmony across their social media and in-person presence:

> ROWAN: If what you present on social media is different from what you look like, I feel like you could get really insecure about, like, meeting people in real life. Like, if someone's seen your photo and they're like, "Oh you don't look like that." . . . I've seen some pictures of people and I'm like, " . . . What? I saw you yesterday, that is not what you look like."

In his work, Festinger outlined two forms of social comparison: *upward comparisons* where people compare themselves to others they view as superior to them in some way, which motivates them to achieve similar results and *downward comparisons* in which, for a person to feel better about themselves, they compare themselves to those they consider to be worse off.[36] As Festinger explained, "If some other person's ability is too far from his own, either above or below, it is not possible to evaluate his own ability accurately by comparison with this other person."[37] In other words, people seek out comparisons with similar rather than dissimilar others. According to this argument, the teens in my study would be likelier to compare themselves to their peers rather than influencers or celebrities. Because Instagram is notoriously understood as a highlight reel, "the end result is that comparisons with Instagram 'peers' are most often upwards in direction (Fardouly et al., 2017), resulting in dissatisfaction with one's own body and appearance."[38] But in the quote above, Rowan articulates a rupture in processes of social comparison, as they employ what Lavrence and Cambre call the "digital forensic gaze." The act of "gazing" in this way describes the practice of assessing user-generated digital images to decide whether or not they've been edited.[39] Rowan—and my two other interviewees, as you'll hear below—feel they can confidently figure out when their peers' self-images have been heavily edited because they don't match their in-person appearance. This may potentially—optimistically(?)—stop social comparison in its tracks, as teens like Rowan might know there's no point comparing their appearances to ones that have been digital enhanced and therefore literally are not real. Contrary to Tiggemann and Anderberg's fear that comparisons with peers via Instagram images results in "dissatisfaction with one's own body and appearance," perhaps in instances where photo editing is too unrealistic teens may not engage in social comparisons at all.

However, on a more pessimistic note, Lavrence and Cambre explain that people also turn this gaze onto themselves when we ask what in our own appearances might be "fixed" through editing software.[40] My own research participants clearly used the digital forensic gaze, assessing both their own and other people's images to identify when something may have been edited and to look for things in their own images with the *potential* to be edited. As Ria notes:

RIA: When I see influencers, I think I've lost caring about it because it's just expected now. But I do find it a bit weird when it's people I know because I see them as all right when I see them in real life.

Crucial in Ria's comment is that, not only does she scrutinize social media posts to check for editing, just as Kiana and Rowan do, but she also finds herself measuring the necessity of such practices ("I see them as all right when I see them in real life"). Echoing some of the findings discussed in chapters 3 and 4, my three interview participants articulate a highly meaningful distinction between social media and real life, by which Ria means face-to-face settings. This conscious separation is evidently powerful to her, as it plays into her experiences of the "digital forensic gaze," via her assessment of other people's appearances and her own.[41] While research by Kleemans et al. showed that adolescent girls were largely unable to distinguish edited from non-edited images of people's faces and bodies, their study did not account for other ways teens might be able to spot editing—for example, by knowing someone in a face-to-face setting and then doing a mental comparison to their social media posts.[42] In other words, while teens might not be able to look at a picture of someone and definitively say, in that moment, whether it had been edited, there are other ways of achieving this goal.

Returning to a point I made earlier, my participants powerfully described variations in the levels of digital photo editing people engage in and the degree of acceptability society grants each level. Rowan summarizes these sentiments this way:

ROWAN: I think it really does depend on how you do it and how severe it is. Because I think, right now, editing your waistline or your hips is a bit more taboo. Like, if you told someone that, they'd go, "Oh, what did you do that for?" . . . But if you just, like, put like a filter on and made your skin smoother or maybe, like, I don't know, you made your skin more tanned or more pale or whatever, depending on, you know, where you're going, I feel like that's a lot less taboo. Like, people say, "Oh yeah, I did a bit of face tuning," and everyone's just like, "Yeah, okay, whatever." So I think, facially, it's a lot different than if you physically changed your body.

For Rowan, and as McGovern et al. note, some forms of digital photo editing are underpinned by a desire to showcase "photos of oneself that present their 'best' physical appearance," which "can also involve self-presentation methods such as selecting the best photos and editing one's appearance in said photos."[43] Rowan feels that, while it's accepted among their peers to put your best self forward on image-based social media platforms, the practice becomes more taboo when the *level* of digital photo editing takes a person into the realm of the inauthentic. For Rowan, this would profoundly alter their sense of self, precisely why they avoid doing it:

> ROWAN: I feel like if I did edit a photo, that photo would then feel a bit, like, wrong. I wouldn't like looking at it, because I would know that, well, I've just changed myself, like, for someone else, so what's the point? . . . If you, like, look at a picture of yourself, and like, look in the mirror and you see, like, a disparity, I feel like that could create, like, quite a weird sense of self.

Very much led by my research participants, in what follows, I devise a typology of digital photo editing. The categorizations link to the technical aspects of the editing process (the extent of change within an image) but also invoke some moral categorizations, according to how "serious" (or socially acceptable) the type of editing is. *Light touch editing* involves lightly altering aspects of an image, like blurring out acne and other perceived "flaws," and may be used in combination with filters. This type of editing may also involve changing the background of an image (e.g., the removal of other people captured within the frame). *Heavy duty editing* involves heavily altering aspects of an image, like adjusting a person's body shape to, say, shrink or enlarge elements of it. And *transformational editing* involves changing a person or setting to the point where it is borderline unrecognizable. For example, some photo editing apps replace a person's face, hair, and other parts of their body, as opposed to changing them in a light-touch or even heavy-duty manner.

Although Rowan has never edited any of their own photos, their friends have engaged in what the above typology would class as light touch and therefore socially acceptable editing:

ROWAN: I don't think any of my friends edit their photos to, like, an extreme extent. I think it's just like, maybe removing like a blemish or making the lighting look nice. But I don't think any of them have, like, altered their body shape or anything like that.

To return to a comment I made at the start of this section, I admit that I was surprised by my participants' overall acceptance of light touch digital photo editing. I'm not sure where my initial assumption came from—maybe because I didn't grow up with such technologies myself or because more "extreme" forms of body work like cosmetic surgery (which I discuss below) weren't as cheap or widely available when I was their age. My assumption might've also come from concerns about the research scenario: that they would tell me what they thought I wanted to hear (that editing is somehow morally "wrong"). But their thoughts, though obviously not representative of all teens, tell me I was right to steer clear of questions about the effects of digital photo editing on their body image and senses of self, as this would've masked the fascinating and complex realities our conversations unearthed.

"Slim-thick, as it was": Race and/in the New Beauty Standard

Not only did the teens from Willow Sixth Form describe *levels* of acceptable digital photo editing, but they also told me about the *types* of digital adjustments people make to their faces and bodies. These changes, as my participants explain, relate to dominant beauty standards within English society. By *beauty standards*, I refer to the norms and rules dictating what beauty looks like, and I talk about how it appears in my participants' and their peers' eyes. But there is, of course, no singularly recognized beauty standard. For example, much existing research on photo editing (either in older media formats like magazine advertisements or those from the digital realm) describes the "thin ideal" for some women's bodies. The thin ideal is "typically associated with Western culturally idealised standards of beauty" which "stipulate that appearance is central to one's value and role in society."[44] Within this context, "a thin body is ideal" because it (supposedly) "assures success and life satisfaction."[45] Afful and Ricciardelli explain that the thin ideal has led to "cultural assumptions that fat bodies are 'deviant,' unattractive, and unhealthy . . . and therefore should be hidden."[46] In 2011, Meyer et al. noted a substantial worsening of the thin ideal in American culture, comparing the so-called perfect size eight characteristic of the 1980s to the significantly smaller size double zero offered by retailers in the late 2000s.[47] But, for my research participants, the thin ideal now feels rather out of date.

As Ria explains, as a Congolese teen she feels today's beauty standard in England is to have "a slim waist and then a big bum and really thin legs." Crucially, though, she remarks that these are physical qualities "it's not naturally possible to have." Kiana—an Indian-British, female 17-year-old—made a similar remark:

> KIANA: I've grown up and been on social media a long time, and the beauty standard has definitely changed because they used to be, like, wanting to be really, really skinny and now there's people that we know that are, like, "Oh, we want a Brazilian Butt Lift (BBL)" or something. Things have drastically changed a lot.

Kiana notes that, while contemporary beauty standards are still "quite Eurocentric," "there's also influence from different parts of the world." Kiana makes a particularly interesting comment about BBLs, "a surgical procedure in which fat is removed from various parts of the body and then injected back into the buttocks."[48] For Kiana and Ria, this type of procedure counters the older thin ideal they felt was depicted in the traditional media texts they consumed when they were children and previously on social media. However, going back to Ria's earlier quote, this look—slim waist, big bum, thin legs (to use her phrases)—isn't biologically achievable because it draws from too many contexts. White, non-binary 17-year-old Rowan made a near-identical remark, despite their having a different racial and gender identity than Kiana and Ria:

> ROWAN: I think, if I generalize in, like, teenagers, especially at my school, I think it's definitely skinny waist, big boobs, narrow shoulders, narrow ribcage. Slim-thick, as it was. Like, you're supposed to be skinny here, but not skinny there, but in reality, you can't have that. If you have a—excuse my language—if you have a big arse then it's like, you're not going to be really skinny, because that's just not how it works.

Rowan also notes how beauty standards vary not only in terms of identity markers like race and gender but also according to a person's social group(s). For example, Rowan feels that people of all genders who go to the gym "will edit themselves differently to people who don't," as they may be likelier to pay close attention to editing their muscularity.

Important for Kiana is that the new beauty standard—which she says is "borrowed" from a combination of "countries and cultures"—contains desirable looks that she herself possesses but was bullied for having when she was younger. She also noted how differently she felt about her appearance while living in England in contrast to when she has visited her family in India. She feels the ideal body type in an Indian context is to be "skinny" and that this earns you compliments from those who subscribe to this beauty ideal. But because she wouldn't describe her own body in this way, she would feel "insecure" while in that geographic context or if her Instagram or TikTok algorithms began treating her as though she was physically situated in India and/or wanted to view content from Indian creators:

> RIA: With TikTok and Instagram, you can see people from all over the world so you may see this person who's getting masses of compliments because they're skinny because you're in an Eastern—so if I was back in India, I'd probably be a bit insecure.

Ria then went on to describe a shift away from the thin ideal in England, where she feels more comfortable in her own skin:

> RIA: I think people who used to fit into that one category of being skinny, like super-skinny, and on Pinterest there'll be those really skinny girls, they've now kind of . . . it's not a shift but it's like socially acceptable to have a bit of fat or something or big boobs. Yeah, so that's like a new thing that's come in.

At face value, it might seem like a good thing that my participants feel beauty standards have shifted away from the thin ideal. But as Kiana and Ria note, this standard has simply been replaced by another perhaps even more pernicious one. Kiana and Ria feel that the new body image standard is literally impossible. It can only be achieved via digital photo editing and is therefore not real in the sense that the person's body simply does not look like it does in an edited image or could only be achieved or via expensive plastic or cosmetic surgery procedures:

> RIA: Because our bodies genetically . . . like people's bodies genetically may never be the ideal body standard and having

that image out there can be quite rough to see, like, online— slim waist, big hips, big boobs—and genetically you know you may never be able to achieve that, that can be quite damaging.

Social concerns about digital photo editing are also accompanied by worries that teens are seeking to replicate the look they achieve via editing through cosmetic surgery procedures. In England, media headlines like "How girls are now begging surgeons to change their faces so they look like their edited pictures on Instagram" bolster fears about the supposed dangers of photo editing technologies.[49] These claims are coupled with anecdotes from cosmetic surgeons, who report that patients often bring filtered Instagram images to their consultations and ask for the same results.[50] Some writers even report a rise in teens seeking "back-to-school" cosmetic surgery.[51] Unlike plastic surgery, cosmetic surgery procedures are entirely elective and are "carried out solely to change a healthy person's appearance to achieve what they feel is a more desirable look."[52] They are classed as either *surgical* (which involves the skin being cut, like rhinoplasty) or *non-surgical* (less invasive procedures like lip fillers).[53] While the uptake of cosmetic surgery procedures typically rises annually for complex reasons like destigmatization, the British Association of Aesthetic Plastic Surgeons (BAAPS) reveals that around half of British surgeons report no rise in teen inquiries.[54] And yet these anxieties persist.

The lack of evidence that teens are undertaking more cosmetic surgery in England does not, of course, mean they aren't aware of it. I directly asked Kiana and Ria if there are conversations among their peers about getting certain procedures, either the surgical options or those that are more cosmetic (like injectables).

Kiana replied: "Yes, a lot of girls who would be deemed as more skinny have said that they'd want a BBL just for the big bum." And Ria said: "Some people want nose jobs because they're trying to get a smaller, slimmer nose, one that's a button nose, so they'll try and remove their nose bridge. That's been going round quite a lot." Kiana also connects certain surgery trends to a desire to achieve the current beauty standard, which she feels represents a move away from whiteness and is more—to use Tolentino's phrase— "ambiguously ethnic": "I think a lot more people are insecure about their lips, people wanting to change their eye shape, which I think could go a bit wrong, trying to look like other ethnic groups."[55]

Eadie, Emma, and Tilly—three of my 17-year-old workshop participants—interestingly drew on what I would describe as deterministic news media framing—mirrored in the abovementioned articles about teens and cosmetic surgery—to shape their proposed article on digital photo editing. The title was "Unreachable Façade," and the tagline read, "How Impossible Beauty Standards Are Detrimental to Universal Body Image." Frankie and Hannah's article was strikingly similar: its proposed headline was "Photoshop Phenomenon: Is Photoshop Killing our Kids?" There are three key things to note about their articles.

First, deterministic news media framing about matters like digital photo editing was clearly recognizable to the teens from Willow Sixth Form, demonstrating its perniciousness in contemporary English society; this is precisely why this book seeks to move away from either-or designations when it comes to assessing technology use among young people. Eadie, Emma, Frankie, Hannah, and Tilly all in some way borrowed deterministic framing in their article drafts:

- "The *impact* on mental health" (Eadie, Emma and Tilly; Figure 3)
- "How do filters *effect* [*sic*] our self-esteem?" (Eadie, Emma and Tilly; Figure 3)
- "Chipping away at teen's [*sic*] mental health" (Frankie and Hannah; Figures 4 and 5)
- "Crippling self esteem issues" (Frankie and Hannah; Figures 4 and 5)

The knowing, ironic use of such framing via emulation is exceptionally powerful and revealing: it was fascinating to me that the five teens innately knew how to frame their articles. I showed no examples that used this style of writing, and the substantive content of their proposed magazine articles did not actually match this reductive headline (which I maintain was not deliberately reductive but was instead a knowing nod to news media framing of teens and technology).

Second, all research participants from Willow Sixth Form in some way—either via their workshop participation or interview data—highlighted the *impossibility* of what they described as the "new normal" in visual depictions of female body image. While the thin bodies depicted via mainstream media have of course long been described as unattainable—and rightly so—the teens in my research pointed to something a little different: the new beauty standards are also impossible because they are digitally generated. This sentiment nods to broader social crises around trust and legitimacy in relation to media.[56] Today, visual imagery—particularly digital visuals—is seen as somewhere between trustworthy and suspect.

Third, their articulations direct us once again to conceptualize digital photo editing practices as having highly paradoxical outcomes: my participants indicate that, in order to be helpful, digital photo editing must also be harmful. While light touch digital photo editing can be helpful because it enables you to hide your so-called flaws, masking those insecurities with editing tools makes them less visible to other teens, thus upholding the same societal beauty standards that informed their insecurities to begin with (and, indeed, perpetuating new and perhaps even more pernicious ones).

Not only is there a lack of evidence that teens are undertaking more cosmetic surgery procedures in the UK, but such articles and studies share a normative framing that cosmetic and plastic surgery are morally wrong. This standpoint was, interestingly, shared by Kiana, Ria and Rowan, who were all largely critical of cosmetic surgery and those seeking it (in contrast to their views on digital photo editing, which were more empathetic). Through research published in 2022, however, Chow notes profound cultural differences in attitudes toward cosmetic procedures. Instead of being "prey to beauty ideals" and victims of "consumerist cultures," the young Chinese women in Chow's research were not working toward "impossible feminine ideals" or "perfection."[57] Instead, "they are far more realistic; they want to look somewhat younger, better, and sometimes more themselves—some of them mention how the surgeries and injections make them more authentic and unique, as if the interventions have brought out something already inside themselves. In general, they consider the post-intervention selves more confident and happy."[58]

Chow's research is rare in highlighting the *pleasures* of cosmetic surgery and other forms of beauty work for Chinese women, especially those who are single and ageing.[59] The women in this

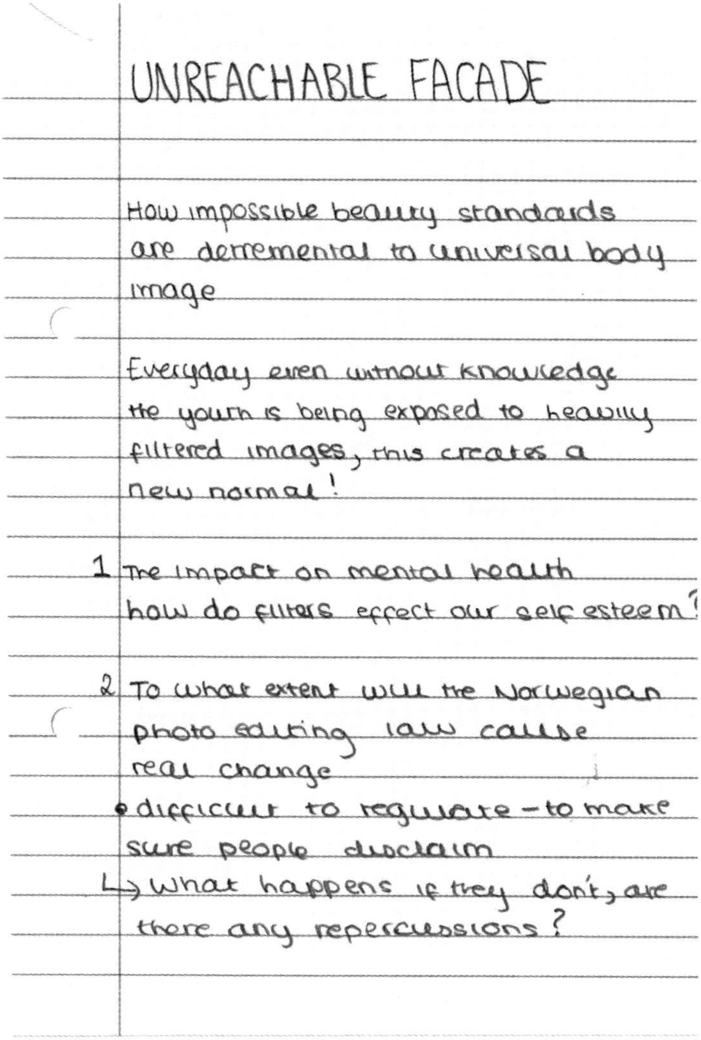

UNREACHABLE FACADE

How impossible beauty standards
are detremental to universal body
image

Everyday even without knowledge
the youth is being exposed to heavily
filtered images, this creates a
new normal!

1 The impact on mental health
how do filters effect our self esteem?

2 To what extent will the Norwegian
photo editing law cause
real change
● difficult to regulate - to make
sure people disclaim
↳ What happens if they don't, are
there any repercussions?

FIGURE 3. A photograph of the first page of a draft magazine article created by English teenagers Eadie, Emma, and Tilly, informing potential readers about how "impossible beauty standards" may be "detrimental" to body image.

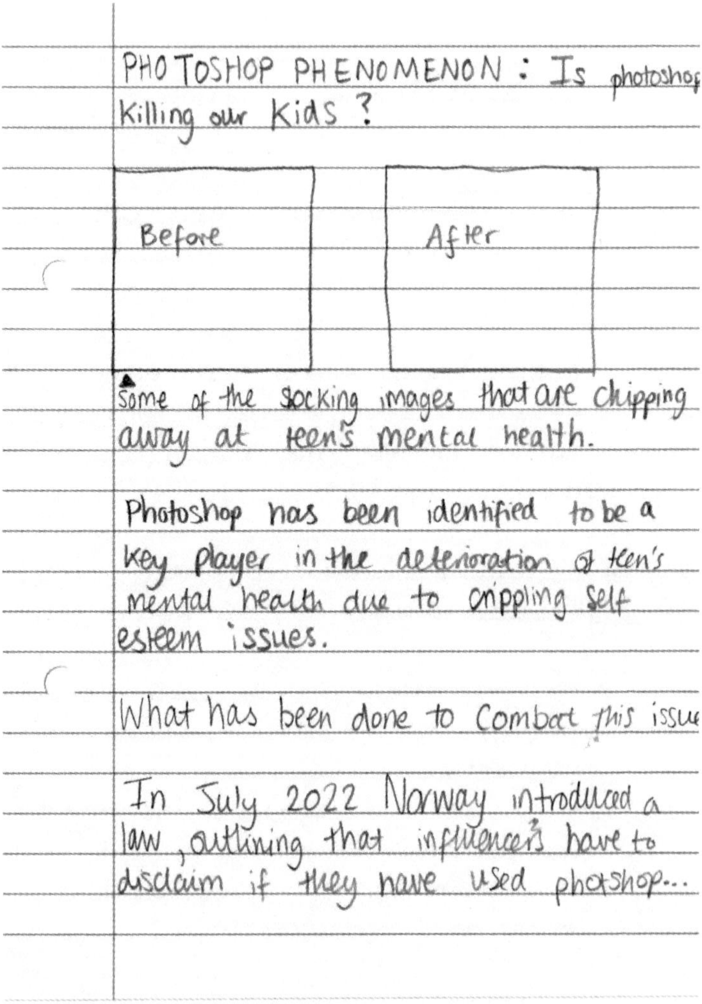

PHOTOSHOP PHENOMENON : Is photoshop
Killing our Kids ?

Before	After

Some of the socking images that are chipping
away at teen's mental health.

Photoshop has been identified to be a
key player in the deterioration of teen's
mental health due to crippling self
esteem issues.

What has been done to Combat this issue

In July 2022 Norway introduced a
law, outlining that influencers have to
disclaim if they have used photoshop...

FIGURE 4. A photograph of the first page of a draft magazine article created
by English teenagers Frankie and Hannah, asking potential readers whether
digital photo editing is "chipping away at teen's [sic] mental health."

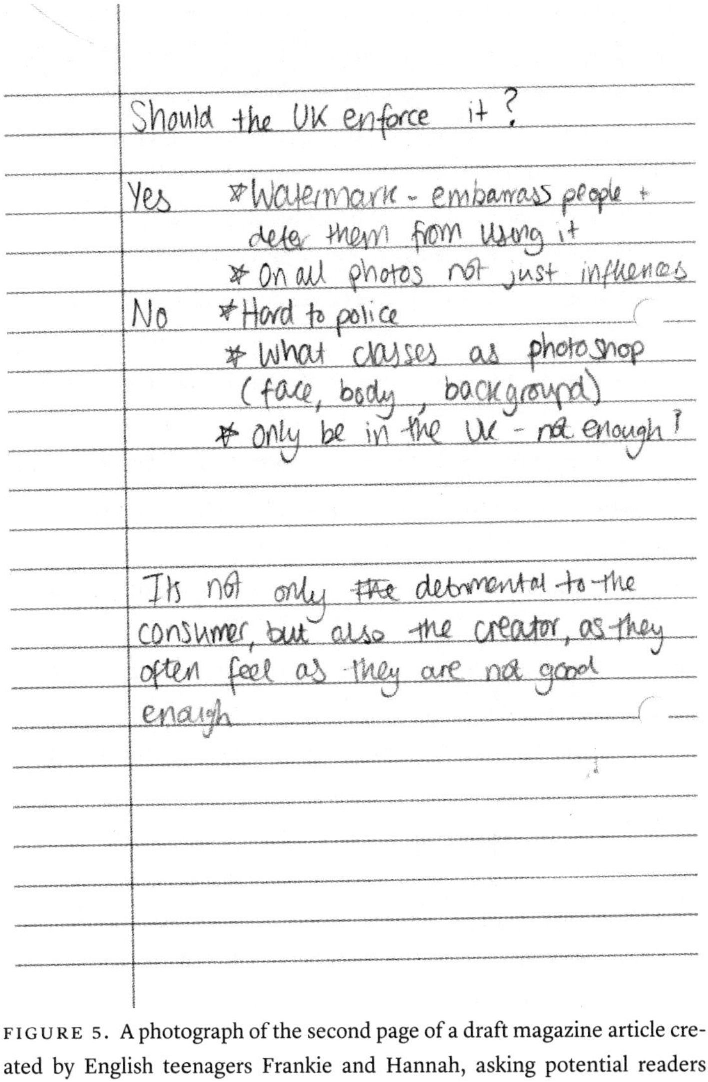

Should the UK enforce it?

Yes   * Watermark - embarrass people + deter them from using it
         * On all photos not just influences

No   * Hard to police
         * What classes as photoshop (face, body, background)
         * only be in the UK - not enough?

Its not only the detrimental to the consumer, but also the creator, as they often feel as they are not good enough

FIGURE 5. A photograph of the second page of a draft magazine article created by English teenagers Frankie and Hannah, asking potential readers whether the UK should also enforce the Norwegian photo editing law.

particular demographic already subvert cultural norms that they ought to be married by a certain age, before they become *shengnü* which, as Chow explains, translates to "left-over women."[60] Their cosmetic surgery procedures and body work are not done with the intention of finding of a husband, but are instead done "for themselves, and for fellow 'sisters' who would appreciate and share the same."[61] Chow's participants are not aiming to be "perfect"; a finding that runs counter to other research.[62] Kiana and Ria also both talked about a conscious rejection of crafting images of perfection on Instagram, famed for demanding "Instagrammable" aesthetics from its users.[63] Kiana says: "Well, on Instagram now I think I've become more chilled a bit. I've started posting all kinds of pictures, just weird funny pictures. I don't know, I feel like it's a way of me being more fun with it. My pictures don't have to be 100 percent perfect." Similarly Ria said: "I don't really post on Instagram but it's quite literally a private Instagram for your friends. It's more chill and you don't have to look a certain way because people already know what you look like."

Kiana and Ria's words can be conceptually connected to the recent rise of an app called BeReal, which positions itself as the anti-Instagram. Once a day, BeReal notifies its users that they have two minutes to post a pair of pictures taken simultaneously, one from their smartphone's front-facing selfie camera and the other from the rear camera.[64] The selling point is that the photos posted to BeReal are supposedly more authentic, as you've had to take them in the moment and can't craft or edit them in the way you might for your Instagram posts. You can still post a BeReal after the two-minute window has closed, but your friends will know that you haven't done it in time; that you haven't "been real." And users can only view their friends' pictures if they have shared their own. It's hard to say what BeReal's fate will be: days before I submitted this manuscript for its first full review, a *New York Times* writer declared that Gen Z was "over being real." But the rapid popularity of this app is still noteworthy, as it nods to the "sense of disillusionment" with the highly curated and calibrated platforms teens like Kiana, Ria, and Rowan have grown up with.[65] The politics of perfection for today's teens, then, are evidently shifting and complex.

From the Thin Ideal to Slim-Thick: The New Body Image Standard

To be an influencer, you have to meet the standards that society sets. So, I wouldn't really say influencers are the problem, I'd say society is the problem. . . . Western countries are so deeply rooted in capitalism, I feel like it does come from, like, companies, and all that. They're constantly showing you these products, like, change this about yourself, do this with yourself, do that, do this, and you'll look better, everyone will like you more.

ROWAN, 17

While previous chapters have focused on secretive communicative practices young people engage in on social media, this chapter has been slightly different. It has not focused on secret communication per se (as in the sharing of words and similar on social media) but has instead examined the secretive behind-the-scenes processes that go into many visually communicative posts: digital photo editing. It has also queried the current platform policies and wider laws around this practice, given recent technological shifts and social concerns, all of which factor into teens' relationships with visual imagery. I close this chapter with the quote above, taken from my interview with Rowan. In many respects, Rowan is right: though there are frequent accusations that digital photo editing is "changing the way we see ourselves," the teens in my study describe substantially more complex processes of identity formation than this quote would allow.[66] My participants shared with me their reflections on body types in traditional media imagery, on their peers' appearances, and on the beauty norms from particular geographical contexts. Kiana and Ria also described how their families' comments factored into their body image, again indicating the array of factors that make up their identities:

KIANA: I think some ethnic families are very judgmental on bodies. The first thing they'll pick out is your body, so I think that has an effect on me, like, doubting the way I look.

RIA: Yes, I think it's quite toxic, they'll always find out insecurities and thoughts you have, and you start stress eating and you put on weight, they'll make you feel horrible for it. So you try and avoid listening to them, you try not to hear them.

And so, while it's obviously important to ask what's new about social media, plenty of things aren't new at all—like influences from our families or the saturation of beauty products in everyday life, to name only two of the many examples my participants gave me. In our rush to solve seemingly new problems about digital photo editing and contemporary beauty standards among young people, we can't forget about these much older problems and contextual factors. As Rowan put it, society is, in many ways, the problem. Then again, we can't ignore my participants' annoyance at celebrities and influencers, and even their peers, who set what they each described as impossible beauty standards: ones that either literally aren't real because they have been digitally manipulated or that they cannot possibly verify because they don't interact with famous folks in everyday settings.

My research with the teens at Willow Sixth Form unearthed several kinds of social comparison between themselves and celebrities and influencers (who they view exclusively via screens) and between themselves and their peers (who they see in face-to-face settings). For example, I noticed that teens found it difficult to compare their bodies to those of celebrities and influencers, in part because they assumed these images were highly edited (in a way that distorts the face or body beyond what could reasonably be considered realistic). But digital photo editing profoundly alters the process of social comparison. What I call transformational editing involves editing a photo to the point where an aspect of a person becomes borderline unrecognizable, leading people to compare themselves to images that are often not real. In 1954, Festinger explained that people are less likely to compare themselves to those with abilities "too far"—from "either above or below"—from their own.[67] This part of his theory continues to have an extent of applicability to the teens in my research, who recognized that celebrities and influencers were not real, in their words, as their self-images were perceived as likelier to be edited than their peers' and that their appearance may have been modified via cosmetic surgery procedures. This may therefore limit teens' social comparison with such posts. The teens I spoke to also felt they could confidently figure out whether their peers' self-images had been heavily edited, as unrealistic social media posts would not match their in-person appearances. Optimistically speaking, this practice of recognition may stop social comparison in its tracks, as teens might see that there's little point in comparing their appearances to ones that have been digitally enhanced and therefore are not real. Contrary to Tiggemann and Anderberg's fear that comparisons with peers via Instagram images results in "dissatisfaction with one's own body and appearance," perhaps in instances where photo editing is *too* unrealistic, teens may not engage in social comparisons at all.

Festinger wrote his theory of social comparison about people's opinions and abilities rather than their physical appearances, and so his theory cannot be neatly applied to the new context I describe here. I am also somewhat less interested in measuring the direction of comparison and its supposed effects on a person than I am in understanding the objects of comparison. While all my research participants in some way compared themselves to others when we spoke, the research underpinning this chapter is largely focused on what teens' social comparisons are; where they come from; how they link to identity markers like gender, race, and beauty; and what they tell us about young lives today. The teens in my research spoke of a shift away from the so-called thin ideal which dominated media texts in England and elsewhere in the late 2000s. In 2011, for example, Meyer et al. noted a substantial worsening of the thin ideal in American culture, comparing the so-called perfect size-eight characteristic of the 1980s to the significantly smaller size, double zero, offered by retailers in the late 2000s.[68] But for my participants, there is a new beauty standard which they say is "borrowed" from a combination of "countries and cultures," and often contains now-desirable looks my participants were bullied for in their younger years (particularly those who are of color). This new body image ideal was described by one of my participants, Rowan, as "slim-thick": "skinny waist, big boobs, narrow shoulders, narrow ribcage," with facial features derived from various ethnic contexts. This new standard has been described as "ambiguously ethnic" and is often achieved via digital photo editing, cosmetic surgery, or a combination between the two and is therefore almost impossible for English teens like those in my study to achieve, perhaps making it even more pernicious than the thin ideal.[69] Of course, body image ideals are contextually bounded, and the ones my participants describe may not resonate with the readers of this book. I do, however, find it fascinating that my three interviewees—who differed in terms of gender identity and ethnicity—described an almost identical beauty standard in separate conversations.

Other research in this area produces inconclusive and at times competing findings on the relationship between young people and digital photo editing, and crucial to note is that studies have thus far predominantly "focused on samples of young white women living in Western countries."[70] As Fardouly and Vartanian rightly state, this means research on digital photo editing is "needed on more diverse samples."[71] And while the research findings described in this chapter offer only a small snapshot into young people's lived realities, my pilot project did its job of telling me where to look next and what questions to ask. Crucially, it taught me that we need to learn so much more about this phenomenon to counter what I would consider to be troubling narratives of the Great Teenage Body Image Debate. Further, and as I argued in the introduction to this chapter, my participants' experiences indicate that, in order to be helpful, digital photo editing must also be harmful. That is, light touch digital photo editing can be helpful because it enables my participants and their peers to hide their insecurities. But, paradoxically, masking those insecurities with editing tools makes them less visible to other teens, thus upholding the same societal beauty standards that informed their insecurities to begin with.

It therefore feels fitting to close this chapter with a quote from Rowan:

> ROWAN: I mean, if I just summed up my thoughts in general, I think it is just, it's not necessarily photo editing that's causing the supposed downfall of mental health in teenagers.

6 *Platform Paradoxes*

Recommendations and Reflections

As I finalize this book, I am also WhatsApping Tom Divon about a new TikTok filter. It's called Bold Glamour, and it alters the appearance of a person's face while they record a video. I tried it out for myself and, I won't lie, I quite liked what I saw. It sharpened my jaw line, plumped up my lips, and thinned out my nose (a feature I have always been quite conscious of). It bears all the hallmarks of what Tolentino calls *Instagram face*: the "single, cyborgian face" that seems to dominate images of "professionally beautiful women" on Instagram. For Tolentino, the issue is not that we—particularly women or those who are feminine-presenting—are starting to literally look the same. The problem is that in-app filters and editing tools like FaceTune adjust our facial features in much the same way, creating a homogenous look among their users and flattening our differences:

> It's a young face, of course, with poreless skin and plump, high cheekbones. It has catlike eyes and long, cartoonish lashes; it has a small, neat nose and full, lush lips. It looks at you coyly but blankly, as if its owner has taken half a Klonopin and is considering asking you for a private-jet ride to Coachella. The face is distinctly

white but ambiguously ethnic.... "We're talking an overly tan skin tone, a South Asian influence with the brows and eye shape, an African-American influence with the lips, a Caucasian influence with the nose, a cheek structure that is predominantly Native American and Middle Eastern."[1]

Older in-app filters on, say, Instagram and Snapchat were a bit glitchy: "Passing a hand in front of your face would interrupt the 'magic,'" whereas Bold Glamour "is incredibly life-like. Users can move and gesticulate on-screen without breaking the illusion."[2] It's true that filters have shifted from playfulness to realism over the last few years: "The introduction of selfie filters initially produced conspicuous, playful forms of editing animated by the novelty of the apps, (i.e., dog face filter)," whereas we have recently seen a move toward "subtler, ambient forms of editing, where it is not always obvious."[3] Bold Glamour, it seems, is simply *too* good, fueling concerns that people won't be able to spot its use.[4] Beauty brand Dove even came out with a campaign to #TurnYourBack on Bold Glamour, reminding people that "no filter should tell you how to look."[5] Clearly, the discourse is that Bold Glamour goes too far: older filters were glitchy enough to be deciphered, whereas this one might genuinely dupe people. And this, we are told, probably won't be great for our senses of self, as we will be comparing our appearances to a standard that transcends reality.

Social concerns about Bold Glamour are tough to assess. At one level, they probably shouldn't be dismissed: popularly used filters should not homogenize our physical appearances, flatten our differences, or foreground one norm of beauty. The use of a filter inevitably invites self-reflection and (perhaps) social comparison, and so I think it's reasonable to worry about how people might feel when they use or view Bold Glamour. Though it's hyperbolic to say filters and editing tools are ruining young people's self-esteem, it's also unwise to brush concerns off as overreactions. But at the same time, assuming Bold Glamour will pull the wool over people's eyes is somewhat condescending and strips us of our digital literacy skills. Social worries about technologies can also reduce opportunities for pleasure—maybe it's *fun* to use Bold Glamour and maybe, in the grand scheme of things, it's not that big of a deal. Clearly, the reason anxieties about Bold Glamour are tough to assess is because the filter is not simply good or bad, helpful or harmful, positive or negative. Individuals will not respond to the same technological innovations in quite the same way, and so Bold Glamour's relationship with its users and viewers will depend on their own identities, which—quite beautifully, I think—are all unique.

It's tough to know how to disentangle social media from other parts of young lives. While 17-year-old Molly told me "You spend so much of your time on social media that it becomes your second life," this isn't the case for all young people around the world. And so, when we ask about young people's relationships with platforms, we must also ask about their identity markers, their geography, who they surround themselves with, their health conditions, and much, much more if we truly wish to work toward a rounded understanding of them. I return to a quote from Orben here, which I have cited throughout this book: academic studies seeking to examine the effects of a particular technology "as a whole"—like asking whether Instagram has caused a rise in reported cases of eating disorders—are largely "ineffective" as they are "far too broad to merit robust conclusions."[6] Studies of this kind are flawed by their very design in that they rest on the deterministic (and incorrect) assumption "'that technologies possess intrinsic powers that affect all people in all situations the same way.'"[7] Studies seeking to measure media effects also fail to account for the other parts of a person's life that help to form the connections between technologies and their complex human identities. And this is just as much the case for studies seeking to examine the positive effects of new technologies as it is for those trying to understand their harms. Learning from some of the earliest internet researchers, my epistemological stance is to ask about the *relationship* between young people and social media, instead of uncritically assigning more power to one side or the other; I maintain an awareness that such dynamics are inconsistent, endlessly fluctuating, and unevenly weighted.

Often—and to make things substantially more complicated— the young people in my research have relationships with certain social media platforms and cultures that might best be described as *paradoxical*. This concept does not attend to either-or outcomes of technological use "(desirable vs. undesirable, anticipated vs. unanticipated, direct vs. indirect)," as such categories are "overly broad and do not adequately reflect the specific content and pressures of the cultural contradictions of technology."[8] As Mick and Fournier note, either-or paradigms ultimately do nothing to advance theories on technological adoption.[9] A paradox, then, has been understood in this book as "the idea that polar opposite conditions can simultaneously exist, or at least can be potentiated, in the same thing," though the concept has of course been discussed in different ways over the years.[10] Among all the young people I have spoken to, I have noticed that it is sometimes only by doing something risky—or even downright harmful—on social media that pleasure and enjoyment can be achieved. To phrase this as my participants might: engaging with like-minded, stigmatized others can make me feel less alone, while also exposing me to things that make me feel worse; asking for people to tell me their secrets through anonymous apps makes me feel excited, while also exposing me to harm; embracing pseudonymity on social media can make me feel safe, but also makes me worry about the identities of those around me; editing my selfies can bring me self-confidence, while also making me feel bad about myself.

The platform paradoxes I outline in this book do not, of course, define all young people's experiences. My case studies offer stories and snapshots of specific demographics at specific moments in time. And while I have sought diversity in my research—for example, by working with a range of school types within different geographical areas and carefully considering my participants' identity markers—I do not claim to generalize across these demographics and certainly not across all young people. I have also avoided generalizing across all platforms: social media are now so broad that the term itself is becoming meaningless without clear identification of the facet to which you are referring—technologies, policies, cultures, demographics, legalities, economics, among many other things. But the paradoxes I describe below came through with such strength in my research data that I find myself wondering how many more might be out there.

PARADOX I. Using social media to engage with content relating to mental health—whether that's through scrolling or posting—is risky. This is because young people might see content they perceive to be harmful, whether or not it breaks a given platform's rules. There is a chance that the things they will be shown on social media via recommendation systems—along with the things they seek out—might not be pleasant. But it can be worth the reward to take this risk; indeed, to exist as helpful spaces for those with mental health conditions, perhaps social media platforms *need* to be harmful, or at the very least risky, because engaging with mental health–related content is itself a risky endeavor. This does not mean people should be stopped from engaging with mental health content altogether, of course. Instead, the realities outlined above suggest we need to embrace paradoxes, as other modes of thinking and policing—like patchwork technical moderation, discussed in chapter 2—are too limiting.

PARADOX II. The teens in my research find anonymous apps to be stressful, especially when they are used in school-based settings. Anonymous apps invoke stress for several reasons, and the first is that they offer a form of *networked anonymity*, where message recipients understand that they are somehow networked with their sender but aren't 100 percent sure who that person is.[11] This means the apps are not always beneficial for a teen's social safety: as they attempt to decipher who said what, they don't feel safe with those around them. Second, anonymous apps make teens feel like they are constantly being watched. This is particularly the case when they are used in school settings as tools for teens to spread gossip about each other. However, teens also find the apps to be intriguing and enticing, so much so that they are willing to accept these risks in a bid to derive some pleasure. Put differently, in order to be fun and engaging, anonymous apps necessitate displeasures for their users, especially for the teens in my research. Participation in anonymous apps therefore involves a highly intricate, entangled, and evolving negotiation between risk and reward, with neither emerging as the clear winner.

PARADOX III. Identity concealment on social media, like using a pseudonym, offers teens significant personal and social safety. Social safety is understood here to mean protection from the risks associated with embarrassing identity disclosures among a young person's peers, while personal safety echoes more traditional understandings of what safety means for young people, and includes protection from things like threats, grooming, identity theft, and catfishing. But while identity concealment is used by teens to avoid harm, the prospect of *other* people being able to do the same thing (i.e., conceal their identities) is risky. For example, malign actors like groomers, bullies, and catfishers who benefit from pseudonymity present teens with personal safety concerns. This means that, paradoxically, anonymity—understood in chapter 4 to refer to the spectrum of identity concealment on offer across platforms—is at once a threat and a method of protection for the teens in my research.

PARADOX IV. The growth, ease-of-use and affordability of digital photo editing tools has led to worries that this process is "changing the way we see ourselves."[12] Such concerns are typically applied to teenage girls, in part because they engage in this practice more frequently than those of other genders and ages.[13] The participants in my research are highly aware of the popularity of digital photo editing and have developed sophisticated techniques for spotting it. My research findings again combine to suggest paradoxical experiences of digital photo editing as, in order to be helpful, digital photo editing must also be harmful. That is, light touch digital photo editing—which, for them, is more socially acceptable than other forms—can be helpful because it enables my participants and their peers to hide their insecurities. But masking those insecurities with editing tools, even if only with a light touch, makes them less visible to other teens, which therefore upholds the same societal beauty standards that informed their insecurities to begin with.

. • .

There are, of course, other words I could have used instead of *paradox*. *Duality* doesn't seem to fit, as this term implies only two competing experiences, which is too limiting a framework when talking about young people and social media. Similar limitations apply to the phrase *contradictory*, which describes two things that cannot both be true (the opposite of the point I am trying to make in this book). Paradox thus seems to be the term that comes closest to describing the defining feature of young peoples' experiences of social media. While thinkers are by no means in complete agreement, one common definition holds that a *paradox* is "a set of mutually inconsistent propositions, each of which seems true."[14] Paradoxes, it is commonly said, involve contradictions that "at least on the surface, have nothing wrong with them," and yet it is only by putting them together that "a tension arises."[15] This feels true for my research participants: social media must be harmful, or at the very least risky, to be helpful to those struggling with their mental health; anonymous apps demand that participants experience displeasure to reap rewards; identity concealment is a threat teens must contend with in order for it to become a mechanism to achieve different forms of safety; practices of digital photo editing have to be harmful in order to be helpful, as editing tools mask "flaws" and work to uphold the same societal beauty standards that informed their insecurities to begin with.

Paradoxes are helpful in moving debates about young people and social media forward precisely because they push us beyond binary modes of thinking: positive vs. negative, good vs. bad, helpful vs. harmful. They force us to "rethink the way things seem to us, because they expose two or more commonsense beliefs that contradict each other."[16] A defining argument of this book is that squeezing social media into categories like good or bad means denying young people's lived realities, which are so much more complicated than we may ever know. A platform paradox approach also means acknowledging that we will never fully solve certain problems in the social media debate, and knowing that that's okay.

Recommendations and Concluding Reflections

In a 2017 journal article, Livingstone and Third reminded readers that the internet was invented by and for adults and then inherited by children and young people: "Although children and young people are simultaneously hailed as pioneers of the digital age and feared for as its innocent victims, the World Wide Web—and the Internet more generally—has been largely conceived, implicitly or explicitly, as an adult resource in terms of provision, regulation and ideology."[17]

It is not young people's fault that the digital technologies they use—many of which they have become reliant on—were not all designed with their safety, needs, and preferences in mind. I have researched young people's experiences of social media since around 2017 and am often called upon by the press, policymakers, tech companies and other interested people to explain the unidirectional risks of new technologies. Not only do I reject this simplistic causational framing in my responses, but I also struggle to suggest solutions or next steps. While I am a deeply pragmatic person and usually *want* to do this, I falter for a few reasons: one is my doubt that quick fixes and tweaks could solve the deeply rooted structural issues characterizing social media use; and another is that, as Livingstone puts it, "what for an adult observer may seem risky, is for a teenager often precisely the opportunity they seek."[18] And this conundrum "complicates straightforward policy attempts to maximise the former while minimizing the latter."[19]

Further, and as Vickery argues, young people do not strictly need to rely on adults to mitigate risks when they use social media.[20] They are often the best placed to understand the intricacies of a particular platform and how it is or is not serving their interests. While there are of course lots of things young people don't know, when it comes to social media, they know substantially more than we as adults give them credit for. As an example, for some of Vickery's research participants, especially those with marginalized identities, the supposedly risky behaviors of "talking to strangers and spending a lot of time playing games" laid bare the "social benefits" of these practices.[21] I feel strongly that our duty is to keep in mind the contextual boundedness of risk, continually considering that what an adult considers to be risky may differ from what a child or young person thinks, and that the wrong decisions about risk minimization can in fact cause the same—or even worse—harms than we had initially intended to reduce.[22]

My hope in publishing this book, then, is that we can lean on the empirical data it shares—which was designed, implemented, and represented with and by young voices—to tease out some practical recommendations. The suggestions I outline below can hopefully be used to aid in our societal understanding and ethical, evidence-based treatment of today's young, networked lives:

1. Avoid the use of 'social media' as a catch-all term.

This approach necessitates an admittedly difficult but largely necessary move away from the broad use of the phrase social media in moments when we are referring to something specific. Take Instagram as an example: I often hear accusations that the platform is bad for its young users' mental health, but where do these concerns lie? Are they located in the act of posting (and curating and editing) images or in viewing them? Are they situated in posts we seek out, or those that are recommended to us? Is the most concerning content found in feeds, stories, or direct messages? Do the comments people leave on our posts come into play at all? Or should we be more worried about the volume of time we are spending on Instagram and about many people's seemingly constant access to the platform via smart devices? Moving forward, we must ensure we are asking the right *kinds* of questions of the social media-mental health connection to elicit reliable and actionable answers.

2. Avoid making claims of newness about social media.

In my job, I am often called upon to talk about new technologies and explain how scared they should or should not make us feel. In my replies to such requests, I find myself leaning on literature from fields like sociology and anthropology to find analog predecessors and offer reassurances that, though we used to worry about this or that new invention, the hype eventually died down. This means we already have many of the tools to help us make sense of new technologies and to know how worried we really need to be. Precisely as Livingstone and Das note, when new technologies emerge, the repertoire we use to describe them need not change every time.[23] And while some concerns are truly novel and thus require fresh investigation, researchers can sometimes avoid dedicating vast resources to answering them: "Although tales of past panics are often met with amusement today, current concerns routinely engender large research investments and policy debate."[24] In their 2020 book *Parenting for a Digital Future*, Livingstone and Blum-Ross advise journalists and policymakers who may be "tempted by hyperbole" about new technologies to "avoid polarizing and extreme formulations of problems" and to instead "recognize and reflect" people's "lived realities and offer positive directions, informed guidance, and balanced solutions": a perspective I wholeheartedly share.[25]

3. Avoid catastrophizing at new developments related to social media.

Social media platforms—and especially platform companies—are far from perfect or risk-free, as I hope this book has outlined. To be crystal clear, I do think there are lots of things we need to worry about in relation to social media and young people. But I would advise readers to steer away from catastrophization as a first reaction. Consider, say, the teenager having a bad time at school or sixth form; the young adult regretting the course they chose at university; the slightly older young adult who can't save for a mortgage because their rent is so high; the person about to leave young adulthood who just got a life-changing medical diagnosis. What if social media is fun for them, providing some light relief in an otherwise difficult time in their lives? I would sincerely love to know how many times "I am never deleting this app" has been posted as a reply to TikTok posts, because I bet it's a very, very high figure. What if social media provides laughter and respite and joy not only when people need it the most but in a more mundane and everyday sense? What if it brings people closer to those in a similar situation and makes them feel less alone? For autistic youth, as Alper explains, social media can provide crucial space "to find autism acceptance, challenge mischaracterizations of disabled people, and further develop their autistic identities."[26] And so, if we insist on sticking only to binary terms then, reader, we must stop only asking about the bad.

4. Work toward a future-proofed e-safety education structure for schools.

E-safety—an initiative intended to provide the safe and responsible use of internet technologies—is taught across all grade levels at English schools. Such teachings emphasize the *content* available to children online; the ways they and other parties *conduct* themselves online; the *contact* children may have with other internet users or parties; and the *contracts* that exist between children and usually private sector organizations.[27] E-safety is currently taught as part of Relationship, Health and Sex Education (RHSE), and charities and third-sector organizations like the National Society for the Prevention of Cruelty to Children (NSPCC), Internet Matters, and Childnet offer resources for educators to use. However, through my research, I have found that such resources alone cannot equip educators with the confidence necessary to deliver effective e-safety sessions. Their under-confidence derives from the fast-paced nature of digital technologies: AI and chatbots, social media platforms and shopping apps, among many other examples seem to move so quickly that, by the time educators have worked out what the current "it" apps are, children have moved on, making e-safety sessions feel out-of-date. Livingstone and Blum-Ross make the same argument: "Many of the professionals tasked with guiding and supporting families (health visitors, social workers, educators, local government, librarians, general practitioners, consumer protection, even law enforcement, etc.) struggle to keep up with the latest developments, research and advice regarding the digital environment."[28]

The issue of under-confidence extends beyond the school gates and into the home, as children and young people—"frequently at the vanguard of digital adoption trends"—lack guidance from adults in their lives due to a lack of understanding.[29] This point can be made in relation to anonymous apps, which rise and fall so quickly in popularity that it feels impossible for adults to keep up (in chapter 3 I therefore outlined a typology of apps to assuage under-confidence about knowing what the "it" app is at any given moment). I advocate for the co-creation of a set of future-proofed resources designed *with* instead of *for* children and young people to be used across English schools and colleges in their e-safety teaching. Resource development should focus less on the content taught and instead concentrate on how resources are scaffolded in order to offer flexibility and responsiveness to changing digital environments: the key source of educators' under-confidence.

5. Following guidance from the 5Rights Foundation, services should not integrate with—or offer functionalities from— other services that do not meet the same safety criteria.
The embedded nature of anonymous apps like YOLO and other examples mentioned throughout this book pose unique risks to young people's safety. This is because smaller apps that are integrated within bigger apps are not necessarily held to the same safety standards and risk being read as a seal of approval with regards to safety.[30] Citing Heidegger, Orben notes that "many

philosophers and researchers believe that technological innovations and change is rapid and seems unstoppable: 'No one can foresee the radical changes to come. But technological advance will move faster and faster and can never be stopped.'"[31]

While anonymous apps' popularity may seem fast and thus difficult to control, largely because their popularity is characterized by a "rise and fall" rhetoric, it is crucial to remember anonymous app companies use almost the same formula for each new product, making it fairly easy to forecast their consequences. But their sometimes meteoritic rise in popularity without the necessary safeguards makes anonymous apps, as Maddox puts it, fundamentally "experimental" in nature.[32] And I do not believe children and young people should continue to be the subjects of this social experiment.

This particular suggestion emerges from a tragic event when, in June 2020, 16-year-old Carson James Bride devastatingly died by an act of suicide. Shortly after, his mother, Kristine Bride, filed a class-action lawsuit against Snapchat, YOLO, and LMK for breaking consumer protection laws, arguing that the anonymous apps failed to enforce the same safety policies they promoted to their users.[33] The lawsuit revealed that

> on June 7, 2020, after receiving numerous abusive, harassing, and upsetting messages on YOLO, Carson searched YOLO's website and other websites searching for "YOLO reveal," "YOLO username reveal hacks," and other keyword searches in an effort to find out who was sending abusive messages to him. . . . On June 23, 2020, the morning of Carson's death, the last web history found from his phone shows that Carson was again searching "Reveal YOLO Username Online" which reflects his final painstaking attempt to find out who was sending abusive YOLO messages to him.[34]

Following this lawsuit, Snap Inc. announced it would prevent YOLO and LMK from integrating into Snapchat.[35] Anonymous apps are therefore a perfect example of "how social media platforms have historically been developed with a 'move fast and break things' attitude," an approach "first articulated by Meta CEO Mark Zuckerberg."[36] But there still seems to be no consequences for anonymous app-adjacent tragedies like Carson's.

6. Commit to more ethical mental health content moderation processes.

Social media companies are famously opaque about what their rules really are. While users are given a vague set of community guidelines to follow, human content moderators are given extensive, hidden-from-public-view rulebooks from which to make decisions about flagged users and content. And the automated moderation systems operating in the background of platforms have their own behavioral guidelines. I do not necessarily advocate for platforms publishing all their rules; for example, while sociologically informative, publishing a list of all banned hashtags on a platform may push people further underground. But we—researchers, social media users, concerned citizens—do not know nearly enough about some of these rules, and we do not have sufficient say in the consequences for rule-breaking, which, needless to say, then becomes far more severe in cases involving people who are struggling with their mental health. My pragmatic suggestions for platforms are therefore as follows: (a) Only remove mental health–related accounts—by which, I mean those dedicated to sharing content about mental health, like meme accounts or those run by identifiable individuals who use their account, for part or all of the time, to discuss mental health—as an absolute last resort after all other avenues have been demonstrably explored and with ample warning. I would also like to see the criteria for banning an account on mental health grounds clearly articulated to users across social platforms; it is a decision that should not be taken lightly. And (b) if content reduction techniques are applied to such accounts (per, for example, Meta's policy, announced in January 2024), platforms should only seek to do so with reasonable warning and explanation. After all, tampering with a person's social media content without telling them why is surely itself a form of harm.

. . .

I close this book by reflecting on one final question: Why is it important to move beyond "tiresome binary debates" about social media and young people?[37] It matters because social media use among young people cannot always be neatly slotted into either-or designations like good or bad, helpful or harmful, positive or negative. When it comes to young people and social media, it's not either/or—it's both/and. This means the knowledge academics like myself produce about young people must, however tricky it may prove to be, represent their realities as accurately as possible. Our social imaginings of young people—particularly from the context from which I write, in England—are already "at best limited, at worst offensive."[38] In 2020, Thurlow et al. published research on the framing of teens' technology use in image banks (online repositories which "source the news media with much of its imagery").[39] The researchers observed a number of dominant clichés about teens and technology in image banks, including an over-representation of young women, a centering of technological artifacts over relationships and relationality, and contradictory relationships between "the verbal copy of newspaper stories and the images selected."[40] This final point resonates with my own experiences in writing newspaper and magazine articles: I try to make a nuanced, evidence-led contribution only to find that a picture of a sad-looking teenage girl staring at her smartphone graces the article, alongside a clickbaity, panic-driven headline. Image banks matter, Machin argues, because a very small handful of them "effectively produce a globalizing 'visual language' with a vision of the world that is pre-structured along formulaic, clichéd and consumer-driven lines."[41] And as Stuart Hall would tell us, representation—be it through image banks, articles, books, or any other communication channel—*matters*.

Moving beyond "tiresome binary debates" about social media and young people matters because the knowledge we produce feeds into the policing of content on platforms and their rules about the identities users can and cannot maintain.[42] It matters because this policing plays a part in how young people negotiate their identities across platforms, how they grow and learn in their networked worlds. It matters because young people's lives are closely governed, and what we say about their relationships with social media has a bearing on the future of their networked worlds. It also matters because either-ors flatten cultural and contextual differences. In 1996, "there were some eighty million Internet users around the world, eighty per cent of whom lived in North America and Europe." But today, "there are more than five billion people on the Internet, roughly two-thirds of them from countries in the Global South. India and China now account for about half the world's mobile-data traffic; [and] the fastest-growing population of users is in Africa."[43]

Broad claims about media use "come to be read as normative reference points for studies of childhood and media in all social contexts," which is a problem, because what is good for one young person in one context may not be for another.[44] And avoiding "tiresome binary debates" about social media and young people matters, perhaps most crucially, because this kind of framing does not produce an accurate or respectful picture of their lives.[45] It matters that we speak factually about young, networked lives, putting their needs ahead of our desires for a clickbaity title, a bigger audience, or a lucrative book deal (which mine, I assure you, was not). Panics are profitable: they make headlines and they can lead to academic prestige, especially within what Orben calls the "industrialized age of science, in which researchers work in more precarious positions and need to find research funding to support their existence."[46] But in an era where panics are profitable, I urge readers to commit to the calm, contextualized examination of empirical evidence and to unapologetically challenge dominant framing and rhetorics wherever necessary. Although doing this—and, by extension, attending to the paradoxes I have described throughout this book—is not quite as easy as labeling something good or bad or weighing up the pros and cons, this practice is necessary to breathe empirical life and critical depth into our understanding of the contemporary realities of young lives online. What matters to me, more than any other outcome of this book's publication, is that it represents my participants' experiences with great ethical care and that maybe, one day, our words can together help to make a positive social change.

Interview Participant Demographic Information

(British Academy Small Grant Research)

I asked my research participants to choose a new name for the study and to tell me their age, pronouns, and ethnicity (only if they wanted to, of course). Other identity markers like their sexual orientation emerged, if at all, through the course of the interviews, as did details like their hobbies and interests. The total number of participants for this study was 36.

Name	Pronouns	Age	Sexual Orientation	School Name	Ethnicity	Hobbies and Interests
Alexandra	She/her	17	Undisclosed	Jaynes Sixth Form College	White British	Wants to go to film school after Sixth Form
Alisha	She/her	17	Undisclosed	Jaynes Sixth Form College	White British	Keen to pursue a career in medicine after Sixth Form
Arthur	He/him	17	Undisclosed	Jaynes Sixth Form College	White British	Musical theater (" and theatre in general"), sport, and education
Asher	He/him	14	Undisclosed	Mason-Oakes Academy	White British	Gaming and talking to friends on Discord
Bart	He/him	17	Undisclosed	Jaynes Sixth Form College	White British	Playing football for a local team and playing the drums in a band
Bella	She/her	17	Heterosexual	Jaynes Sixth Form College	White British	Planning on pursuing a career in journalism, ideally broadcast journalism
Bonnie	She/her	17	Bisexual	Jaynes Sixth Form College	White British	Enjoys reading feminist literature "a bit obsessively" and horse riding
Charlie	She/her	16	Undisclosed	Jaynes Sixth Form College	White British	Wants to study theology at a Northern British university
Chloe	She/her	17	Undisclosed	Jaynes Sixth Form College	Black British	Aspiring lawyer with a keen interest in feminist literature

Name	Pronoun	Age	Sexuality	School	Ethnicity	Notes
Claire	She/her	17	Undisclosed	Jaynes Sixth Form College	White British	More reticent, but said she sits in the "middle" level of popularity at the Sixth Form
Clyde	He/him	18	Gay	Jaynes Sixth Form College	White British	Academically interested in politics and philosophy and does dance as a hobby
Darren	He/him	14	Undisclosed	Mason-Oakes Academy	White British	Became too nervous to share many details
Gabe	He/him	16	Undisclosed	Jaynes Sixth Form College	White British	"Anything really. I'm not fussed, I'll do anything."
Harry	He/him	13	Undisclosed	Mason-Oakes Academy	White British	Soccer and gaming
Jack	He/him	14	Heterosexual	Mason-Oakes Academy	White British	Rugby and "appearance upkeep"
Jamal	He/him	14	Undisclosed	Mason-Oakes Academy	White British	Painting and "outdoorsy" things
James	He/him	13	Undisclosed	Mason-Oakes Academy	White British	Playing rugby and soccer, with help from his dad
Jeremy	He/him	13	Undisclosed	Mason-Oakes Academy	White British	Gaming and sports
Jess	She/her	17	Undisclosed	Jaynes Sixth Form College	White British	Walking her dogs and exercising

(continued)

Name	Pronouns	Age	Sexual Orientation	School Name	Ethnicity	Hobbies and Interests
Joseph	He/him	14	Undisclosed	Mason-Oakes Academy	White British	More reticent, but shared that he's "got brown hair"
Kelsey	They/them	17	Undisclosed	Jaynes Sixth Form College	White British	Watching anime and singing
Lamar	He/him	14	Undisclosed	Mason-Oakes Academy	Mixed race	Computer programming and gaming
Lee	He/him	14	Undisclosed	Mason-Oakes Academy	White British	Playing golf and gaming
Lyrica	She/her	17	Undisclosed	Jaynes Sixth Form College	Asian British	Music and music production, acting, and theater; "quite a stereotypical creative person"
Maddie	She/her	17	Undisclosed	Jaynes Sixth Form College	White British	Keen to pursue a career in psychology, specifically criminal psychology; following sports on social media
Milly	She/her	17	Heterosexual	Jaynes Sixth Form College	White British	Spending time at the gym
Molly	She/her	17	Undisclosed	Jaynes Sixth Form College	White British	Discovering new music—which she enjoys doing as part of her "everyday routine"—and learning Spanish; *definitely* not applying to Oxbridge"
Monica	She/her	17	Undisclosed	Jaynes Sixth Form College	White British	"Couldn't live without music" and enjoys reading fiction

Name	Pronouns	Age		School	Ethnicity	Description
Osas	He/him	13	Undisclosed	Mason-Oakes Academy	Black British	Loves basketball and was about to leave for a summer basketball camp around the time of our interview
Richard	He/him	13	Undisclosed	Mason-Oakes Academy	White British	Drawing, gaming, and mountain biking
Samuel	They/them	14	Unsure	Mason-Oakes Academy	White British	Biking and spending time with friends
Smith	He/him	17	Undisclosed	Jaynes Sixth Form College	Asian British	Says there's "nothing interesting" to know about him other than his favorite color (dark red) and desire to pursue medicine at university
Steve	He/him	17	Undisclosed	Jaynes Sixth Form College	White British	Enjoys flying, has his glider solo pilot's license, and is part of the Scouting movement
Tom	He/him	13	Undisclosed	Mason-Oakes Academy	White British	Enjoys golfing and playing basketball in his spare time and his favourite subject at school is math
Tyrone	He/him	14	Undisclosed	Mason-Oakes Academy	White British	"Going out with the lads," biking, and listening to music
Victoria	She/her	16	Undisclosed	Jaynes Sixth Form College	White British	Reading, writing, and streaming music on her phone

Workshop and Interview Participant Information

(Strategic Research Support Fund Pilot Study)

Name	Pronouns	Age	School Name	Ethnicity
Eadie	She/her	17	Willow Sixth Form	White British
Emma	She/her	17	Willow Sixth Form	White British
Frankie	She/her	17	Willow Sixth Form	White British
Hannah	She/her	17	Willow Sixth Form	White British
Kiana	She/her	17	Willow Sixth Form	Congolese
Ria	She/her	17	Willow Sixth Form	Indian British
Rowan	They/them	17	Willow Sixth Form	White British
Tilly	She/her	17	Willow Sixth Form	White British

Research Methods and Ethical Considerations Underpinning Chapters 3 and 4

Research Funding and Questions

In early 2018, I was lucky enough to secure a Small Grant from the British Academy to qualitatively explore young people's views of anonymous apps.[1] After receiving clearance from the University of Sheffield's Research Ethics Committee (UREC) and passing my Disclosure and Barring Service (DBS) check, my plan was to go into English schools to conduct my fieldwork. But then the pandemic hit. After a 15-month locked-down hiatus, I finally went into two schools to interview willing participants, either individually or in pairs, about their views of anonymous apps. When I initially emailed the two schools to gauge their interest in participating in my research, I stressed that prospective interviewees only needed to have an *opinion* about anonymous apps and did not need to use the apps or have direct experiences of them to speak to me.[2] This meant my participants and I discussed anonymity and pseudonymous communication across a range of platforms and spaces, including Xbox Live, Discord, Reddit, Omegle, Instagram, TikTok, Snapchat, YouTube, Twitter, and Facebook and did not limit ourselves to anonymous apps. This also ensured social media non-users—through choice, access limitations, or something else—could have their voices heard. The research was shaped by four initial questions:

RQ1: How do teens use anonymous apps, and do their experiences resonate with press discourses about cyberbullying and other social issues?

RQ2: Why are teens moving away from established social media platforms like Facebook and turning to anonymous apps?

RQ3: How are teens' identities (age, gender, religious background, ethnicity, social class, amongst possible others) shaping, and being shaped by how they use anonymous apps?

RQ4: What do parents/carers and educators know about anonymous apps, and how do they communicate their views of the apps to young people?

Research Sites

From 2019 through 2020, I ran several workshops with University of Sheffield's Widening Participation team to help me trial the suitability of the workshop task I had devised and to help me network with stakeholders from potential research sites. The team's aim is to provide avenues into higher education for those with identities it considers to be underrepresented. This might mean students live in neighborhoods where not many people go to university, that they have declared disabilities, or that they are previous recipients of free school meals. Among other things, the team invites students to participate in dedicated classes at the university, and the connections I made through these workshops led me to two research sites, both of which are located outside of Sheffield: Jaynes Sixth Form College and Mason-Oakes Academy (these names have been pseudonymised). I also have some data from a religion-based secondary school (11–16) in the Midlands, England, where most students are also Black, Asian and Minority Ethnic (BAME). This data is also presented in chapter 3, though it only includes reflections on workshop data and informal (but approved-for-publication) conversations with educators. This is because my fieldwork at this site fell through during the pandemic. I sought an institutional spread to ensure a diversity of experiences and to expose myself to lots of different perspectives.

In chapter 3, I introduced readers to students from Jaynes Sixth Form College: a non-paid-for education institution based in the North of England. Jaynes welcomes students from secondary schools within a commutable distance and prepares these 16- to 19-year-olds to complete their A-Levels and offers BTEC and CTEC courses (more practice-driven qualifications than A-Levels) as well. The college primarily focuses on supporting students' progression to university. In chapter 4, readers met some of the students from Mason-Oakes Academy, a non-paid-for all-boys secondary school located in the North of England. The school accepts students who live within a particular catchment area (a geographic radius from the school) between the ages of 11–16. Both Jaynes and Mason-Oakes are located in a Northern British city widely considered to be working-class, with its roots in the Industrial Revolution. The city has a majority-White population and in the 2019 general election was a Labour party stronghold.

Participant Demographics

Of my 21 participants from Jaynes Sixth Form College, I had one Black-British participant, two Asian-British participants, and 18 who were White British. Fourteen participants used she/her pronouns, six used he/him, and one used they/them. All participants were aged 13 or 14 at the time we spoke. Of my 15 participants from Mason-Oakes, I had one Black-British participant, one mixed-race participant, and 13 who were White British. One of my participants used they/them pronouns and the rest used he/him pronouns. All participants were aged 13–18 at the time we spoke.

Familiarization Workshops

The visits to my field sites involved me delivering an initial workshop activity to those I planned to interview, as a way for me to ease them into the research scenario and get to know them better. After a round of introductions and some scene-setting, I began the workshop by splitting participants into small groups and asking them to design their ideal anonymous app. I asked them what app they felt there was room for in the current marketplace, what their app's core demographic might be, and how its users would be protected from harm. Groups were asked to use large sheets of paper and brightly colored pens to come up with some branding for their proposed app and to consider how its users would navigate their way through the app's interface. Each workshop participant was given a £20 One4All shopping voucher, regardless of whether they felt comfortable enough to proceed to the interview stage of the research. I do not include the workshop data in this book as these research findings will be published elsewhere.

Interviewing and Safeguarding Principles

After the workshops, teens were invited to participate in qualitative, semi-structured interviews with myself. The interviews were scheduled either on the day of the workshop or on the next day or two. I interviewed a total of 21 students from Jaynes Sixth Form College, following an introductory visit, an online talk (May 2021), and three research visits between June 2021 and April 2022. Following a phone call and email exchange with senior teaching staff at the school, during two research visits in July 2021, I interviewed a total of 15 students from Mason-Oakes Academy.

I devised two versions of the interview guide: one for teens and another for adults. The intended interview length for students—up to 30 minutes—aimed to avoid disruption to their education and to avoid being overly prescriptive; however, most interviews lasted just shy of an hour.[3] To inform teens that their interview quotes might be used for academic research, I emailed copies of the Information Letter, Participant Information Sheet, and Participant Consent Form to my contact at each of the students' schools. These materials were sent to the schools no less than two weeks before each interview was planned, allowing time for students and teachers to ask questions. Both schools' policies required consent from parents/carers, and so I also sent a separate Parental Consent Form. Students were asked to choose a new name for the research so that I could write about their quotes anonymously in any published materials, like this book. I devised two copies of the Participant Information Sheets for young people: one aimed at 11- to 14-year-olds, and one aimed at 15- to 18-year-olds. The interviews were always held in a quiet room that was free from interruptions. At Jaynes Sixth Form College, I was not required to have a member of staff in the room during the interviews, and none of my participants' parents or carers requested this (which they had the option to do via the Consent Form). However, the room had windows and was constantly observable by adults working at the school.[4]

At Mason-Oakes Academy, I was required to have a member of staff in the room with me during each interview, and I reflect on the implications of this in chapter 4. For example, although the teacher respectfully worked on their laptop and was very unintrusive, there were occasions when students would look behind them at the teacher before saying something. This was something I was warned of in an earlier interview with Ray, a 40-something male safeguarding lead for a school trust in Northern England. Ray correctly anticipated that students would look at their teacher to "check for acknowledgement or permission to speak" and that if I wanted a "real ethnographic feel," I wouldn't get it with somebody else in the room. That said, several teens seemed fairly unaffected by their teacher's presence, indicated by their use of swear words and by talking openly about sexual encounters. They also whispered to me about a meme account someone set up for their school on Instagram which, for reasons I discussed extensively in chapter 4, they didn't want their teacher to know about.

Data Analysis

My interview transcripts were imported into NVivo and analyzed thematically, broadly adhering to instructions provided by Braun and Clarke and based on previous experience of conducting thematic analysis on qualitative datasets.[5] Data were analyzed *inductively*, though some segments of the transcripts were not coded at all as there was not "anything of relevance" for my research questions.[6] That said, some segments were tagged with many different codes, as a number of different meanings were evident in that data.[7] I was conscious that I worked alone on this research and thus did not have a second coder to work with. To remedy this, I would truly say I lived with my data: I didn't only read and re-read my transcripts, I listened to the recordings over and over again while I went on walks, tidied my home, and took the train to and from work. The thematic analysis helped me, to borrow Braun and Clarke's words, not just to summarize and represent my data but to capture my "analytic take" and to make *meaning* from what I had in front of me.[8] I had captured so much information and needed to know what my take was, informed by their words but also in relation to broader theories and debates about young people and social media.

Although all interviews presented across chapters 3 and 4 were from the same funded research project (British Academy Small Grant SRG18R1\180909), I thematically analyzed the datasets separately. This was not my initial intention, but as I explain in chapters 3 and 4, because the pupils from Mason-Oakes

Academy had less direct experience of anonymous apps than those from Jaynes Sixth Form College, the former set of interviews were more focused on identity negotiations across social media platforms writ large. The initial codes applied *across* the datasets via a thematic analysis were thus too distinct to yield rigorous results, and so I coded the datasets separately, arriving at initial codes, meta-codes, and eventually, a list of main themes for each of the two schools. This gave me fascinating insights and led me to split my discussion of each school into two separate chapters (3 and 4, respectively).

For the interviews conducted with pupils from Mason-Oakes Academy, after an initial sweep of all transcripts and eliminating codes that were overly descriptive (for example, "time spent on social media" or "motivations for joining [insert name of platform]"), I landed on 67 initial codes and 13 meta-codes across all transcripts, with some codes appearing more frequently than others (for example, "naming" was the most commonly used code across the transcripts and "popularity" was the least common. Quite interestingly, "popularity" was a substantially more common code across the Jaynes Sixth Form College transcripts). Following a process of review and refinement, these meta-codes fell into four core themes:

1. Achieving personal safety on social media.
2. Achieving social safety on social media.
3. Societal discourses of anonymity.
4. Contradictory emotions and experiences toward social media.

The third most common code was "contradictions." These were instances in which the teens pointed to the contradictory nature of their digital lives; for example, when they feel something is both good and bad and can't quite disentangle those things. I coded these instances as "contradictory" during my initial sweep and wanted to capture this here, as the notion of *contradictions* evidently evolved into the *paradoxes* I conceptualize through this book.

I followed the same coding process for my interviews with students from Jaynes Sixth Form College and landed on 73 initial codes and 15 meta-codes across all transcripts. Again, not all codes appeared equally across the dataset, though some of the less common ones—for example, "screenshots"—ended up playing important roles within themes and told unique and vital stories. I therefore made sure I didn't disregard the less common codes in my re-telling of teens' stories. Following a process of review and refinement, these 15 meta-codes fell into four core themes:

1. Gossip and rumor spreading on anonymous apps.
2. Gendered experiences of anonymous apps.
3. Popularity and navigating social relationships as teens.
4. Contradictory emotions and experiences toward anonymous apps.

At first, it may seem clearer how the themes developed from my interviews with Mason-Oakes Academy pupils mapped onto the structure and argumentation of the chapter in which they are presented (chapter 4). The themes played somewhat less of an ordering or structuring role in the chapter where I discuss my conversations with Jaynes Sixth Form College pupils (chapter 3), as I split the narrative into sub-sections titled: Why Are Anonymous Apps So Popular? and Why Do Anonymous Apps Fail? I made this creative decision because anonymous apps are fairly under-researched academically, especially within media and communications studies and sociology, and so chapter 3 engages in scene-setting in a way chapter 4 does not. But the themes I arrived at thoroughly underpin the chapter's main arguments, with the fourth theme—contradictory emotions and experiences toward anonymous apps—playing a starring role in the book's broader contribution to knowledge. A final note is that the second theme—gendered experiences of anonymous apps, which captured codes like "surveillance" and "sexuality" within its umbrella—is in the process of becoming its own academic journal article.

Research Methods and Ethical Considerations Underpinning Chapter 5

Research Funding and Questions

The content in this chapter is based on a pilot project I conducted across June and July 2022, funded by my department's Strategic Research Support Fund and ethically approved by the University of Sheffield's Research Ethics Committee (UREC).[1] The pilot study was a smaller, adapted version of a project I proposed to Instagram's Research Award scheme, where myself and Professor Ruth Holliday were named as finalists but unfortunately did not receive the funding.[2] The research asked how British teens aged 16–18 feel about their own and other people's photo editing habits on social media, particularly on visual platforms like Instagram. The underpinning research questions were as follows:

RQ1: How do teens use digital filters and editing tools in their everyday lives?

RQ2: How do teens feel about their own and other people's use of photo editing, regardless of whether they engage in this practice?

RQ3: How would teens feel if the Norwegian photo editing law made its way to the UK?

Research Site

My research was conducted at a private (fee-paying) English sixth form, making it very different from the schools described in chapters 3 and 4. Willow primarily prepares its 16- to 18-year-old students to complete their A-Levels, a common qualification in England which can be used for entry into universities. The sixth form is located in a city with a majority-White population and has a social stereotype of being one of the wealthier parts of Northern England—especially compared with the other Northern cities I've mentioned thus far—housing plenty of historical buildings and other tourist attractions. Willow's fees sit at around £5,000 per academic term and there are three terms per school year.

Participant Demographics and Recruitment

Of my eight workshop participants from Willow Sixth Form, I had one Congolese participant, one Indian-British participant, and six who were White British. Seven participants used she/her pronouns, and one used they/them. All participants were aged 17 at the time we spoke. I asked my contact at this school to help me identify potential participants for my research; crucially, I asked that participants *self-select* for this study, given the potential for the discussions of sensitive issues (e.g., body image). In the research described in chapters 3 and 4, I did not make this kind of request and instead allowed the schools to handle participant recruitment in a way they felt was suitable.

Familiarization Workshop

My pilot study used two qualitative research methods: a group workshop and semi-structured interviews. Like the research described in chapters 3 and 4, I conducted a workshop with the teens I planned to interview as a way for them to get to know me better and to encourage deeper critical thinking about the topic. The workshop lasted an hour and involved one main activity followed by presentations from each group. Students were split into pairs and asked to map out a framework for an article to be published in a magazine like *Teen Vogue*. They were told their article should respond to the new Norwegian photo editing law, described in chapter 5, and which I introduced to them at the start of the session. Students were then given clear instructions about what to include (e.g., title, tagline, angle, sub-section headings, etc.) and were later asked to feed their work back to the rest of the group. The documentation produced by students during the workshop was used as a conversational prompt during the interviews, though it was primarily used as supplementary descriptive data in chapter 5. This was because, unlike my interview transcripts, workshop materials were not subjected to rigorous thematic (or other) modes of analysis.

Workshop participants were then asked to follow up via email if they wished to participate in either an individual or paired interview in order to say more about their views on digital photo editing.[3] I had a very short time frame in which to conduct my workshop and interviews: I received my research funding in May 2022 and the term at Willow Sixth Form ended in early July 2022. As a result, I was only able to conduct follow-up interviews with three teens. The three interviews lasted just shy of an hour each and were all conducted online during a free hour of the students' teaching days. In agreement with my contact at the sixth form and in consultation with participants' parents, a teacher was not required to be present for the interviews. Each workshop participant was given a £20 One4All shopping voucher, regardless of whether they felt comfortable enough to proceed to the interview stage of the research.

Interviewing and Safeguarding Principles

To inform participants that their interview quotes and materials produced during the workshop might be used for academic research, I emailed copies of an Information Letter, Participant Information Sheet and Participant Consent Form to my contact at Willow Sixth Form. These materials were sent to the school around two weeks before the workshop was planned, allowing time for students and teachers to ask questions. The sixth form did not require informed consent from participants' parents/carers, however my contact kindly emailed relevant parents/carers to inform them that the research was taking place and to ask that they contact the sixth form or myself with any queries. Students were asked to choose a new name for the research so that I could write about their quotes anonymously in any published materials, like this book. Given the subject matter, there was a risk of psychological distress in this project. To ensure appropriate protection and well-being of the participants, a member of the safeguarding team was present in the workshop and was also available on-site during and immediately after the interviews. Willow Sixth Form offers various forms of support for teens experiencing body image issues and eating disorders and was therefore well equipped to speak to any students who felt they may be struggling or who found themselves triggered by the research.

Data Analysis

The process of inductive thematic analysis for my interviews with Willow Sixth Form students followed the same principles and processes as those described in appendix C and, as such, this section will be much shorter. While I conducted a smaller number of interviews for this particular project compared with the others described in this book, it was still important for me to engage in a rigorous process of data analysis and, crucially, to make *meaning* from my conversations with teens and to arrive at my "analytical take."[4] The workshop data I share in chapter 5 intended to aid in my analysis and offer contextualization and was therefore not subjected to a thematic analysis.

After an initial sweep of all transcripts uploaded to NVivo and after eliminating codes that were overly descriptive, I landed on thirty-two initial codes and eight meta-codes across all transcripts, with some codes appearing more frequently than others. For example, "comparisons" was the most common meta-theme, capturing smaller codes within it, which is why Festinger's social comparison theory and similar concepts became so crucial in my analysis.[5] As I describe in chapter 5, I noted profound comparisons between my interviewees and their peers and between my interviewees and celebrities/influencers. I also highlighted comparisons in beauty and related norms between different periods of time to now and between the different standards governing societal norms according to our identities. The meta-code "mental health" also came up a lot, reminding me to tell readers that process of coding these transcripts was somewhat more emotionally demanding than the others. It was difficult to read teens' words and not look inwards, as a woman who grew up with similar media and other cultural touchpoints and who still shares some of the experiences my participants described, despite our age gap. Following a process of review and refinement, these meta-codes fell into three core themes:

1. Norms around acceptability in digital photo editing.
2. Identity markers and/in contemporary beauty standards.
3. Paradoxical emotions and experiences toward social media.

The third theme reflects how my thinking had evolved between my two projects (those described in chapters 3 and 4 versus chapter 5). As some time had passed and I had already analyzed much of the data presented in this book, I no longer thought of young people's experiences of social media in terms of contradictions and had moved on to paradoxes, arriving at this as an analytical theme in itself by the time I spoke to the teens at Willow.

Notes

Introduction: Social Media in Young Lives

1. Bella is not her legal name and is instead the name she chose for herself to protect her identity.

2. Following lessons from Nguyễn and Pendleton (2020) and Appiah (2020), I will use *Black* and *White* as racial designators throughout this book. Not capitalizing the *W* in White allows whiteness to be the norm; race becomes "something that only other people have" (Appiah, 2020).

3. Please see chapter 3 and appendix C for a thorough contextual description of Jaynes Sixth Form College, which has been renamed to avoid identification.

4. Please see appendix A for a full list of participants' names and demographic details.

5. Constine, 2018.

6. Internet Matters, 2022.

7. Constine, 2019.

8. Livingstone, 2008, 408.

9. See for example Baym, 2015.

10. Livingstone, 2020.

11. Smith, 2018.

12. Mick and Fournier, 1998, 124.

13. Mick and Fournier, 1998, 140.

14. I say more about this body of work in chapter 1.

15. In May 2022, the Pew Research Center made the fascinating decision to overhaul how it reports on generations; the center now avoids inappropriate

designations of generational labels, warning readers that they "should not expect to see a lot of new research coming out of Pew Research Center that uses the generational lens" (Parker, 2023).

16. Prensky, 2001, 1.

17. Prensky, 2001.

18. Banaji, 2011; Helsper and Eynon, 2010, 517; Livingstone, 2007.

19. Third, 2016, no pagination, quoted in Livingstone and Third, 2017, 668.

20. Banaji, 2017, 191.

21. See Gerrard (2023) for a longer discussion of this issue.

22. Instant messaging is defined as real-time text-based communication sent via digital devices, and bulletin board systems are software that allow users to dial in to exchange messages with each other, share files, and play games, among other networked activities.

23. McLelland et al., 2017, 56.

24. McLelland et al., 2017, 57.

25. boyd and Ellison, 2007, 211.

26. Miltner and Gerrard, 2022, 50.

27. See Miltner and Gerrard (2022) for a critique of the Myspace nostalgia discourse.

28. boyd and Ellison, 2007.

29. van der Nagel, 2018.

30. I qualify the word *real* here as social media very much forms part of our real, everyday lives, and so I reject a distinction between our "real" lives and those we play out on social media. That said, this is a term my participants frequently used and, crucially, it is how they often feel when using social media as they consciously seek a separation between different spaces and identities. I therefore do not qualify this term throughout but do so here to acknowledge its complexities.

31. Ofcom, 2022b.

32. Burgess et al., 2017, 1.

33. Gerrard, 2023.

34. Humphreys, 2018, 19.

35. Humphreys, 2018, 13.

36. Humphreys, 2018, 68.

37. Gillespie, 2010.

38. Gillespie, 2010, 359.

39. Gillespie, 2010, 358.

40. See for example Bruns, 2008.

41. Writers like Marwick (2013), though, rightly note that many of the newer technologies described as "participatory" in the mid-2000s existed before terms like this were coined, and include wikis, online journals, and blogs.

42. Jermyn and Holmes, 2006, cited in Livingstone and Das, 2013, 106.

43. Gillespie, 2010, 358.

44. Gillespie, 2015.

45. boyd, 2014, 8.

46. boyd, 2014, 5.

47. boyd, 2014, 16.

48. Gillespie, 2015, 1.

49. "Internet research" is broadly defined as "research which utilizes the Internet to collect information through an online tool," or which studies "how people use the Internet" (Buchanan, 2011, 90).

50. 5Rights Foundation, n.d.(b).

51. 5Rights Foundation, n.d.(a).

52. Banaji, 2015, 2.

53. Banaji, 2017, 191.

54. Jeffrey and Dyson, 2008, cited in Banaji, 2015, 4.

55. Sarwatay and Raman, 2022, 548.

56. Sarwatay and Raman, 2022, 548.

57. Cohen, 1972/2002; Drotner, 1999; Marwick, 2008.

58. Livingstone and Third, 2017, 658.

59. Patelis, 2013, 121–122.

60. Haines, 2021.

61. City University London, 2021.

62. Vandenbosch et al., 2022, 4.

63. Buckingham and Jensen, 2012, 423.

1. From Moral and Media Panics to Platform Paradoxes

1. Baym, 2015; Walsh, 2020.

2. Drotner, 1999, 610.

3. Gruenberg, 1935, cited in Orben, 2020, 1144.

4. Hall, 1973/2009. Reception studies were met with some tension within academia—for example, some accused them of being perhaps *too* celebratory.

5. The encoding/decoding model of communication was founded by Stuart Hall (1932–2014), a Jamaican-born British Marxist, cultural theorist, and activist.

6. Banaji, 2017, 191.

7. Banaji, 2017, 191, emphasis in original.

8. Nemer and Freeman, 2015.

9. Senft and Baym, 2015.

10. Nemer and Freeman, 2015, 1832.

11. Cohen, 1972/2002, 1.

12. Orben, 2020, 1147.

13. Orben, 2020, 1147.

14. Baym, 2015, 47–48.

15. Grimes et al., 2008, 51, quoted in Orben, 2020, 1147.

16. Baym, 2015, 32.

17. Hunt, 1997; McRobbie and Thornton, 1995.

18. *Independent*, 1988 and *The Times*, 1992 in Hunt, 1997, 639.

19. Hall et al., 1978.

20. Hall et al., 1978, vii.

21. Hunt, 1997, 630.

22. McRobbie and Thornton similarly noted the changing nature of journalistic practice over the years: where moral panics were once the "unintended outcome," they were now "a goal" (1995, 560).

23. Buckingham and Jensen, 2012, 417.

24. Drotner, 1999, 594.

25. Buckingham and Jensen, 2012, 417.

26. Buckingham and Jensen, 2012, 417.

27. Buckingham and Jensen, 2012, 419.

28. Hall et al., 1978, 16.

29. See pages xxxiv–xxxvi of Cohen (1972/2002) for Cohen's reflections on this critique.

30. Cohen, 1972/2002; Goode and Ben-Yehuda, 1994; Hall et al., 1978.

31. Buckingham and Jensen, 2012, 418.

32. Drotner, 1999, 615.

33. Marwick, 2008.

34. Mick and Fournier, 1998, 140.
35. Mick and Fournier, 1998, 124.
36. Mick and Fournier, 1998, 125.
37. Haimson et al., 2021.
38. Haimson et al., 2021, 1.
39. Yeshua-Katz and Martins, 2013.
40. Yeshua-Katz and Martins, 2013, 500.
41. Yeshua-Katz and Martins, 2013, 506, emphasis in original.
42. Yeshua-Katz and Hård af Segerstad, 2020.
43. Yeshua-Katz and Hård af Segerstad, 2020, 1.
44. Yeshua-Katz and Hård af Segerstad, 2020, 1.
45. Livingstone and Das, 2013, 105.
46. Goffman, 1963/1990.
47. Goffman, 1963/1990, 12.
48. Goffman, 1963/1990, 13, 14.
49. Goffman, 1963/1990, 15.
50. Goffman, 1963/1990, 14.
51. Goffman, 1963/1990, 12.
52. Kanai, 2017, 9 in Tiidenberg et al., 2021, 202.
53. Goffman, 1963/1990, 102.
54. Goffman, 1963/1990, 103.
55. Goffman, 1963/1990, 103.
56. Goffman, 1963/1990, 103.
57. Benselin and Ragsdell, 2016; Kennedy, 2016.
58. Young and Quan-Haase, 2013, 481.
59. Watson and Valtin, 1997, 432.
60. Nussbaum, 2007.
61. Johnson, 2010.
62. Warren and Laslett, 1977, 44.
63. Warren and Laslett, 1977, 44.
64. Warren and Laslett, 1977, 44.
65. Simmel, 1950, 331.
66. Warren and Laslett, 1977, 47.
67. Bok, 1989, cited in Finkenauer et al., 2002, 123.
68. Warren and Laslett, 1977, 45.
69. Livingstone and Third, 2017, 664.

70. Raynes-Goldie, 2010.
71. Raynes-Goldie, 2010.
72. Westin, 1967, 7.
73. Parent, 1983 in Nissenbaum, 2010, 97.
74. Trepte et al., 2017, 2.
75. Livingstone and Third, 2017, 662.
76. Third et al., 2014, 40, quoted in Livingstone and Third, 2017, 662.
77. Tiggemann, 2022, 173.
78. Tiggemann, 2022, 173.
79. Festinger, 1954.
80. Festinger, 1954, 120.

2. Moderating the Mental Health Crisis

Note: Some of the empirical research data presented in this chapter also appears in a peer-reviewed academic publication, which contains a discussion of ethical and methodological processes and considerations (Gerrard, 2018).

1. Crawford, 2019.
2. Devine, 2022.
3. Milmo, 2022.
4. Milmo, 2022.
5. Gerrard and Gillespie, 2019.
6. Crawford, 2019.
7. Odgers, 2024, citing Martínez-Alés, 2022.
8. Büchi and Hargittai, 2022, 1.
9. Gillespie, 2018, 46.
10. Gillespie et al., 2020, 2.
11. Meaker, 2022.
12. Meaker, 2022.
13. Hern, 2019.
14. Milosevic, 2017.
15. Milosevic, 2017, 5.
16. Bramwell, 2019.
17. For a full list, see Gerrard, 2022.
18. Gerrard and Gillespie, 2019.
19. Livingstone et al., 2013, 305.

20. World Health Organization, 2022, 66.
21. World Health Organization, 2022, 44.
22. Gerrard and McCosker, 2020; McCosker and Gerrard, 2020.
23. Hwang et al., 2009, 1116.
24. Goffman, 1963/1990.
25. Goffman, 1963/1990, 12.
26. Goffman, 1963/1990, 15.
27. Goffman, 1963/1990, 14.
28. Cockerham, 2021, 9.
29. Cockerham, 2021, 11.
30. Cockerham, 2021, 10.
31. Cockerham, 2021, 16.
32. Covid: Calls for . . ., 2020.
33. Tiidenberg et al., 2021, 182.
34. Tiidenberg et al., 2021, 52.
35. Tiidenberg et al., 2021, 52.
36. Tiidenberg et al., 2021, 58.
37. Tiidenberg et al., 2021, 59.
38. Marwick and boyd, 2010; Tiidenberg et al., 2021, 60.
39. Tiidenberg et al., 2021, 183.
40. Tiidenberg et al., 2021, 183.
41. Tiidenberg et al., 2021.
42. Tiidenberg et al., 2021, 206.
43. Goffman, 1963/1990, 31.
44. Suzor, 2016.
45. Ging and Garvey, 2018.
46. Ging and Garvey, 2018; Boero and Pascoe, 2012, 40.
47. Boero and Pascoe, 2012, 29.
48. Zappavigna, 2012, 101.
49. Goffman, 1963/1990, 31-32.
50. Barinka, 2022.
51. Chancellor et al., 2016.
52. Chancellor et al., 2016, 3.
53. Johnson and Jajodia, 1998, cited in Marwick and boyd, 2014, 1058.
54. Johnson and Jajodia, 1998, cited in Marwick and boyd, 2014, 1058.
55. u/linedryonly, 2018.

56. Gerrard, 2018.

57. Hendry, 2020, 1, emphases in original.

58. Gerrard, 2018.

59. Gerrard, 2018.

60. Cobb, 2017, 195, emphasis in original.

61. Ang, 1991.

62. Maris, 2021, 4819.

63. Maris, 2021, 4820.

64. u/linedryonly, 2018.

65. Beat, n.d.

66. Yeshua-Katz and Hård af Segerstad, 2020.

67. Yeshua-Katz and Hård af Segerstad, 2020, 1.

68. Feuston et al., 2020, 12.

69. Feuston et al., 2020, 12.

70. Feuston et al., 2020, 11.

71. Feuston et al., 2020, 2.

72. Scott et al., 2023.

73. Gerrard and Gillespie, 2019.

74. Crawford, 2019.

75. Meaker, 2022.

76. Tyler and Slater, 2018, 723.

77. Benselin and Ragsdell, 2016.

78. Striphas, 2015, 407.

79. Gerrard, 2018.

80. For a copy of this image, see Gerrard, 2018.

81. Gerrard and Gillespie, 2019.

82. Ofcom, 2022b.

83. TikTok Newsroom, 2021.

84. Malik, 2024; Meta Newsroom, 2024.

85. Mailk, 2024.

86. Gillespie, 2022, 1.

87. Gillespie, 2022, 2.

88. Gillespie, 2022, 2.

89. Gillespie, 2022, 6.

90. Gillespie, 2022, 2.

91. Meta Newsroom, 2024.

92. Horwitz, 2023.

93. Horwitz, 2023.

94. Martin et al., 2000, 209.

95. Cockerham, 2021, 16.

96. Tyler, 2020, 17–18.

97. Oluwole, 2023.

98. Livingstone and Blum-Ross, 2020, 192.

99. Livingstone and Third, 2017, 663.

100. Livingstone, 2008, 407.

101. Livingstone, 2020.

102. Yeshua-Katz and Hård af Segerstad, 2020, 1.

103. Grimes et al., 2008 in Orben, 2020, 1153.

104. Mick and Fournier, 1998, 140.

3. *Amuse Me or Abuse Me* on Anonymous Apps

Note: The empirical research data presented in this chapter has not been published elsewhere. However, theoretical concepts arising from this project can be found in a contribution to an academic publication (Gillespie et al., 2020) and in a *WIRED* article (Gerrard, 2021).

1. This might mean students live in neighborhoods where not many people go to university, that they have declared disabilities, or that they are previous recipients of free school meals.

2. Gerrard, 2020.

3. Orr, 2014.

4. Orr, 2014.

5. Bell, 2017.

6. Madi, 2017.

7. Bell, 2017.

8. Cassin, 2018.

9. Lunden, 2019.

10. Constine, 2019.

11. Madi, 2017.

12. Madi, 2017.

13. Milosevic, 2017, 138.

14. Bachmann et al., 2017, 254.

15. Bachmann et al., 2017, 255, emphasis added.

16. Sharon and John, 2018, 2.

17. Ma et al., 2017.

18. Sharon and John, 2018, 5.

19. Sharon and John, 2018, 2.

20. Bachmann et al., 2017, 255.

21. Readers should see appendix C for a far more thorough description of the methods and ethical considerations underpinning this research.

22. I invite readers to look through appendix A for a full list of participants' names and other crucial demographic details, along with information about their hobbies and interests.

23. Ma et al., 2017.

24. Sharon and John, 2018.

25. Cutler, 2014.

26. Internet Matters, 2020.

27. Robson, 2018.

28. Internet Matters, 2020.

29. Davis, 2012, 1528.

30. Watson and Valtin, 1977, 448.

31. Solís et al., 2015.

32. Warren and Laslett, 1977, 49.

33. Watson and Valtin, 1997, 432.

34. Warren and Laslett, 1977, 44.

35. Warren and Laslett, 1977, 44.

36. Warren and Laslett, 1977, 45.

37. Watson and Valtin 1997.

38. Watson and Valtin 1997.

39. Dundes, 1965.

40. Knibbs, 2014.

41. Burgess et al., 2017, 1.

42. Robson, 2013, cited in Milosevic, 2017, 70.

43. Milosevic, 2017, 71.

44. Cox, 2015, quoted in Bayne et al., 2019, 98.

45. Hatmaker, 2021.

46. Yik Yak, 2021.

47. Sardá et al., 2019, 562.

48. Donath, 1999, 51.

49. Buxton, 2018.

50. For a longer discussion of the concept of "popularity-by-surprise," see Gerrard, 2020.

51. Suler, 2004, 321.

52. Englander et al., 2017.

53. Anti-Bullying Alliance, n.d.

54. Englander et al., 2017.

55. Milosevic, 2016, 5166.

56. Sheanoda et al., 2021.

57. Miller and Slater, 2000.

58. Hine, 2015, 33.

59. Livingstone and Third, 2017, 667–668.

60. Hine, 2015, 33.

61. Suler, 2004, 322.

62. Milosevic, 2016, 5167.

63. Pew Research Center, 2014.

64. Ofcom, 2022a, 53.

65. Li, 2007.

66. Nichols, 2018.

67. Nichols, 2018, 74.

68. Jaynes, 2020.

69. Jaynes, 2020, 1378.

70. Assessment and Qualifications Alliance (AQA), 2019.

71. Watson and Valtin, 1997.

72. Skeggs, 1997; Tyler, 2008 cited in Jaynes, 2020, 1384.

73. van der Nagel, 2018.

4. Personal and Social Safety in Anonymous Communication

Note: The empirical research data presented in this chapter has not been published elsewhere.

1. Livingstone and Third, 2017, 658.

2. Bachmann et al., 2017, 241.

3. See for example UK Government and Parliament, 2021.

4. Bachmann et al., 2017.

5. Turkle, 1995/2011, 12. Turkle's early work must always be read in the context in which it was written: the dawn of a new communication technology characterized by significantly less pessimism about the tech world and it so-called impacts on our lives than we see today. It is perfectly normal for new technologies to be greeted with such excitement, only for public perception to be neutralized as those technologies become more embedded into society.

6. Marwick, 2013, 25.

7. Patelis, 2013, 121–122.

8. Byttow, 2015.

9. Hogan, 2013.

10. Wallace, 1999, 25.

11. Gibbs et al., 2015.

12. Gibbs et al., 2015.

13. Patelis, 2013, 121–122; Hogan, 2013, 292, emphasis added.

14. McNicol, 2013, 201.

15. Kennedy, 2016.

16. van der Nagel and Frith, 2015.

17. Bayne et al., 2019, 93.

18. Erikson, 1968.

19. Kroger, 2006.

20. Ragelienė, 2016.

21. Goffman, 1956.

22. Hall, 1996.

23. Hine, 2015.

24. Warren and Laslett, 1977, 45.

25. Bok, 1989, quoted in Finkenauer et al., 2002, 123.

26. Simmel, 1950, 331.

27. Finkenauer et al., 2002.

28. Finkenauer et al., 2002, 128.

29. Finkenauer et al., 2002.

30. Gibbs et al., 2015.

31. Mick and Fournier, 1998, 140.

32. Mick and Fournier, 1998, 140.

33. Duffy and Chan, 2019, 119.

34. Duffy and Chan, 2019, 119, emphases in original.

35. Duffy and Chan, 2019, 121.

36. Duffy and Chan, 2019.

37. Duffy and Chan, 2019.

38. Fourteen-year-old White-British Asher, who uses he/him pronouns, was interviewed alongside his two friends, Joseph and Lee. Theirs was another fun interview, likely due to the three friends' close relationship. Asher's main hobby is gaming and talking to his friends on Discord. He also uses Instagram and Snapchat but especially enjoys using TikTok: "I'm just on there all the time. I get such a laugh on there." While Asher uses "nicknames and stuff" on social media, he didn't tell me which accounts are pseudonymized and which aren't.

39. Suler, 2004.

40. Livingstone and Blum-Ross, 2020, 191.

41. Bayne et al., 2019, 99.

42. Black et al., 2016, 21.

43. UK Government and Parliament, 2021.

44. Patelis, 2013.

45. Marwick and Hargittai, 2018.

46. Marwick and Hargittai, 2018.

5. At-Home Photoshopping and the New War on Body Image

Note: Some empirical research data presented in this chapter also appears in Duffy and Gerrard (2022).

1. In the class, I grade students' work anonymously and so they were asked to remove identifying markers where possible. Kait had therefore blurred her own and Freya's faces out of the image and redacted her Instagram username.

2. Festinger, 1954.

3. Toward the end of the essay, Freya explained that she had started eating normally again (i.e., in a way that was typical for her).

4. Although Photoshop is a distinct software owned by the Adobe company, I use a lowercase *p* here and throughout in places where I emphasize the embeddedness of this term—which has, in many respects, lost its affiliation to the Adobe brand—into contemporary culture. Where I refer to Photoshop *the product*, I capitalize the *P*.

5. The Photoshop product was initially released by the Knoll brothers in 1987 and then sold to Adobe in 1988 (Lavrence and Cambre, 2020).

6. Advertising Standards Authority (ASA), 2023.

7. Competition and Markets Authority (CMA), 2022.

8. McGovern et al., 2022, 505.

9. Warren et al., 2005, 241.

10. Haines, 2021.

11. Harrison and Hefner, 2014; Kleemans et al., 2016.

12. Chow, 2022, 1455.

13. Hall, 1997, 15.

14. Hall, 1997, 61.

15. Hall, 1973/2009.

16. Hall, 1973/2009.

17. Tiggemann, 2022, 173.

18. Tiggemann, 2022, 173.

19. Lindholm, 2013, 363.

20. Orvell, 1989, 146, quoted in Lindholm, 2013, 363–364.

21. Thumim, 2012, 4.

22. Shiffman, 2021.

23. Shiffman, 2021, emphasis in original.

24. Lis and Shalev, 2012.

25. Matera, 2017.

26. Okoye, 2021.

27. UK Parliament, 2021.

28. UK Parliament, 2021.

29. Vandenbosch et al., 2022, 3.

30. Danthinne et al., 2019.

31. Danthinne et al., 2019.

32. Paraskeva et al., 2017, cited in Danthinne et al., 2019, 659.

33. Festinger, 1954, 117.

34. Tiggemann, 2022, 173.

35. Tiggemann, 2022, 173.

36. Festinger, 1954.

37. Festinger, 1954, 120.

38. Tiggemann and Anderberg, 2020, 2185.

39. Lavrence and Cambre, 2020.

40. Lavrence and Cambre, 2020.

41. Lavrence and Cambre, 2020.

42. Harrison and Hefner, 2014; Kleemans et al., 2016.

43. McGovern et al., 2022, 505.

44. Warren et al., 2005, 241.

45. Warren et al., 2005, 241.

46. Afful and Ricciardelli, 2015, 463.

47. Meyer et al., 2011, 222.

48. Elmhirst, 2021.

49. Crouch and Oliver, 2021.

50. Manavis, 2019.

51. Kekatos, 2018.

52. National Health Service (NHS), 2018.

53. NHS, 2018.

54. Abraham and Zuckerman, 2011; British Association of Aesthetic Plastic Surgeons (BAAPS), 2019; International Society of Aesthetic Plastic Surgery (ISAPS), 2019; Walker et al., 2019.

55. Tolentino, 2019.

56. Bennett and Livingston, 2020.

57. Chow, 2022, 1459.

58. Chow, 2022, 1459.

59. Chow, 2022.

60. Chow, 2022, 1451.

61. Chow, 2022, 1462.

62. See for example Gill, 2021.

63. Leaver et al., 2020.

64. Herrman, 2022.

65. Duffy and Gerrard, 2022.

66. Haines, 2021.

67. Festinger, 1954, 120.

68. Meyer et al., 2011, 222.

69. Tolentino, 2019.

70. Vandenbosch et al., 2022, 4.

71. Fardouly and Vartanian, 2016, 1.

6. Platform Paradoxes: Recommendations and Reflections

1. Tolentino, 2019.

2. Ruggeri, 2023.

3. Lavrence and Cambre, 2020, 2.

4. Fitchen, 2023.

5. Oglivy, n.d.

6. Grimes et al., 2008, cited in Orben, 2020, 1153.

7. boyd, 2014, 15, quoted in Orben, 2020, 1146.

8. Mick and Fournier, 1998, 140.

9. Mick and Fournier, 1998, 140.

10. Mick and Fournier, 1998, 124.

11. Sharon and John, 2018.

12. Haines, 2021.

13. City University London, 2021.

14. Cuonzo, 2014, 2, emphasis in original.

15. Cuonzo, 2014, 6.

16. Cuonzo, 2014, 17.

17. Livingstone and Third, 2017, 658.

18. Livingstone and Helsper, 2007, cited in Livingstone, 2008, 397.

19. Livingstone, 2008, 397.

20. Vickery, 2017, 9–10.

21. Vickery, 2017, 256.

22. Vickery, 2017, 7.

23. Livingstone and Das, 2013, 105.

24. Orben, 2020, 1143.

25. Livingstone and Blum-Ross, 2020, 192.

26. Alper, 2023, 71.

27. 5Rights Foundation, n.d.(b).

28. Livingstone and Blum-Ross, 2020, 191.

29. Livingstone and Third, 2017, 666.

30. 5Rights Foundation and Gerrard, 2022.

31. Heidegger, 1966, 51, quoted in Orben, 2020, 1151.

32. Maddox, 2022.

33. Laharia, 2021.

34. Bride v. Snap, 2021, 20–22.

35. Bride v. Snap, 2021, 20–21.

36. Maddox, 2022.

37. Buckingham and Jensen, 2012, 423.

38. Thurlow et al., 2020, 546.

39. Thurlow et al., 2020, 529.

40. Thurlow et al., 2020, 546.

41. Machin, 2004, cited in Thurlow et al., 2020, 532.

42. Buckingham and Jensen, 2012, 423.

43. Kapur, 2024.

44. Banaji, 2015, 6.

45. Buckingham and Jensen, 2012, 423.

46. Orben, 2020, 1148.

Appendix C. Research Methods and Ethical Considerations Underpinning Chapters 3 and 4

1. The British Academy, n.d.

2. This distinction was reflected in my thematic analysis, through which I split codes into "opinions" and "experiences" of anonymity or anonymous apps (a distinction that quickly became complex, and which I later refined).

3. See Bradford and Cullen, 2012, and Krueger and Casey, 2015.

4. Gill et al., 2008.

5. Braun and Clarke, 2021; 2022.

6. Braun and Clarke, 2022, 53.

7. Braun and Clarke, 2022, 53.

8. Braun and Clarke, 2022, 35; Braun and Clarke, 2021.

Appendix D. Research Methods and Ethical Considerations Underpinning Chapter 5

1. Approval number: 047192.

2. Meta Research, 2021.

3. I have used the paired interview model in past research (described in chapters 3 and 4) and found it to be very helpful for teens who were nervous or shy.

4. Braun and Clarke, 2021; Braun and Clarke, 2022, 35.

5. Festinger, 1954.

References

5Rights Foundation. (n.d.(a)). Risky-by-design: Introduction. https://www
.riskyby.design/introduction

5Rights Foundation. (n.d.(b)). Risky-by-design: The risks. https://www
.riskyby.design/risks

5Rights Foundation and Gerrard, Y. (2022). Risky-by-design: Anonymity.
https://www.riskyby.design/anonymity

Abraham, A., and Zuckerman, D. (2011). Adolescents, celebrity worship, and
cosmetic surgery. *Journal of Adolescent Health*, *49*(5): 453–454.

Advertising Standards Authority (ASA). (2023, March 23). Influencers' guide
to making clear that ads are ads. https://www.asa.org.uk/resource
/influencers-guide.html

Afful, A. A., and Ricciardelli, R. (2015). Shaping the online fat acceptance
movement: Talking about body image and beauty standards. *Journal of
Gender Studies*, *24*(4): 453–472.

Alper, M. (2023). *Kids across the spectrums: Growing up autistic in the digital age.*
MIT Press.

Ang, I. (1991). *Desperately seeking the audience.* Routledge.

Anti-Bullying Alliance. (n.d.). Our definition of bullying. https://
anti-bullyingalliance.org.uk/tools-information/all-about-bullying
/understanding-bullying/definition

Appiah, K. A. (2020, June 18). The case for capitalizing the *B* in Black. *The
Atlantic*. https://www.theatlantic.com/ideas/archive/2020/06/time-to-
capitalize-blackand-white/613159/

Assessment and Qualifications Alliance (AQA). (2019, July 1). Level 3 extended project qualification: specification. https://filestore.aqa.org.uk/subjects/AQA-W-7993-SP-19.PDF

Bachmann, G., Knecht, M., and Wittel, A. (2017). The social productivity of anonymity. *Ephemera: Theory and Politics in Organization*, *17*(2): 241–258.

Banaji, S. (2011). Disempowering by assumption: Digital natives and the EU Civic Web Project. In M. Thomas. (Ed.), *Deconstructing Digital Natives: Young People, Technology, and the New Literacies* (pp. 49–66). Routledge.

Banaji, S. (2015). Behind the high-tech fetish: Children, work and media use across classes in India. *International Communication Gazette*, *77*(6). 519–532. https://eprints.lse.ac.uk/61686/1/_lse.ac.uk_storage_LIBRARY_Secondary_libfile_shared_repository_Content_Banaji%2C%20S_Behind%20high-tech%20fetish_Banaji_Behind%20high-tech%20fetish_2015.pdf

Banaji, S. (2017). *Children and media in India: Narratives of class, agency and social change*. Routledge.

Barinka, A. (2022, October 26). Meta's Instagram users reach 2 billion, closing in on Facebook. *Bloomberg*. https://www.bloomberg.com/news/articles/2022-10-26/meta-s-instagram-users-reach-2-billion-closing-in-on-facebook

Baym, N. K. (2015). *Personal connections in the digital age*. (2nd edition). Polity.

Bayne, S., Connelly, L., Grover, C., Osborne, N., Tobin, R., Beswick, E., and Rouhani, L. (2019). The social value of anonymity on campus: A study of the decline of Yik Yak. *Learning, Media and Technology*, *44*(2): 92–107.

Beat. (n.d.). Statistics for journalists. https://www.beateatingdisorders.org.uk/media-centre/eating-disorder-statistics/

Bell, K. (2017, July 23). How Sarahah became one of the most popular iPhone apps in the world. *Mashable*. https://mashable.com/article/the-story-of-sarahah-app

Bennett, W., and Livingston, S. (2020). *The disinformation age: Politics, technology, and disruptive communication in the United States*. Cambridge University Press.

Benselin, J. C., and Ragsdell, G. (2016). Information overload: The differences that age makes. *Journal of Librarianship and Information Science*, *48*(3): 284–297.

Black, E. W., Mezzina, K., and Thompson, L. A. (2016). Anonymous social media: Understanding the content and context of Yik Yak. *Computers in Human Behavior, 57*: 17–22.

Boero, N., and Pascoe, C. J. (2012). Pro-anorexia communities and online interaction: Bringing the pro-ana body online. *Body and Society, 18*(2): 27–57.

Bok, S. (1989). *Secrets: On the ethics of concealment and revelation.* New York.

boyd, d. (2014). *It's complicated: The social lives of networked teens.* Yale University Press.

boyd, d., and Ellison, N. B. (2007). Social network sites: Definition, history, and scholarship. *Journal of Computer-Mediated Communication, 13*(1): 210–230.

Bradford, S., and Cullen, F. (2012). *Research and research methods for youth practitioners.* Routledge.

Bramwell, K. (2019, May 30). Instagram: "I don't want people to be ashamed of their scars." *BBC News.* https://www.bbc.co.uk/news/health-48431858

Braun, V. and Clarke, V. (2021). One size fits all? What counts as quality practice in (reflexive) thematic analysis? *Qualitative Research in Psychology, 18*(3): 328–352.

Braun, V. and Clarke, V. (2022). *Thematic analysis: A practical guide.* Sage.

Bride v. Snap. (2021, May 10). United States District Court, Northern District of California (San Francisco Division). Civil Action No.: 3:21-cv-3473. https://digitalcommons.law.scu.edu/cgi/viewcontent.cgi?article=3460&context=historical

British Academy. (n.d.). BA/Leverhulme Small Research Grants Awards 2018–19. https://www.thebritishacademy.ac.uk/funding/ba-leverhulme -small-research-grants/past-awards/2018-19/

British Association of Aesthetic Plastic Surgeons (BAAPS). (2019). Cosmetic surgery: Teens just "'not bovvered." https://baaps.org.uk/media/press_releases/1296/cosmetic_surgery_teens_just_not_bovvered/

Bruns, A. (2008). *Blogs, Wikipedia, Second Life, and beyond: From production to produsage.* Peter Lang.

Buchanan, E. (2011). Internet research ethics: Past, present, and future. In M. Consalvo and C. Ess (Eds.), *The Handbook of Internet Studies* (pp. 83–108). Wiley-Blackwell.

Büchi, M., and Hargittai, E. (2022). A need for considering digital inequality when studying social media use and well-being. *Social Media + Society, 8*(1): 1–7.

Buckingham, D. and Jensen, H.S. (2012). Beyond 'media panics': Reconceptualising public debates about children and media. *Journal of Children and Media, 6*(4): 413–429.

Burgess, J., Marwick, A., and Poell, T. (2017). Editors' introduction. In *The Sage Handbook of Social Media* (pp. 1–10). Sage.

Buxton, M. (2018, April 13). Can Lipsi succeed where other anonymous messaging apps have failed? *Refinery29.* https://www.refinery29.com /en-us/2018/04/196146/lipsi-anonymous-app

Byttow, D. (2015, April 29). Sunset. *Medium.* https://medium.com/secret-den /sunset-bc18450478d5

Cassin, E. (2018, February 26). Sarahah: Anonymous app dropped from Apple and Google stores after bullying accusations. *BBC Trending.* https://www .bbc.co.uk/news/blogs-trending-43174619

Chancellor, S., Pater, J.A., Clear, T., Gilbert, E., and De Choudhury, M. (2016). #thyghgapp: Instagram content moderation and lexical variation in pro-eating disorder communities. *Proceedings of the 19th ACM Conference on Computer-Supported Cooperative Work and Social Computing, CSCW '16.* http://www.munmund.net/pubs/cscw16_thyghgapp.pdf

Chow, Y.F. (2022). More than perfect: Cosmetic surgery and ageing single women in contemporary China. *European Journal of Cultural Studies, 25*(5): 1448–1466.

City University London. (2021). 90% of young women report using a filter or editing their photos before posting. *ScienceDaily.* https://www.sciencedaily .com/releases/2021/03/210308111852.htm

Cobb, G. (2017). "This is not pro-ana": Denial and disguise in pro-anorexia online spaces. *Fat Studies, 6*(2): 189–205.

Cockerham, W.C. (2021). *Sociology of mental disorder.* (11th edition). Routledge.

Cohen, S. (1972/2002). *Folk devils and moral panics: The creation of the Mods and Rockers.* Routledge.

Competition and Markets Authority (CMA). (2022, November 3). Hidden ads: Being clear with your audience. https://www.gov.uk/government /publications/social-media-endorsements-guide-for-influencers /social-media-endorsements-being-transparent-with-your-followers

Constine, J. (2018, June 14). Snapchat launches privacy-safe Snap Kit, the un-Facebook platform. *TechCrunch.* https://techcrunch.com/2018/06 /14/snapchat-snap-kit/

Constine, J. (2019, May 8). #1 app YOLO Q&A is the Snapchat platform's 1st hit. *TechCrunch*. https://techcrunch.com/2019/05/08/download-yolo-app/

Covid: Calls for gyms to be classed as "essential" to avoid future lockdown. (2020, October 31). *BBC News*. https://www.bbc.co.uk/news/uk-wales-54689877

Cox, G. (2015, September 9). Yik Yak's privacy policy may not be what you think. *University Press*. https://www.upressonline.com/2015/09/yik-yaks-privacy-policy-may-not-be-what-you-think/.

Crawford, A. (2019, 22 January). Instagram "helped kill my daughter." *BBC News*. https://www.bbc.co.uk/news/av/uk-46966009

Crouch, G., and Oliver, O. (2021). How girls are now begging surgeons to change their faces so they look like their edited pictures on Instagram. *Daily Mail*. https://www.dailymail.co.uk/news/article-9533193/How-girls-begging-surgeons-change-faces-look-like-edited-pictures.html.

Cuonzo, M. (2014). *Paradox*. MIT Press.

Cutler, K-M. (2014, February 3). Anonymity's moment: Secret is like Facebook for what you're really thinking. *TechCrunch*. https://techcrunch.com/2014/02/03/anonymitys-moment-secret-is-like-facebook-for-what-youre-really-thinking/

Danthinne, E.S., Giorgianni, F.E., and Rodgers, R.F. (2020). Labels to prevent the detrimental effects of media on body image: A systematic review and meta-analysis. *International Journal of Eating Disorders*, *53*(5): 647-661.

Das, R., and Ytre-Arne, B. (2021). Audiences' communicative agency in a datafied age: Interpretative, relational and increasingly prospective. *Communication Theory*, *31*(4): 779-797.

Davis, K. (2012). Friendship 2.0: Adolescents' experiences of belonging and self-disclosure online. *Journal of Adolescence*, *35*(6): 1527-1536.

Devine, K. (2022, September 30). The digital trail that sheds light on final months of Molly Russell's life. *Sky News*. https://news.sky.com/story/the-digital-trail-that-sheds-light-on-final-months-of-molly-russells-life-12707478

Donath, J.S. (1999). Identity and deception in the virtual community. In M.A. Smith and P. Kollock (Eds.), *Communities in Cyberspace* (pp. 27-58). Routledge.

Drotner, K. (1999). Dangerous media? Panic discourses and dilemmas of modernity. *Paedagogica Historica: International Journal of the History of Education*, 35(3): 593–619.

Duffy, B. E., and Chan, N. K. (2019). "You never really know who's looking": Imagined surveillance across social media platforms. *New Media and Society*, 21(1): 119–138.

Duffy, B. E., and Gerrard, Y. (2022, 5 August). BeReal and the doomed quest for online authenticity. *WIRED*. https://www.wired.com/story/bereal -doomed-online-authenticity/

Dundes, A. (1965). Here I sit—a study of American Latrinalia. *Kroeber Anthropological Society Papers*, 34: 91–105.

Elmhirst, S. (2021, February 9). Brazilian butt lift: Behind the world's most dangerous cosmetic surgery. *The Guardian*. https://www.theguardian .com/news/2021/feb/09/brazilian-butt-lift-worlds-most-dangerous -cosmetic-surgery

Englander, E., Donnerstein, E., Kowalski, R., Lin, C. A., and Parti, K. (2017). Defining cyberbullying. *Paediatrics*, 140(2): S148-S151.

Erikson, E. H. (1968). *Identity: Youth and crisis*. W. W. Norton.

Fardouly, J., and Vartanian, L. R. (2016). Social media and body image concerns: Current research and future directions. *Current Opinion in Psychology*, 9: 1–5.

Fardouly, J., Pinkus, R. T., Vartanian, L. R. (2017). The impact of appearance comparisons made through social media, traditional media, and in person in women's everyday lives. *Body Image*. 20: 31–39.

Festinger, L. (1954). A theory of social comparison processes. *Human Relations*, 7: 117–40.

Feuston, J. L., Taylor, A. S., and Piper, A. M. (2020). Conformity of eating disorders through content moderation. *Proceedings of the ACM on Human-Computer Interaction*, 4(CSCW1), 40: 1–28. DOI: *10.1145/3392845*

Finkenauer, C., Engels, R. C. M. E., and Meeus, W. (2002). Keeping secrets from parents: Advantages and disadvantages of secrecy in adolescence. *Journal of Youth and Adolescence*, 31(2): 123–136.

Fitchen, L. (2023, February 28). "This is a problem": A new hyper-realistic TikTok beauty filter is freaking people out. *VICE*. https://www.vice.com /en/article/pkg747/tiktok-beauty-filter-bold-glamor-problem

Gerrard, Y. (2018). Beyond the hashtag: Circumventing content moderation on social media. *New Media and Society*, *20*(12): 4492–4511.

Gerrard, Y. (2020). "Too good to be true": The challenges of regulating tech startups. In T. Gillespie, P. Aufderheide, E. Carmi,Y. Gerrard, R. Gorwa,A. Matamoros-Fernández, S.T. Roberts, A. Sinnreich, and S. Myers West. Expanding the debate about content moderation: Scholarly research agendas for the coming policy debates. *Internet Policy Review*, *9*(4). DOI: 10.14763/2020.4.1512.

Gerrard, Y. (2021, May 5). Social apps that go suddenly viral put kids at risk. *WIRED*. https://www.wired.com/story/opinion-social-apps-that-go -suddenly-viral-put-kids-at-risk/

Gerrard, Y. (2022). Social media moderation: The best-kept secret in tech. In D. Rosen (Ed.), *The Social Media Debate: Unpacking the Social, Psychological, and Cultural Effects of Social Media* (pp. 77–95). Routledge.

Gerrard, Y. (2023, 21 August). Why are 'photo dumps' so popular? A digital communications expert explains. *The Conversation*. https:// theconversation.com/why-are-photo-dumps-so-popular-a-digital -communications-expert-explains-210486

Gerrard, Y., and Gillespie, T. (2019, 21 February). When algorithms think you want to die. *WIRED*. https://www.wired.com/story/when-algorithms-think-you-want-to-die/

Gerrard, Y., and McCosker, A. (2020, 4 November). The perils of moderating depression on social media. *WIRED*. https://www.wired.com/story /opinion/the-perils-of-moderating-depression-on-social-media/

Gibbs, M., Meese, J., Arnold, M., Nansen, B., and Carter, M. (2015). #Funeral and Instagram: death, social media, and platform vernacular. *Information, Communication and Society*, *18*(3): 255–268.

Gill, P., Stewart, K., Treasure, E., and Chadwick, B. (2008). Conducting qualitative interviews with school children in dental research. *British Dental Journal*. 204(7): 371–374.s

Gill, R. (2021). Being watched and feeling judged on social media. *Feminist Media Studies*, *21*(8): 1387–1392.

Gillespie, T. (2010). The politics of "platforms." *New Media and Society*, *12*(3): 347–364.

Gillespie, T. (2015). Platforms intervene. *Social Media + Society*, *1*(1): 1–2.

Gillespie, T. (2018). *Custodians of the internet: Platforms, content moderation, and the hidden decisions that shape social media.* Yale University Press.

Gillespie, T. (2022). Do not recommend? Reduction as a form of content moderation. *Social Media + Society, 8*(3): 1–13.

Gillespie, T., Aufderheide, P., Carmi, E., Gerrard, Y., Gorwa, R., Matamoros-Fernández, A., Roberts, S. T., Sinnreich, A., and Myers West, S. (2020). Expanding the debate about content moderation: Scholarly research agendas for the coming policy debates. *Internet Policy Review, 9*(4): 1–29.

Ging, D., and Garvey, S. (2018). "Written in these scars are the stories I can't explain": A content analysis of pro-ana and thinspiration image sharing on Instagram. *New Media and Society, 20*(3): 1181–1200.

Goffman, E. (1956). Embarrassment and social organization. *American Journal of Sociology, 62*(3): 264–271.

Goffman, E. (1963/1990). *Stigma: Notes on the management of spoiled identity.* Penguin.

Goode, E., and Ben-Yehuda, N. (1994). *Moral panics: The social construction of deviance.* Blackwell.

Grimes, T., Anderson, J. A., and Bergen, L. (2008). *Media violence and aggression: Science and ideology.* Sage.

Gruenberg, S. M. (1935). Radio and the child. *The Annals of the American Academy of Political and Social Science, 177*(1): 123–128.

Haimson, O. L., Liu, T., Zhang, B. Z., and Corvite, S. (2021). The online authenticity paradox: What being "authentic" on social media means, and barriers to achieving it. *Proceedings of the ACM on Human-Computer Interaction, 5*(423): 1–18.

Haines, A. (2021). From "Instagram face" to "Snapchat dysmorphia": How beauty filters are changing the way we see ourselves. *Forbes.* https://www.forbes.com/sites/annahaines/2021/04/27/from-instagram-face-to-snapchat-dysmorphia-how-beauty-filters-are-changing-the-way-we-see-ourselves

Hall, S. (1973/2009). Encoding/decoding. In S. Thornham, C. Bassett and M. Marris (Eds.), *Media Studies: A Reader* (pp. 28–38). (3rd edition). Edinburgh University

Hall, S. (1996). Who needs "identity"? In S. Hall and P. du Gay. (Eds.), *Questions of Cultural Identity* (pp. 1–17). Sage.

Hall, S. (Ed.) (1997). *Representation: cultural representations and signifying practices*. Sage.

Hall, S., Critcher, C., Jefferson, T., Clarke, J., and Roberts, B. (1978). *Policing the crisis: Mugging, the state, and law and order*. Macmillan.

Harrison, K. and Hefner, V. (2014). Virtually perfect: Image retouching and adolescent body image. *Media Psychology*, *17*(2): 134–153.

Hatmaker, T. (2021, August 16). Yik Yak returns from the dead. *TechCrunch*. https://techcrunch.com/2021/08/16/yik-yak-is-back/

Heidegger, M. (1966). *Discourse on thinking*. Harper and Row.

Helsper, E. J., and Eynon, R. (2010). Digital natives: Where is the evidence? *British Educational Research Journal*, *36*(3): 503–520.

Hendry, N. A. (2020). Young women's mental illness and (in-)visible social media practices of control and emotional recognition. *Social Media + Society*, *6* (4): 1–10.

Hern, A. (2019, February 4). Instagram to launch "sensitivity screens" after Molly Russell's death. *The Guardian*. https://www.theguardian.com /technology/2019/feb/04/instagram-to-launch-sensitivity-screens -after-molly-russell-death

Herrman, J. (2022, May 10). This new social app is boring, in a good way. *New York Times*. https://www.nytimes.com/2022/05/10/style/bereal-app-social-media.html

Hine, C. (2015). *Ethnography for the internet: embedded, embodied and everyday*. Bloomsbury.

Hogan, B. (2013). Pseudonyms and the rise of the real-name web. In J. Hartley, J. Burgess, and A. Bruns. (Eds.), *A Companion to New Media Dynamics* (pp. 290–307). Wiley.

Horwitz, J. (2023, November 2). His job was to make Instagram safe for teens. His 14-year-old showed him what the app was really like. *Wall Street Journal*. https://www.wsj.com/tech/instagram-facebook-teens-harassment-safety-5d991be1

Humphreys, L. (2018). *The qualified self: Social media and the accounting of everyday life*. MIT Press.

Hunt, A. (1997). "Moral panic" and moral language in the media. *British Journal of Sociology*, *48*(4): 629–648.

Hwang, J. M., Cheong, P. H., and Feeley, T. H. (2009). Being young and feeling blue in Taiwan: Examining adolescent depressive mood and online and offline activities. *New Media and Society*, 11(7): 1101–1121.

Internet Matters. (2022, October 27). Parents' guide: What is Yolo app and is it safe? https://www.internetmatters.org/hub/guidance/parents-guide-what-is-yolo-app-and-is-it-safe/

Internet Matters. (2020, November 18). What is the Tellonym app? https://www.internetmatters.org/hub/esafety-news/what-is-the-tellonym-app/

International Society of Aesthetic Plastic Surgery (ISAPS). (2019). ISAPS International survey on aesthetic/cosmetic procedures. https://www.isaps.org/wp-content/uploads/2019/12/ISAPS-Global-Survey-Results-2018-new.pdf.

Jaynes, V. (2020). The social life of screenshots: The power of visibility in teen friendship groups. *New Media and Society*, 22(8): 1378–1393.

Jeffrey, C., and Dyson, J. (2008). *Telling young lives: Portraits of global youth.* Temple University Press.

Jermyn, D., and Holmes, S. (2006). The audience is dead; long live the audience! Interactivity, "telephilia" and the contemporary television audience. *Critical Studies in Television*, 1(1): 49–57.

Johnson, B. (2010, January 11). Privacy no longer a social norm, says Facebook founder. *The Guardian*. https://www.theguardian.com/technology/2010/jan/11/facebook-privacy

Johnson, N. F. and Jajodia, S. (1998). Exploring steganography: Seeing the unseen. *Computer*, 31(2): 26–34.

Kanai, A. (2017). Girlfriendship and sameness: Affective belonging in a digital intimate public. *Journal of Gender Studies*, 26(3): 293–306.

Kapur, A. (2024, January 29). Can the internet be governed? *The New Yorker*. https://www.newyorker.com/magazine/2024/02/05/can-the-internet-be-governed

Kekatos, M. (2018). The rise of teenagers who want "back-to-school surgery." *Daily Mail*. https://www.dailymail.co.uk/health/article-5888949/Plastic-surgeons-warn-rise-teenagers-want-school-surgery.html

Kennedy, H. (2016). *Post, mine, repeat: Social media data mining becomes ordinary.* Palgrave Macmillan.

Kleemans, M., Daalmans, S., Carbaat, I., and Anschütz, D. (2016). Picture perfect: The direct effect of manipulated Instagram photos on body image in adolescent girls. *Media Psychology, 21*(1): 93–110.

Knibbs, K. (2014, February 19). We read the Whisper and Secret fine print so you don't have to. *The Daily Dot.* https://www.dailydot.com/debug/whisper-secret-privacy-policies/

Krueger, R. A., and Casey, M. A. (2015). *Focus groups: A practical guide for applied research.* (5th edition). Sage.

Kroger, J. (2006). *Identity development: adolescence through adulthood.* (2nd edition). Sage.

Laharia, U. (2021, May 13). Snapchat suspends Q&A apps YOLO and LMK after mother sues for teen's suicide. *Newsweek.* https://www.newsweek.com/snapchat-suspends-q-apps-yolo-lmk-after-mother-sues-teens-suicide-1591285

Lavrence, C., and Cambre, C. (2020). "Do I look like my selfie?": Filters and the digital-forensic gaze. *Social Media + Society, 6* (4): 1–13.

Leaver, T., Highfield, T., and Abidin, C. (2020). *Instagram: Visual social media cultures.* Polity.

Li, Q. (2007). New bottle but old wine: A research of cyberbullying in schools. *Computers in Human Behavior, 23*(4): 1777–1791.

Lindholm, C. (2013). The rise of expressive authenticity. *Anthropological Quarterly, 86*(2): 361–395.

Lis, J., and Shalev, S. (2012, March 20). Knesset passes bill banning use of underweight models in advertising. *Haaretz.* https://www.haaretz.com/2012-03-20/ty-article/knesset-passes-bill-banning-use-of-underweight-models-in-advertising/0000017f-e631-da9b-a1ff-ee7f753f0000

Livingstone, S. (2007). Interactivity and participation on the internet: Young people's response to the civic sphere. In P. Dahlgren. (Ed.), *Young Citizens and New Media: Learning for Democratic Participation* (pp. 103–124). Routledge.

Livingstone, S. (2008). Taking risky opportunities in youthful content creation: Teenagers' use of social networking sites for intimacy, privacy and self-expression. *New Media and Society, 10*(3): 393–411.

Livingstone, S. (2020). More online risks to children, but not necessarily more harm: EU Kids Online 2020 survey. *Media@LSE Blog.* https://blogs.lse.ac

.uk/medialse/2020/02/11/more-online-risks-to-children-but-not
-necessarily-more-harm-eu-kids-online-2020-survey/

Livingstone, S., and Blum-Ross, A. (2020). *Parenting for a digital future: How hopes and fears about technology shape children's lives.* Oxford University Press.

Livingstone, S., and Das, R. (2013). The end of audiences? Theoretical echoes of reception amid the uncertainties of use. In J. Hartley, J. Burgess, A. Bruns (Eds.), *A Companion to New Media Dynamics* (pp.104–121). Wiley-Blackwell.

Livingstone, S., and Helsper, E. J. (2007). Taking risks when communicating on the internet: The role of offline social-psychological factors in young people's vulnerability to online risks. *Information, Communication and Society, 10*(5): 619–44.

Livingstone, S., and Third, A. (2017). Children and young people's rights in the digital age: An emerging agenda. *New Media and Society, 19*(5): 657–670.

Livingstone, S., Ólafsson, K., and Staksrud, E. (2013). Risky social networking practices among "underage" users: Lessons for evidence-based policy. *Journal of Computer-Mediated Communication, 18*(3): 303–320.

Lunden, I. (2019, January 31). After bans from Apple and Google, Sarahah debuts Enoff, an iOS app for anonymous feedback at work. *TechCrunch.* https://techcrunch.com/2019/01/31/after-bans-from-apple-and-google-sarahah-debuts-enoff-for-anonymous-feedback-at-work/

Ma, X., Andalibi, N., Barkhuus, L., and Naaman, M. (2017). People are either too fake or too real: Opportunities and challenges in tie-based anonymity. *Proceedings of the 2017 CHI Conference on Human Factors in Computing Systems,* Denver, CO, 6–11 May 2017: 1781–1793.

Machin, D. (2004). Building the world's visual language: The increasing global importance of image banks in corporate media. *Visual Communication, 3*(3): 316–336.

Maddox, A. (2022, July 14). Sendit, Yolo, NGL: Anonymous social apps are taking over once more, but they aren't without risks. *The Conversation.* https://theconversation.com/sendit-yolo-ngl-anonymous-social-apps-are-taking-over-once-more-but-they-arent-without-risks-186647

Madi, M. (2017, August 7). Sarahah: The honesty app that's got everyone talking. *BBC News.* https://www.bbc.co.uk/news/av/world-middle-east-40846321

Malik, A. (2024, January 9). Meta to restrict teen Instagram and Facebook accounts from seeing content about self-harm and eating disorders. *TechCrunch*. https://techcrunch.com/2024/01/09/meta-to-restrict-teen-instagram-and-facebook-accounts-from-seeing-content-about-self-harm-and-eating-disorders/

Manavis, S. (2019). How Instagram's plastic surgery filters are warping the way we see our faces. *New Statesman*. https://www.newstatesman.com/science-tech/social-media/2019/10/how-instagram-plastic-surgery-filter-ban-are-destroying-how-we-see-our-faces

Maris, E. (2021). The imagined industry. *International Journal of Communication*, *15*: 4819–4839.

Martin, J. K., Pescosolido, B. A., and Tuch, S. A. (2000). Of fear and loathing: The role of "disturbing behavior," labels, and causal attributions in shaping public attitudes toward people with mental illness. *Journal of Health and Social Behavior*, *41*(2): 208–223.

Martínez-Alés, G., Jiang, T., Keyes, K. M., and Gradus, J. L. (2022). The recent rise of suicide mortality in the United States. *Annu. Rev. Publ. Health*. *5*(43): 99–116.

Marwick, A. E. (2008). To catch a predator? The MySpace moral panic. *First Monday*, *13*(6). DOI: https://doi.org/10.5210/fm.v13i6.2152

Marwick, A. (2013). Online identity. In J. Hartley, J. Burgess and A. Bruns. (Eds.), *Companion to New Media Dynamics* (pp. 355–364). Blackwell.

Marwick, A. E., and boyd, d. (2010). I tweet honestly, I tweet passionately: Twitter users, context collapse, and the imagined audience. *New Media and Society*, *13*(1): 114–133.

Marwick, A. E., and boyd, d. (2014). Networked privacy: How teenagers negotiate context in social media. *New Media and Society*, *16*(7): 1051–1067.

Marwick, A. E., and Hargittai, E. (2018). Nothing to hide, nothing to lose? Incentives and disincentives to sharing information with institutions online. *Information, Communication and Society*, *22*(12): 1697–1713.

Matera, A. (2017, October 3). Photoshop is now illegal in France. *Teen Vogue*. https://www.teenvogue.com/story/photoshop-is-now-illegal-in-france

McCosker, A., and Gerrard, Y. (2020). Hashtagging depression on Instagram: Towards a more inclusive mental health research methodology. *New Media and Society*, *23*(7): 1899–1919.

McGovern, O., Collins, R., and Dunne, S. (2022). The associations between photo-editing and body concerns among females: A systematic review. *Body Image*, *43*: 504–517.

McLelland, M., Yu, H., and Goggin, G. (2017). Alternative histories of social media in Japan and China. In J. Burgess, A. Marwick and T. Poell (Eds.), *The Sage Handbook of Social Media* (pp. 53–68). Sage.

McNicol, A. (2013). None of your business? Analyzing the legitimacy and effects of gendering social spaces through system design. In G. Lovinik and M. Rasch (Eds.), *Unlike Us Reader: Social Media Monopolies and their Alternatives* (pp. 200–219). Amsterdam: Institute of Network Cultures.

McRobbie, A., and Thornton, S. L. (1995). Rethinking "moral panic" for multi-mediated social worlds. *The British Journal of Sociology*, *46*(4): 559–574.

Meaker, M. (2022, October 5). How a British teen's death changed social media. *WIRED*. https://www.wired.co.uk/article/how-a-british-teens -death-changed-social-media

Meta Newsroom. (2024, January 9). New protections to give teens more age-appropriate experiences on our apps. https://about.fb.com/news /2024/01/teen-protections-age-appropriate-experiences-on-our-apps/

Meyer, M. D. E., Fallah, A. M., and Wood, M. M. (2011). Gender, media, and madness: Reading a rhetoric of women in crisis through Foucauldian theory. *The Review of Communication*, *11*(3): 216–228.

Mick, D. G., and Fournier, S. (1998). Paradoxes of technology: Consumer cognizance, emotions, and coping strategies. *Journal of Consumer Research*, *25*(2): 123–143.

Miller, D., and Slater, D. (2000). *The Internet: An ethnographic approach*. Oxford: Berg.

Milmo, D. (2022, September 30). 'The bleakest of worlds': How Molly Russell fell into a vortex of despair on social media. *The Guardian*. https://www .theguardian.com/technology/2022/sep/30/how-molly-russell-fell-into-a-vortex-of-despair-on-social-media

Milosevic, T. (2016). Social media companies' cyberbullying policies. *International Journal of Communication*, *10*: 5164–5185.

Milosevic, T. (2017). *Protecting children online? Cyberbullying policies of social media companies*. MIT Press.

Miltner, K. M., and Gerrard, Y. (2022). "Tom had us all doing front-end web development": A nostalgic (re)imagining of Myspace. *Internet Histories*, 6(1–2): 48–67.

National Health Service (NHS). (2018). Plastic surgery. https://www.nhs.uk /conditions/plastic-surgery/

Nemer, D., and Freeman, G. (2015). Empowering the marginalized: Rethinking selfies in the slums of Brazil. *International Journal of Communication*, 9: 1832–1847.

Nguyễn, A. T. and Pendleton, M. (2020, March 23). Recognizing race in language: Why we capitalize "Black" and "White." Center for the Study of Social Policy. https://cssp.org/2020/03/recognizing-race-in-language-why-we-capitalize-black-and-white/#:~:text=For%20these%20reasons%2C%20we%20require,as%20real%2C%20existing%20racial%20identities.

Nichols, K. (2018). Moving beyond ideas of laddism: Conceptualising "mischievous masculinities" as a new way of understanding everyday sexism and gender relations. *Journal of Gender Studies*, 27(1): 73–85.

Nissenbaum, H. (2010). *Privacy in context: technology, policy, and the integrity of social life*. Stanford University Press.

Nussbaum, E. (2007, February 2). Say everything. *New York Magazine*. https:// nymag.com/news/features/27341/

Odgers, C. L. (2024, March 29). The great rewiring: Is social media really behind an epidemic of teenage mental illness? *Nature (Book Review)*, 628: 29–30. https://www.nature.com/articles/d41586-024-00902-2#ref-CR8

Ofcom. (2022a, March 30). Children and parents: Media use and attitudes report 2022. https://www.ofcom.org.uk/research-and-data/media -literacy-research/childrens/children-and-parents-media-use-and -attitudes-report-2022

Ofcom. (2022b, 14–18 July). Children's online user ages quantitative research study. https://www.ofcom.org.uk/__data/assets/pdf_file/0015/245004 /children-user-ages-chart-pack.pdf

Oglivy. (n.d.). Our work: #TurnYourBack, Dove. https://www.ogilvy.com /work/turnyourback

Okoye, C. (2021, December 8). Legislation aims to promote mental health through realistic advertising images. *Boston Globe*. https://www

.bostonglobe.com/2021/12/08/metro/legislation-aims-promote-mental
-health-through-realistic-advertising-images/

Oluwole, V. (2023, June 28). Kenya tops global TikTok usage charts, shaping news trends. *Business Insider Africa*. https://africa.businessinsider.com /local/lifestyle/kenya-tops-global-tiktok-usage-charts-shaping-news -trends/wthlmg5

Orben, A. (2020). The Sisyphean cycle of technology panics. *Perspectives on Psychological Science, 15*(5): 1143–1157.

Orr, G. (2014, November 12). How a community art project with postcards became an international hit. *The Independent*. https://www.independent .co.uk/arts-entertainment/art/features/how-a-community-art-project -with-postcards-became-an-international-hit-9857220.html

Orvell, M. (1989). *The real thing: Imitation and authenticity in American culture, 1800–1940*. University of North Carolina Press.

Paraskeva, N., Lewis-Smith, H., and Diedrichs, P. C. (2017). Consumer opinion on social policy approaches to promoting positive body image: Airbrushed media images and disclaimer labels. *Journal of Health Psychology, 22*(2): 164–175.

Parent, W. A. (1983). Privacy, morality, and the law. *Philosophy and Public Affairs, 12*(4): 269–288.

Parker, K. (2023, May 22). How Pew Research Center will report on generations moving forward. Pew Research Center. https://www.pewresearch .org/short-reads/2023/05/22/how-pew-research-center-will-report-on -generations-moving-forward/

Patelis, K. (2013). Political economy and monopoly abstractions: What social media demand. In G. Lovinik and M. Rasch. (Eds.), *Unlike us reader: Social media monopolies and their alternatives* (pp. 117–126). Amsterdam: Institute of Network Cultures.

Pew Research Center. (2014, October 22). Online harassment. https:// www.pewresearch.org/internet/2014/10/22/online-harassment/

Prensky, M. (2001). Digital natives, digital immigrants part 1. *On the Horizon, 9*(5): 1–6.

Ragelienė, T. (2016). Links of adolescents' identity development and relationship with peers: A systematic literature review. *Journal of the Canadian Academy of Child and Adolescent Psychiatry, 25*(2): 97–105.

Raynes-Goldie, K. (2010). Aliases, creeping, and wall cleaning: Understanding privacy in the age of Facebook. *First Monday, 15*(1). DOI: https://doi.org/10.5210/fm.v15i1.2775

Robson, S. (2013, August 16). A purple coffin and mourners wearing onesies: Heartbroken family and friends gather at funeral for teenage troll victim Hannah Smith. *Mail Online*. http://www.dailymail.co.uk/news/article-2395484/Hannah-Smith-funeral-Family-friends-gather-cyberbully-victim-Lutterworth.html

Robson, S. (2018, July 18). Schools warn that new app called Tellonym could be "fuelling cyberbullying among teens." *Manchester Evening News*. https://www.manchestereveningnews.co.uk/news/greater-manchester-news/schools-warn-new-app-called-14920680

Ruggeri, A. (2023, March 1). The problems with TikTok's controversial "beauty filters." *BBC Future*. https://www.bbc.com/future/article/20230301-the-problems-with-tiktoks-controversial-beauty-filters

Sardá, T., Natale, S., Sotirakopoulos, N., and Monaghan, M. (2019). Understanding online anonymity. *Media, Culture and Society, 41*(4): 557–564.

Sarwatay, D., and Raman, U. (2022). Everyday negotiations in managing presence: Young people and social media in India. *Information, Communication and Society, 25*(4): 536–551.

Scott, C. F., Marcu, G., Anderson, R. E., Newman, M. W., Schoenebeck, S. (2023). Trauma-informed social media: Towards solutions for reducing and healing online harm. *Proceedings of the 2023 CHI Conference on Human Factors in Computing Systems*. 1–20. https://doi.org/10.1145/3544548.3581512.

Senft, T., and Baym, N. (2015). What does the selfie say? Investigating a global phenomenon. *International Journal of Communication, 9*: 1588–1606.

Sharon, T., and John, N. A. (2018). Unpacking (the) secret: Anonymous social media and the impossibility of networked anonymity. *New Media and Society, 20*(11): 4177–4194.

Sheanoda, V., Bussey, K., and Jones, T. (2021). Sexuality, gender and culturally diverse interpretations of cyberbullying. *New Media and Society, 26*(1): 154–171.

Shiffman, A. (2021, October 5). The Midas retouch: Does Norway's new law signal the end of influencer photoshopping? *VOGUE Scandinavia*. https://www.voguescandinavia.com/articles/photo-editing-law-in-norway

Simmel, G. (1950). The secret and the secret society. In K. W. Wolff (Ed. and trans.), *The Sociology of Georg Simmel*. Free Press.

Skeggs, B. (1997). *Formations of class and gender: Becoming respectable*. Sage.

Smith, M. (2018, March 6). How young are "young people"? And at what age does a person become "old"? *YouGov*. https://yougov.co.uk/topics /politics/articles-reports/2018/03/06/how-young-are-young-people -and-what-age-does-perso

Solís, M. V., Smetana, J. G., and Comer, J. (2015). Associations among solicitation, relationship quality, and adolescents' disclosure and secrecy with mothers and best friends. *Journal of Adolescence, 43*(1): 193–205.

Striphas, T. (2015). Algorithmic culture. *European Journal of Cultural Studies, 18*(4–5): 395–412.

Suler, J. (2004). The online disinhibition effect. *CyberPsychology and Behavior, 7*(3): 321–326.

Suzor, N. (2016, September 18). How does Instagram censor hashtags? *Medium*. https://medium.com/@nicsuzor/how-does-instagram-censor-hashtags-c7f38872d1fd

Third, A. (2016). Researching the benefits and opportunities for children online. Global Kids Online. www.globalkidsonline.net/opportunities

Third, A., Bellerose, D., Dawkins, U., Keltie, E., and Pihl, K. (2014). *Children's rights in the digital age: A download from children around the world*. (2nd edition). Young and Well Cooperative Research Centre and UNICEF.

Thumim, N. (2012). *Self-representation and digital culture*. Palgrave Macmillan.

Thurlow, C., Aiello, G., and Portmann, L. (2020). Visualizing teens and technology: A social semiotic analysis of stock photography and news media imagery. *New Media and Society, 22*(3): 528–549.

Tiggemann, M. (2022). Digital modification and body image on social media: Disclaimer labels, captions, hashtags, and comments. *Body Image, 41*: 172–180).

Tiggemann, M., and Anderberg, I. (2020). Social media is not real: The effect of 'Instagram vs reality' images on women's social comparison and body image. *New Media and Society, 22*(12): 2183–2199.

Tiidenberg, K., Hendry, N. A., and Abidin, C. (2021). *tumblr*. Polity.

TikTok Newsroom. (2021, December 16). An update on our work to safeguard and diversify recommendations. https://newsroom.tiktok.com/en-us /an-update-on-our-work-to-safeguard-and-diversify-recommendations

Tolentino, J. (2019, December 12). The age of Instagram face. *The New Yorker*. https://www.newyorker.com/culture/decade-in-review/the-age-of -instagram-face

Trepte, S., Reinecke, L., Ellison, N. B., Quiring, O., Yao, M. Z., and Ziegele, M. (2017). A cross-cultural perspective on the privacy calculus. *Social Media + Society*, *3*(1): 1–13.

Turkle, S. (1995/2011). *Life on the screen: Identity in the age of the internet*. Touchstone.

Tyler, I. (2008). 'Chav Mum Chav Scum': Class disgust in contemporary Britain. *Feminist Media Studies*, *8*(1): 17–34.

Tyler, I. (2020). *Stigma: the machinery of inequality*. Zed Books.

Tyler, I., and Slater, T. (2018). Rethinking the sociology of stigma. *The Sociological Review Monographs*, *66*(4): 721–743.

u/linedryonly. (2018, November 15). Reddit ban endangered thousands of lives (re: r/ProED). *Reddit*. https://www.reddit.com/r/TrueOffMyChest /comments/9xa1dt/reddit_ban_endangered_thousands_of_lives_re_rproed/

UK Government and Parliament. (2021, September 5). Petition: Make verified ID a requirement for opening a social media account. https://petition .parliament.uk/petitions/575833?reveal_response=yes

UK Parliament. (2021, May 4). Digitally altered body images Bill. https://bills .parliament.uk/bills/2778.

van der Nagel, E. (2018). Alts and automediality: Compartmentalising the self through multiple social media platforms. *M/C Journal*, *21*(2). DOI: https://doi.org/10.5204/mcj.1379

van der Nagel, E., and Frith, J. (2015). Anonymity, pseudonymity, and the agency of online identity: Examining the social practices of r/GoneWild. *First Monday*, *20*(3). DOI: https://doi.org/10.5210/fm.v20i3.5615

Vandenbosch, L., Fardouly, J., and Tiggemann, M. (2022). Social media and body image: Recent trends and future directions. *Current Opinion in Psychology*, *45*: 1–6.

Vickery, J. R. (2017). *Worried about the wrong things: Youth, risk, and opportunity in the digital world*. MIT Press.

Wallace, K. A. (1999). Anonymity. *Ethics and Information Technology*, *1*: 23–35.

Walker, C. E., Krumhuber, E. G., Dayan, S., and Furnham, A. (2019). Effects of social media use on desire for cosmetic surgery among young women. *Current Psychology*, *40*: 3355–3364.

Walsh, J. P. (2020). Social media and moral panics: Assessing the effects of technological change on societal reaction. *International Journal of Cultural Studies*, 23(6): 840–859.

Warren, C., and Laslett, B. (1977). Privacy and secrecy: A conceptual comparison. *Journal of Social Issues*, 33(3): 43–51.

Warren, C. S., Gleaves, D. H., Cepeda-Benito, A., del Carmen Fernandez, M., and Rodriguez-Ruis, S. (2005). Ethnicity as a protective factor against internalization of a thin ideal and body dissatisfaction. *International Journal of Eating Disorders*, 37(3): 241–249.

Watson, A. J., and Valtin, R. (1997). Secrecy in middle childhood. *International Journal of Behavioral Development*, 21(3): 431–452.

Westin, A. (1967). *Privacy and freedom*. Atheneum.

World Health Organization (WHO). (2022). World mental health report: transforming mental health for all. https://www.who.int/publications/i/item/9789240049338

Yeshua-Katz, D., and Hård af Segerstad, Y. (2020). Catch 22: The paradox of social media affordances and stigmatized online support groups. *Social Media + Society*, 6(4): 1–12.

Yeshua-Katz, D., and Martins, N. (2013). Communicating stigma: The pro-ana paradox. *Health Communication*, 28(5): 499–508.

Yik Yak. (2021, August 16). The yak is back. https://yikyak.com/the-yak-is-back

Young, A. L., and Quan-Haase, A. (2013). Privacy protection strategies on Facebook: The internet privacy paradox revisited. *Information, Communication and Society*, 16(4): 479–500.

Zappavigna, M. (2012). *Discourse of Twitter and social media: How we use language to create affiliation on the Web*. Bloomsbury.

Index

harmful content, 35, 41–42, 50, 51, 60, 65–66, 72. *See also* online harmful behaviors; violence and social media

Harrison, K., 167–68

hashtag moderation, 57–59

heavy duty editing, 184

Hefner, V., 167–68

Hendry, N. A., 62

Henrion, G., 82

herding together, 38–39

hidden ads, 166

Hine, C., 100, 138

Holliday, R., 236

Horwitz, J., 72

Humphreys, L., 11

Hunt, A., 28–29

hybrid apps, 87

identity(ies) and social media: autistic, 213; compartmentalizations, 138; vs. confusion, 135; development, 5, 65–66, 85, 135, 161, 198; fragmentation, 127, 138; integration of online/offline, 100–101, 126, 182; marginalized or stigmatized, 33, 38, 127, 162, 212; markers, 125, 130, 154, 155, 159, 170, 187, 200, 205, 206, 223, 240, 253n1; negotiations, 234; performativity, 131; verification, 137

identity concealment, 124–27, 209; being who you want to be on the real-name web, 129–31; conclusion, 158–63; data archived on internet, impact of, 158–63; introduction, 124–29; personal safety: protection from the unknown, 150–58; research

interviews, 131–35; social safety: protection from adults, 145–50; social safety: protection from peers, 135–45

identity disclosures: among peers, 135, 138–39; embarrassing, 21, 42, 44, 134, 138, 151, 161, 209

identity explorations, 139; and anonymous apps, 90–92

image banks, 219–20

image-centric social media platforms, 45. *See also* FaceApp (digital photo editing app); Instagram

image tags, 43

imagined audience theory, 63

imagined industry theory, 63–64

imagined intimacy, 62

imagined surveillance, 146, 147

influencers, 46, 47, 166, 171, 178–79, 197, 198–99, 239

information overload, 68

informed consent, 238

insecurities, 209, 210

Instagram, 11, 14, 25, 155, 212; anonymous app connected to, 104; appearance-based insults on, 114, 117; comparisons with Instagram 'peers,' 181, 200; content moderation policies on, 49–52, 72–73; digital archive on, 94–95; digital photo editing on, 167, 168; evading detection on, 62–63; face, 203; hashtag moderation on, 58–60; naming practices on, 132, 144, 151; personalized recommendations on, 67, 69; portrayal of beauty norms on, 170–71; posts, 146, 164,

Founded in 1893,
UNIVERSITY OF CALIFORNIA PRESS
publishes bold, progressive books and journals
on topics in the arts, humanities, social sciences,
and natural sciences—with a focus on social
justice issues—that inspire thought and action
among readers worldwide.

The UC PRESS FOUNDATION
raises funds to uphold the press's vital role
as an independent, nonprofit publisher, and
receives philanthropic support from a wide
range of individuals and institutions—and from
committed readers like you. To learn more, visit
ucpress.edu/supportus.